THE COMMONWEALTH AND INTERNATIONAL LIBRARY
Joint Chairmen of the Honorary Editorial Advisory Board
SIR ROBERT ROBINSON, O.M., F.R.S., LONDON
DEAN ATHELSTAN SPILHAUS, MINNESOTA
Publisher: ROBERT MAXWELL, M.C., M.P.

SELECTED READINGS IN ANALYTICAL CHEMISTRY
General Editor: R. J. MAGEE

ORGANIC FUNCTIONAL GROUP ANALYSIS
THEORY AND DEVELOPMENT

ORGANIC FUNCTIONAL
GROUP ANALYSIS

Theory and Development

George H. Schenk
Associate Professor of Chemistry
Wayne State University
Detroit, Michigan

ORGANIC FUNCTIONAL GROUP ANALYSIS

THEORY AND DEVELOPMENT

BY

GEORGE H. SCHENK

ASSOCIATE PROFESSOR OF CHEMISTRY
WAYNE STATE UNIVERSITY, DETROIT, MICHIGAN

THE QUEEN'S AWARD
TO INDUSTRY 1966

PERGAMON PRESS

OXFORD · LONDON · EDINBURGH · NEW YORK
TORONTO · SYDNEY · PARIS · BRAUNSCHWEIG

PERGAMON PRESS LTD.
Headington Hill Hall, Oxford
4 & 5 Fitzroy Square, London W.1

PERGAMON PRESS (SCOTLAND) LTD.
2 & 3 Teviot Place, Edinburgh 1

PERGAMON PRESS INC.
44-01 21st Street, Long Island City, New York 11 101

PERGAMON OF CANADA LTD.
207 Queen's Quay West, Toronto 1

PERGAMON PRESS (AUST.) PTY, LTD.
Rushcutters Bay, Sydney, New South Wales

PERGAMON PRESS S.A.R.L.
24 rue des Écoles, Paris 5e

VIEWEG & SOHN GMBH
Burgplatz 1, Braunschweig

Contents

v

Preface

THE DEVELOPMENT of modern organic functional group analysis methods has occurred slowly and as a result of the research of many workers. It is not possible, as in many areas of physics, for example, to represent most of the progress in this field by reprinting the few outstanding papers. It is not even possible to delineate the development of every important functional group analysis method.

To keep the size of the book within reason, the author has chosen to represent progress in functional group analysis by seven selected methods. These have been chosen to represent as many different types of functional group methods as possible. It is freely admitted that these methods are among those which the author is most interested, and that many important methods have been omitted. This selection, however, does insure that much of the treatment will have the depth that an active researcher can contribute.

In choosing the methods and writing the chapters, the author tried to include a number of topics found in J.S. Fritz and G.S. Hammond's book on *Quantitative Organic Analysis*. This volume should therefore be a valuable supplement to the latter. In particular, Chapter 1 and the corresponding papers in Part II serve to update and expand the consideration of their Chapter 2, the details of developing an oximation method. Whereas their treatment of oximation is quite general, Chapter 1 of this volume covers specifically the oximation of acetone and furfural.

Chapter 2 was included in order to illustrate the utility of non-

ix

aqueous titrations and also to show how the determination of the per cent enol gives information which complements the per cent purity found by nonaqueous titration. Chapters 3 and 4 were included to dramatize the powerful analytical advantages in utilizing base catalysis and acid catalysis with the same reagent, acetic anhydride. Chapters 5, 6, and 7 all illustrate novel but extremely useful functional group methods which have received fresh impetus from recent research.

In order to include early papers as well as the most modern papers, the author has deleted many of the tables, figures, and less essential portions of the thirty-one papers in the hopes of giving as much credit as possible to many deserving research workers. Some theoretical papers have been included to show that functional group analysis benefits from basic studies. Wherever possible, instrumental applications of functional group methods have also been mentioned.

The author would like to thank the publishers of the following journals for permission to reprint the original articles, three of which were translated: *Analytical Chemistry, Analyst, Journal of the American Chemical Society, Journal of the Chemical Society (London), Journal of Chemical Physics, Berichte, Analytica Chimica Acta, Bulletin de la Societe Chimique de France, Microchemical Journal,* and *Annali di Chimica Applicata.*

Finally the author would like to acknowledge the assistance and encouragement of his wife without whom this book would have been impossible.

PART 1

PART 1

CHAPTER 1

Determination of the Carbonyl Group: Oximation and Other Methods

THE METHODS for the determination of the carbonyl function are numerous: oximation, bisulfite addition, iodoform, semicarbazone formation, 2,4-dinitrophenylhydrazone formation, and reduction with lithium aluminum hydride or sodium borohydride. Mitchell[20] has reviewed these methods as far as 1951, and recent books by Siggia[25] and Critchfield[7] have included methods which have appeared since then. Oximation is the most general of these methods and will be discussed at length in this chapter. This method involves the reaction of hydroxylamine, usually added as hydroxylamine hydrochloride, with the aldehyde or ketone to form the corresponding oxime:

$$\underset{R}{\overset{R}{\diagdown}}C{=}O + NH_2OH \rightarrow \underset{R}{\overset{R}{\diagdown}}C{=}N{-}OH + H_2O$$

EARLY OXIMATION METHODS

Oximation appears to be one of the older organic analytical methods. Brochet and Cambier[4] appear to have been the first to record an oximation method when they reported the oximation of formaldehyde in 1895. (In contrast, the quantitative addition of strong acids such as hydrochloric acid to epoxide groups was not reported until 1930.) Unfortunately, Brochet and

3

Cambier gave no analytical data and very few details; in addition their paper focused on the condensation of methylamine with formaldehyde instead of the oximation of formaldehyde.

The real beginning of the development of the oximation method can be traced to the need for the determination of citral, $C_9H_{15}CHO$, in lemon oil. In 1899 Walther[26] worked out the quantitative determination of citral in lemon oil and gave complete analytical details. The problem Walther faced was that faced by every analyst in devising an oximation method: how to avoid a strongly basic solution so as to prevent decomposition of hydroxylamine and yet keep the pH high enough to maintain a reasonable equilibrium concentration of NH_2OH. The problem can be understood in mathematical terms by rearranging the ionization constant expression for hydroxylamine ($K_b = 1 \times 10^{-8}$):

$$\frac{[NH_2OH]}{[NH_3OH^+]} = \frac{[OH^-]}{K_b} = \frac{[OH^-]}{1 \times 10^{-8}} = \frac{1 \times 10^{-6}}{[H^+]}$$

It is easily seen that at a pH less than 5, less than 10% of the total hydroxylamine will be present as NH_2OH. This sets a lower limit of 5 on the pH for a general method which will be suitable for the determination of ketones having low oxime formation constants. Walther solved the problem by using a sodium bicarbonate buffer to maintain the pH at 7 to 8. Unfortunately, the carbon dioxide liberated during the reaction of hydroxylamine hydrochloride and formaldehyde apparently carried off free hydroxylamine so that he obtained 7–8% citral in oils supposedly containing 5% citral.

The first general oximation method was developed by Bennett[2] in 1909 and applied by Bennett and Donovan[3] to the determination of formaldehyde, acetone, benzaldehyde, cinnamaldehyde, camphor, and carvone in 1922. The essential parts of both papers are reprinted in Part II, Chapters 1 and 2. Bennett partially neutralized the hydroxylamine hydrochloride reagent with sodium hydroxide to the phenolphthalein end point, giving roughly a 4:1 ratio of $[NH_2OH]/[NH_3OH^+]$. His buffer system was thus the hydroxylamine–hydroxylammonium ion species. The difference between a blank and sample titration using 0.5 N sulfuric acid gave the amount of hydroxylamine which had reacted with the carbonyl compound.

The next major contribution to the oximation of carbonyl groups was that of Bryant and Smith[5] in 1935. They used a dilute 2% pyridine solution in ethanol. Their work was important for three reasons: it demonstrated that tertiary amines might be used as the basic component of the buffer, it showed that steric hindrance (as in the case of 2,4-dimethyl-3-pentanone) reduces the equilibrium conversion to the oxime significantly below 100% (unless pyridine is present), and it also demonstrated that steric hindrance reduces the rate of oximation significantly. This paper is reprinted in Part II, Chapter 3.

Bryant and Smith's use of pyridine is worth discussing. In the 95% ethanol solvent, the pyridine is apparently a somewhat weaker base than hydroxylamine, so that the equilibrium in the buffer system is shifted somewhat to the left:

$$NH_3OH^+ + C_5H_5N \rightleftharpoons NH_2OH + C_5H_5NH^+$$

As oximation proceeds, the following occurs:

$$\text{$>$}C=O + NH_3OH^+ + C_5H_5N \rightarrow \text{$>$}C=NOH + C_5H_5NH^+ + H_2O$$

The 0.5 N alcoholic sodium hydroxide titrant neutralizes only the pyridinium ion, not the unreacted hydroxylammonium ion, at the bromophenol blue end point. The amount of titrant consumed is therefore directly equivalent to the amount of reacted hydroxylammonium ion and to the amount of carbonyl compound present.

The use of pyridine as part of the buffer system, in contrast to the hydroxylamine used by Bennett and Donovan, also provides a somewhat more constant concentration of base as the hydroxylamine is constantly reacting with the carbonyl compound. Unfortunately, the presence of pyridine makes the bromophenol blue end point quite vague. Thus, although the use of pyridine permitted a high equilibrium conversion to the oxime, it defeated the purpose by reducing the accuracy and precision of the end point.

OXIMATION EQUILIBRIA AND pH

About this time, Conant and Bartlett[6] and Hammett[15] published theoretical articles on the effect of pH on oximation and semicarbazone equilibria. Both defined an apparent, or conditional, equilibrium constant, K, for an equilibrium involving both protonated and unprotonated species in water:

$$\text{>\hspace{-2pt}C=O} + \left\{ \begin{array}{l} RNH_2 \\ RNH^+ \end{array} \right\} \rightleftharpoons \left\{ \begin{array}{l} \text{>\hspace{-2pt}C=NR} \\ \text{>\hspace{-2pt}C=NHR^+} \end{array} \right\} (+ H_2O)$$

where RNH_2 is unprotonated hydroxylamine or semicarbazide ($H_2NCONHNH_2$), and RNH_3^+ is protonated hydroxylamine or semicarbazide. K and the true equilibrium constant, K_0, were defined as follows:

$$K = \frac{\left[\text{>\hspace{-2pt}C=NR}\right] + \left[\text{>\hspace{-2pt}C=NHR^+}\right]}{\left[\text{>\hspace{-2pt}C=O}\right]\{[RNH_2] + [RHN^+]\}}$$

$$K_0 = \frac{\left[\text{>\hspace{-2pt}C=NR}\right]}{\left[\text{>\hspace{-2pt}C=O}\right][RNH_2]}$$

K depends on the pH whereas K_0 is independent of pH.

To derive a relationship between K and K_0, both papers define an ionization constant, K_a, for protonated hydroxylamine or semicarbazide:

$$K_a = \frac{[RNH_2][H^+]}{[RNH_3^+]}$$

and an ionization constant, K_c, for the ionization of the protonated oximes or semicarbazones:

$$K_c = \frac{\left[\rangle C{=}NR\right][H^+]}{\left[\rangle C{=}NHR^+\right]}$$

Using these definitions, one can derive the relationship between K and K_0 at any pH:

$$K = K_0 \frac{K_a}{K_c}\left\{\frac{K_c + [H^+]}{K_a + [H^+]}\right\}$$

Then, using the data in Table 1, one can calculate the values of K listed in Table 2 at various pH's for acetoxime and acetone semicarbazone.

Table 1. Equilibrium constants for acetoxime
and for some semicarbazones[6]

Compound	K_0	K_c^a	K_a^b
Acetoxime	1×10^6	1×10^{-2}	1×10^{-6}
Acetone semicarbazone	3×10^2	4.6×10^{-2}	2×10^{-4}
Benzaldehyde semicarbazone	3×10^5	1×10^{-1}	2×10^{-4}
Furfural semicarbazone	1×10^5	3.6×10^{-2}	2×10^{-4}
Pinacolone semicarbazone	9×10^1	—	2×10^{-4}

[a] Acidity constant for the ionization of $\rangle C{=}NHR^+$.
[b] Acidity constant for the ionization of RNH_3^+.

Whether oximation or semicarbazone formation will be quantitative (either 99 % or 99.9 %) will depend on the value of K and on the total concentration of both forms of unreacted hydroxylamine (NH_2OH and NH_3OH^+). The latter will be limited to the order of 10^{-2} M by such factors as the volume of the back titration, etc. At a particular pH, such as 4, one can then calculate the equilibrium conversion of acetone to both forms of the oxime by using the definition of K and solving for the appropriate ratio:

$$[10^{-2} \text{ M}] \, 1 \times 10^4 = \frac{100}{1} = \frac{\left[\text{>C=NR} \right] + \left[\text{>C=NHR}^+ \right]}{\left[\text{>C=O} \right]}$$

The calculation above indicates that the reaction is about 99 % complete at equilibrium at pH 4. At pH 5, it can similarly be calculated that the reaction is 99.9 % complete. This illustrates that in water, the oximation equilibrium is somewhat unfavorable for ketones unless the pH is kept at 5 or above. It is also apparent from Tables 1 and 2 that semicarbazone formation is affected less by pH but also falls short of being quantitative for ketones.

Table 2. *Conditional constants for acetoxime and acetone semicarbazone*

pH	K, Acetoxime	K, Acetone semicarbazone
3	1×10^3	5×10^1
4	1×10^4	2×10^2
5	1×10^5	$3 \times 10^2 \, (= K_0)$
6	0.5×10^6	$3 \times 10^2 \, (= K_0)$
7	$1 \times 10^6 \, (= K_0)$	$3 \times 10^2 \, (= K_0)$
8	$1 \times 10^6 \, (= K_0)$	$3 \times 10^2 \, (= K_0)$

MODERN OXIMATION METHODS

The use of pyridine in 95% ethanol as solvent remained the standard for oximation until 1956 when Higiuchi and Barnstein[17] published their hydroxylammonium acetate procedure. Oximation was carried out in glacial acetic acid with this reagent, and perchloric acid in glacial acetic acid was used as the titrant. The use of this reagent was important, because the use of the acetate salt removed the need for a polar solvent like water to dissolve hydroxylamine hydrochloride. The method was important because it was a completely nonaqueous method. The absence of water allowed a favorable equilibrium conversion of ketones to ketoximes and also permitted a sharp end point, something the Bryant–Smith method lacked.

Unfortunately, this method was inconvenient in that it required synthesis of the acetate salt and potentiometric titration of both the reagent blank and the sample. Only in the case of aliphatic ketones was the oxime basic enough to yield a detectable end point.

In 1957 Fritz and Hammond[12] considered the oximation problem from a theoretical viewpoint, and in 1959 Fritz, Yamamura, and Bradford[13] published a completely nonaqueous method, based on those considerations. They dissolved hydroxylamine hydrochloride in methanol and diluted to volume with 2-propanol. Perchloric acid in methyl Cellosolve

$$(CH_3OCH_2CH_2OH)$$

was used as titrant. Their buffer system consisted of adding a tertiary amine, 2-dimethylaminoethanol, to hydroxylamine hydrochloride to establish the following equilibrium:

$$NH_3OH^+ + Me_2NCH_2CH_2OH \rightleftharpoons NH_2OH + Me_2NHCH_2CH_2OH^+$$

The 2-dimethylaminoethanol is a stronger base than hydroxylamine so that the equilibrium is shifted somewhat to the right.

This buffer permits rapid reaction and quantitative conversion of most carbonyl compounds to the oxime. Hindered ketones such as acetophenone required 45–60 min heating at 70°C.

The other important contribution of this method was the extremely sharp end point obtained with the perchloric acid titrant. The potentiometric break appears to be the biggest such break of any oximation method. In addition, a mixed indicator of martius yellow and methyl violet was also found to be suitable for visual titrations.

In 1957, Pesez[21] reported an oximation method based on hydroxylammonium formate dissolved in methanol, with perchloric acid in dioxane as titrant. Ruch, Johnson, and Critchfield[22] modified this method by substituting 2 to 1 methyl Cellosolve–methanol as solvent for the methanol and 0.5 N nitric acid in methyl Cellosolve for the perchloric acid titrant. This modification makes the method superior to the Fritz–Yamamura–Bradford method for the analysis of carbonyl groups in acetals or ketals: the nitric acid titrant is too weak to catalyze the hydrolysis of acetals and ketals in contrast to the stronger perchloric acid. The break at the potentiometric end point is good but not as sharp as that in the Fritz method. Both papers are reprinted in Part II, Chapters 4 and 5.

RATE OF OXIMATION AND pH

Some workers have assumed that under all conditions oximation is a second order reaction involving a rate-determining nucleophilic attack of hydroxylamine on the carbonyl group. As Fritz and Hammond[12] have emphasized, oximation is subject to acid-catalysis, with a third order rate law:

$$\frac{-d\left(\diagup\!\!\diagdown C{=}O\right)}{dt} = k_3 \left(\diagup\!\!\diagdown C{=}O\right) (NH_2OH) (H^+)$$

Jencks[18] has studied the kinetics of oximation of acetone and other compounds and finds two different rate-determining steps, depending on the pH region. His paper is reprinted in Part II, Chapter 6.

In acidic solution (below pH 2–3), the NH_2OH concentration is significantly reduced by protonation (to NH_3OH^+) so that the rate-determining step is the above-mentioned addition of NH_2OH to the carbonyl group to form an intermediate addition compound:

$$HOH_2N: \rightarrow \ \diagdown C{=}O \rightleftharpoons HOHN{-}C{-}OH$$

The acid-catalyzed decomposition of the intermediate to the oxime in acid solution is obviously rapid. The rate law below pH 2–3 will have the form of a pseudo-second order rate law:

$$\frac{-d\left(\diagup\!\!\diagdown C{=}O\right)}{dt} = k_2 \left(\diagup\!\!\diagdown C{=}O\right)(NH_2OH)$$

$$k_2 = 6.8 \times 10^4 \ \text{M}^{-1} \ \text{min}^{-1} \quad \text{(acetone, 25°C)}$$
$$k_2 = 9 \times 10^4 \ \text{M}^{-1} \ \text{min}^{-1} \quad \text{(furfural, 25°C)}$$

When the hydroxylamine concentration is much larger than that of acetone, the reaction becomes a pseudo-first order reaction. The observed rate constant, k_{obs}, will be the product $k_2(NH_2OH)$. Figure 4 in this paper is a plot of k_{obs} vs. pH for the oximation of acetone and furfural. One can calculate k_{obs} using the K_a of 1×10^{-6} M for the ionization of NH_3OH^+, and a given concentration of NH_3OH^+. For the oximation of acetone where $(NH_3OH^+) = 0.0167$ M (Jencks' Figure 4) and a given pH, k_{obs} is calculated as follows:

$$k_{obs} = 6.8 \times 10^4 \ \text{M}^{-1} \ \text{min}^{-1} \ \frac{1 \times 10^{-6} \ \text{M} \ (0.0167 \ \text{M} \ NH_3OH^+)}{(H^+)}$$

at pH 3,

$$k_{obs} = 1.1 \text{ min}^{-1} \quad \text{(acetone, 25°C)}$$

Similar calculations can be made for the oximation of furfural.

These rate constants are of value because they allow the analyst to calculate the time required for quantitative (99.9%) reaction. As long as hydroxylamine is present in twofold excess over the carbonyl compound, it can be assumed that a first order rate law will be fairly valid. At pH 3, the time for quantitative oximation of acetone may be calculated by using the integrated form of the first order rate law:

$$t_{99.9\%} = \frac{1}{1.1 \text{ min}^{-1}} \; 2.3 \log \frac{(100\% \text{ Me}_2\text{CO})_{0\%}}{(0.1\% \text{ Me}_2\text{CO})_{99.9\%}}$$

$$t_{99.9\%} = \frac{6.9}{1.1 \text{ min}^{-1}} = 6.2 \text{ min} \quad \text{(acetone, 25°C, pH 3)}$$

This reaction time is probably satisfactory although it should be remembered that ketones with much smaller rate constants than acetone may have to be analyzed by oximation. However, consideration of equilibrium constants above indicated that the pH should be kept at 5 or above. Obviously, the pH cannot be kept at 3 even though the kinetics are favorable at this pH.

Above pH 4–5, Jencks[18] found evidence for a rate-determining acid-catalyzed dehydration of the intermediate addition compound to the oxime:

$$\text{HOHN} \overset{\displaystyle \diagdown}{\underset{\displaystyle \diagup}{\text{C}}} \text{OH} \overset{\text{H}^+}{\rightleftarrows} \text{HON} = \overset{\displaystyle \diagup}{\underset{\displaystyle \diagdown}{\text{C}}} + \text{H}_2\text{O}$$

The prior addition of NH_2OH to the carbonyl group is obviously rapid since the equilibrium concentration of NH_2OH at this pH is relatively high compared to the region below pH 2–3.

The rate law above pH 4–5 will also have the form of a pseudo-second order rate law:

$$\frac{-d\left(\text{\textbackslash C=O}\right)}{dt} = k_2 \left(\text{\textbackslash COHNHOH}\right) (\text{H}^+)$$

$k_2 = 1.08 \times 10^8$ M^{-1} min^{-1} (acetone, 25 °C)
$k_2 = 2.2 \times 10^6$ M^{-1} min^{-1} (furfural, 25 °C)

where ($>$COHNHOH) is the concentration of the intermediate. If the pH is held constant and hydroxylamine is in large excess, the reaction again exhibits pseudo-first order kinetics with a rate law of this form:

$$\frac{-d\left(\text{\textbackslash C=O}\right)}{dt} = k_{obs} \left(\text{\textbackslash C=O}\right)$$

For the formation of the intermediate from the carbonyl compound and hydroxylamine, Jencks defines an equilibrium constant, K_1:

$$K_1 = \frac{\left(\text{\textbackslash COHNHOH}\right)}{\left(\text{\textbackslash C=O}\right)(\text{NH}_2\text{OH})}$$

$K_1 = 1.0$ M^{-1} (acetone)
$K_1 = 5.2$ M^{-1} (furfural)

From the definition for K_1 follows the relation between k_2 and k_{obs} above pH 4–5:

$$k_{obs} = k_2 K_1 (\text{NH}_2\text{OH}) (\text{H}^+)$$

One can calculate k_{obs} for acetone at a given pH after first using the K_a of 1×10^{-6} for the ionization of NH_3OH^+ to calculate (NH_2OH). For example, for the conditions of Jencks' Figure 4 at pH 6 where (NH_2OH) + (NH_3OH) = 0.0167 M,

(NH$_2$OH) is found to be 0.0084 M and k_{obs} is calculated as follows:

$$k_{obs} = 1.08 \times 10^8 \text{ M}^{-1} \text{ min}^{-1} [1.0 \text{ M}^{-1}] \times$$

$$\times \ (0.0084 \text{ M NH}_2\text{OH}) (10^{-6} \text{ M H}^+)$$

$$k_{obs} = 0.9 \text{ min}^{-1} \quad \text{(acetone, 25°C, pH 6)}$$

Once again, the time for quantitative oximation of acetone can be calculated by using the integrated form of the first order rate law:

$$t_{99.9\%} = \frac{1}{0.9 \text{ min}^{-1}} \ 2.3 \log \frac{(100\% \text{ Me}_2\text{CO})_{0\%}}{(0.1\% \text{ Me}_2\text{CO})_{99.9\%}}$$

$$t_{99.9\%} = \frac{6.9}{0.9 \text{ min}^{-1}} = 7.7 \text{ min} \quad \text{(acetone, 25°C, pH 6)}$$

The reaction time at pH 6 is probably satisfactory although it is slightly longer than the time required at pH 3. However, Table 2 indicates that the conditional equilibrium constant is quite large at pH 6. Thus, if oximation of acetone is to be conducted in aqueous media, pH 6 would be the best compromise between the kinetic and equilibrium requirements. The rate is about 1.5 times greater at pH 5 than at pH 6, but the conditional constant is only half as large at that pH as it is at pH 6.

As the graph for furfural in Jencks' Figure 4 indicates, the effect of pH on rate varies with the carbonyl compound. Obviously a pH of 6 would not be the best compromise for aldehydes like furfural, but the conditional equilibrium constant is likely to be much larger than for ketones like acetone. For a completely general method, a nonaqueous solvent is probably the best choice.

Jencks also found a small increase in the rate of oximation in aqueous solution in the neutral pH region of 6–7 when the concentration of potassium dihydrogen phosphate in the buffer was increased. This was not observed below pH 3, however (cf. Jencks' Figure 4). This was attributed to general acid catalysis by the $H_2PO_4^-$ ion on the rate-determining acid-catalyzed dehydration step:

$$HOHN-\underset{\underset{H-\underset{\lfloor}{O}PO_3H^-}{|}}{\overset{|}{C}}-OH \quad\rightleftharpoons\quad O-PO_3H^{2} + H^+ + H_2O + HON=C$$

FUTURE RESEARCH: NEW APPLICATIONS
AND METHODS

The above discussion has been limited to acid-catalyzed oximation. Jencks[1,18] has indicated that base-catalyzed oximation and semicarbazone formation are both possible above pH 9. He suggests that the intermediate addition compound is dehydrated by base as follows:

$$RN-\underset{\underset{H}{|}}{\overset{|}{C}}-OH \quad\rightleftharpoons\quad RN=C \quad + H_2O + \quad :Base$$

It should therefore be possible to design a method employing base-catalysis, although the instability of hydroxylamine in a base might limit this to semicarbazide. This method might be of use in analyzing compounds such as α, α, α-trifluoroacetophenone which reacts slowly in acid because of the low rate of the acid-catalyzed dehydration of the intermediate.[1] The electron-withdrawing effect of fluorine would make the intermediate quite acidic and therefore susceptible to rapid base-catalyzed dehydration.

Another phase of oximation that might be explored is the titrimetric finish. The requirements of the acid–base titration seriously limit the pH and the buffer systems that might be used for the oximation reaction. If, for example, a simple oxidation-reduction titration were used, the potential of general acid catalysis might be fully realized. If semicarbazide is used, oxidizing agents that react stoichiometrically with it are not difficult to find. For example, iodine oxidizes it stoichiometrically to nitrogen in a phosphate buffer:[6]

$$H_2NNHCONH_2 + 2I_2 + H_2O \xrightarrow{(pH\ 1)} N_2 + CO_2 + NH_4^+ + 3H^+ + 4I^-$$

The stoichiometry of the oxidation of hydroxylamine varies with pH and is more difficult to control.[12] In the presence of MgO or Na_2HPO_4, it is oxidized to nitrous oxide by iodine:

$$2NH_2OH + 2I_2 \rightarrow N_2O + 4H^+ + H_2O + 4I^-$$

In the 10–30 mg range, the results are 1 % low, but in the 60 mg range, the results appear to be as much as 4 % low.

Finally, there is the use of oximation in connection with instrumental methods of analysis that needs further research. Now that functional group research has provided conditions for quantitative oximation of carbonyl compounds, the instrumental analyst may use these methods to convert carbonyl compounds to oximes and analyze the oximes by instrumental methods.

The advantage of doing this is illustrated by an actual method using gas chromatographic analysis. Converting a carbonyl compound quantitatively to the oxime will change the retention time of the compound, so as to resolve its chromatographic peak from that of another non-carbonyl compound whose retention time is similar to the carbonyl compound. A stringent requirement for the oxime is that such a derivative must be stable enough to withstand the temperature of the heated gas chromatographic column. Ketoximes are fairly stable but aldoximes are not. Fales and Luukkainen,[11] whose paper is reprinted in

Part 2, Chapter 7, found that O-methylhydroxylamine could be used to form stable O-methyloximes of both aldehydes and ketones:

$$\text{\textgreater}C{=}O + NH_2OCH_3 \rightarrow \text{\textgreater}C{=}NOCH_3 + H_2O$$

In addition, this derivative was of use in mass spectrometric analysis, in that the fragmentation pattern of various carbonyl compounds was altered considerably. Finally, they also found by NMR spectrometry that the $=NOCH_3$ function has an easily integrated singlet peak at 3.81 ppm (δ). This appears to be amenable to quantitative analysis.

OTHER CARBONYL METHODS

Other functional group methods for the carbonyl group have not received the study and development that oximation has. A few of these methods deserve mention. The well-known addition of sodium bisulfate to aldehydes has been used since 1900. The most recent general method appears to be the modified potentiometric acid–base method of Siggia and Maxey.[24] Their method is useful for aliphatic, aromatic, and unsaturated aldehydes. The unreacted reagent is titrated with sodium hydroxide. Ketones do not interfere if present in amounts less than 10 mole %.

A more modern approach to the determination of aliphatic carbonyl groups is oxidation with peroxytrifluoroacetic acid, as suggested by Hawthorne[16] in 1956:

$$\underset{\displaystyle RCR'}{\overset{\displaystyle O \atop \displaystyle \|}{}} + CF_3CO_3H \rightarrow CF_3CO_2H + \underset{\displaystyle RCOR'}{\overset{\displaystyle O \atop \displaystyle \|}{}} \quad (\text{or } R'COR)$$

The unreacted peroxytrifluoroacetic acid is determined iodometrically.

The iodoform reaction appears to have received almost as

much study as oximation. As originated by Messinger,[19] it was used for the determination of acetone:

$$CH_3COCH_3 + 4OH^- + 3I_2 \rightarrow CHI_3 + CH_3CO_2^- + 3H_2O + 3I^-$$

It was later found that the reaction in aqueous solution gave results that were over 2% high,[10, 20] especially when the iodine was added in 180 sec or less from a pipet. It was suggested that oxidation of acetone to formic acid was responsible.[20] However, Cullis and Hashmi[8] found by paper chromatography that almost 2% of the iodine consumed in the reaction ended up as iodoacetic acid. Goltz and Glew[14] later verified the 2% high error in 50 sec pipetting timbe but found that a 300-sec pipetting time gave results from 99.5 to 100.5% acetone. Dal Nogare, Norris, and Hitchell[10] found that the order of addition and concentration of reagents were important, and also developed a spectrophotometric method for acetone and acetaldehyde by measurement of the iodoform at 347 mμ.

Cullis and Hashmi[8] also studied the order of addition of reagents in the course of their kinetic study of the iodoform reaction of methyl ketones. Their paper, reprinted in Part II, Chapter 8, is perhaps the ultimate study of the iodoform method. Their essential point is that side reactions complicate the determination of methyl ketones other than acetone and seriously affect the stoichiometry.

The rate-determining step of the reaction involves the reaction of an acidic alpha hydrogen with hydroxide ion. Therefore methyl ketones having at least one alpha methylene hydrogen also undergo slow iodination at the methylene carbon and give high results:

$$CH_3COCHR_2 \rightarrow CI_3COCHR_2 \rightarrow CI_3COCIR_2 \rightarrow CHI_3 + R_2IOC_2^-$$

This would indicate that non-methyl ketones, such as diethyl ketone, ought to react slowly, though perhaps not stoichiometrically, with the iodoform reagent. Cullis and Hashmi[9] were able to follow the kinetics of such reactions and reported first order rate constants at 25°C of $3.31 \times 10^3 \text{sec}^{-1}$ for diethyl ketone and $2.30 \times 10^3 \text{sec}^{-1}$ for diisopropyl ketone. The conditions were the same as in Table 2 of their first paper.[8]

These studies suggest that methyl ketones without methylene hydrogens might give stoichiometric results in the iodoform reaction. Using Cullis and Hashmi's conditions, the present author and co-workers[23] found that acetophenone, $CH_3COC_6H_6$, reacted 98.0% in 1 hr with the iodoform reagent. Other such ketones appear to give significantly low results; for example, methyl β-naphthyl ketone reacted only 95.4% in 1.5 hr. A fair conclusion is that the iodoform reaction should probably be limited to the determination of acetone and acetophenone in the absence of other ketones and compounds with similar acidic hydrogens.

REFERENCES

1. ANDERSON, B.M., JENCKS, W.P., *J. Amer. Chem. Soc.* **82**, 1773 (1960).
2. BENNETT, A.H., *Analyst* **34**, 14 (1909).
3. BENNETT, A.H., DONOVAN, F.K., *Ibid.* **47**, 146 (1922).
4. BROCHET, A., CAMBIER, R., *Compt. rend.* **120**, 449 (1895).
5. BRYANT, W.M.D., SMITH, D.M., *J. Amer. Chem. Soc.* **57**, 57 (1935).
6. CONANT, J.B., BARTLETT, P.D., *J. Amer. Chem. Soc,.* **54**, 2881 (1932).
7. CRITCHFIELD, F.E., *Organic Functional Group Analysis*, pp. 60–80, Pergamon Press, New York, 1963.
8. CULLIS, C.F., HASHMI, M.H., *J. Chem. Soc.*, 2512. (1956).
9. CULLIS, C.F., HASHMI, M.H., *Ibid.*, 1548 (1957).
10. DAL NOGARE, S., NORRIS, T.O., MITCHELL, J., *Anal. Chem.* **23**, 1473 (1951).
11. FALES, H.M., LUUKKAINEN, T., *Ibid.* **37**, 955 (1965).
12. FRITZ, J.S., HAMMOND, G.S., *Quantitative Organic Analysis*, pp. 6–21, John Wiley, 1957.
13. FRITZ, J.S., YAMAMURA, S.S., BRADFORD, E.C., *Anal. Chem.* **31**, 260 (1959).
14. GOLTZ, G.E., GLEW, D.N., *Ibid.* **29**, 816 (1957).

15. HAMMETT, L.P., *Physical Organic Chemistry*, p. 335, McGraw-Hill, New York, 1940.
16. HAWTHORNE, M.F., *Anal. Chem.* **28**, 540 (1956).
17. HIGIUCHI, T., BARNSTEIN, C.H., *Ibid.* **28**, 1022 (1956).
18. JENCKS, W.P., *J. Amer. Chem. Soc.* **81**, 475 (1959).
19. MESSINGER, J., *Ber.* **21**, 3366 (1888).
20. MITCHELL, J., Jr., *Organic Analysis*, Vol. 1, pp. 243–307, Interscience, New York, 1953.
21. PESEZ, M., *Bull. soc. chem. France*, 417 (1957).
22. RUCH, J.E., JOHNSON, J.B., CRITCHFIELD, F.E., *Anal. Chem.* **33**, 1566 (1961).
23. SCHENK, G.H., PALMER,T.A., GUTNIKOV, G., Unpublished results, Iowa State University and Wayne State University, 1958, 1960.
24. SIGGIA, S., MAXEY, W., *Anal. Chem.* **19**, 1023 (1947).
25. SIGGIA, S., *Quantitative Organic Analysis via Functional Groups*, 3rd ed., pp. 73–129, Wiley, New York, 1963.
26. WALTHER, J., *Pharm. Centralb.* **40**, 621 (1899).

Analysis of Enolic-type Compounds: Kurt Meyer Bromination and Nonaqueous Titration

COMPOUNDS of the β-diketone or β-ketoester type exist in two main tautomeric forms: the keto and enol forms. In the enol, the oxygens may be oriented *cis* or *trans* to one another so that both a *cis*-enol and a *trans*-enol may exist. The *cis* form is the predominate form, being stabilized by intramolecular hydrogen bonding. Typical structures of the keto and *cis*-enol tautomers of ethyl acetoacetate are as shown:

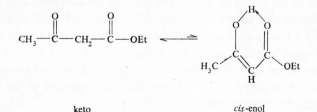

keto   *cis*-enol

Two different types of functional group methods have evolved for the analysis of enolic type compounds. The first to appear was the determination of the per cent enol by bromination of the double bond. Much later, sophisticated spectroscopic techniques such as NMR spectrometric measurement of the —CH_2— and =CH hydrogens replaced this functional group method. The second functional group method was the determination of the per cent purity of the enolic compound by nonaqueous titration of both keto and enol tautomers with a strong base.

BROMINATION OF THE ENOL TAUTOMER

An enol differs from its keto tautomer in having a hydroxyl group, a carbon–carbon double bond, and an ethylenic hydrogen instead of two methylene hydrogens. Some study[11] has been given to the chelation or complexation of iron(III) through the hydroxyl group with the idea of estimating the enol tautomer, but early methods centered on the bromination of the double bond.

In 1911 Kurt Meyer[15] published a direct bromine titration and a back titration bromine method for the determination of the per cent enol in ethyl acetoacetate as well as other compounds. The disadvantages of the direct titration were the instability of the bromine titrant and the difficulty of perceiving the yellow color of the excess bromine. The indirect method was more promising in that the total amount of bromine added did not have to be known; an excess was merely added. The products were hydrogen bromide and the monobrominated, not dibrominated diketone or ketoester. The monobrominated product probably results because of an intramolecular rearrangement of the postulated bromonium ion intermediate:

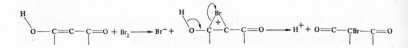

Sodium thiosulfate was quickly titrated into the solution to remove the unreacted bromine. Potassium iodide was then added to displace the bromide ion and to eventually produce iodine and the original tautomeric mixture of enol and keto forms:

$$O{=}C{-}CBr{-}C{=}O \;+\; 2I^-{+}H^+ \longrightarrow I_2 \;+\; Br^- \;+\; HO{-}C{=}CH{-}C{=}O$$

The iodine is then titrated with a standard sodium thiosulfate solution, giving the multiequivalents of iodine and the multiequivalents of the enol tautomer.

Because the thiosulfate could not be added in excess but had to be titrated to remove the excess bromine, there was time for the hydrogen bromide produced to catalyze the further enolization of the keto form. Meyer and Kappelmeier[16] reduced this error by adding immediately an excess of 2-naphthol to remove the unreacted bromine. The unreacted 2-naphthol caused no interference in the final titration as unreacted thiosulfate in Meyer's original method did. This modification was adequate for ethyl acetoacetate and dibenzoylmethane, but inadequate for 5,5-dimethylcyclohexan-1,3-dione. Large variations in the per cent enol of ethyl acetoacetate with a change in solvent were found, ranging from 6.87% in methanol at 0°C to 16.2% in benzene to 32% in carbon disulfide.[15]

In 1938 Cooper and Barnes[2] published an improved modification of the Kurt Meyer method using diisobutylene, C_8H_{16}, to absorb the unreacted bromine:

$$RHC{=}CR_2 + Br_2 \rightarrow RHCBr{-}CBrR_2$$

They claimed that 2-naphthol turned the solution brown, making it difficult to note the disappearance of the yellow color of iodine at the end point. Their paper is reprinted in Part II, Chapter 9. Using 2-naphthol, they obtained from 90.85 to 98.52% enol in dibenzoylmethane. Using diisobutylene, they obtained

16 results in the narrow range of 95.16–96.15%. They did not report results with other compounds, but the author has found that their method works reasonably well for compounds other than 5,5-dimethylcyclohexan-1,3-dione. Their method still has the disadvantage of excess bromine being present during the 15 sec reaction time.

Later, Schwarzenbach and co-workers[20, 21] designed an apparatus to eliminate errors caused by the presence of unreacted bromine. They ran a solution of known concentration of the compound, and a solution of increasing concentration of bromine, at controlled rates through a reaction vessel. The time at which unreacted bromine appeared was determined potentiometrically, and simultaneously the bromine solution was analyzed. They were able to determine the enol content of ketones like cyclohexanone, where the per cent enol is quite low.

In 1945 Eidenoff[4] reported the use of a further modification of the Kurt Meyer method to analyze dilute (10^{-4} M) solutions. He used a chilled bromine solution containing ice, and absorbed the unreacted bromine with aniline hydrochloride after 3 sec. After adding potassium iodide, he allowed the solution to stand for 1.5 hr at 35 °C to permit the slow reaction of iodide and the bromoketone to occur.

In 1954 Gero[10] proposed the use of iodine monochloride since it reacts more rapidly than bromine and does not substitute as readily as bromine. He reported 13.2% enol in ethyl acetoacetate compared to the 6.87% found by Meyer.

The year before, Jarrett, Sadler, and Shoolery[12] reported that NMR spectrometry could be used to determine the relative amounts of enol and keto tautomers in a pure β-diketone. The preferred method involves comparing the peak area of the C=C—H of the enol with one half the peak area corresponding to the two methylene hydrogens of the keto tautomer. (The O—H peak of the enol may be used but this is subject to error if water is present.) Since the NMR measurement cannot disturb the keto–enol equilibrium, it should be more accurate than bromination, which disturbs the equilibrium. It is interesting that the per cent enol in 2,4-pentanedione (acetylacetone) was found to be higher than that found by the Kurt Meyer method. This paper is reprinted in Part II, Chapter 10, because it is an interesting comparison of a functional group method with a sophisticated instrumental method.

NONAQUEOUS TITRATION OF ENOLIC COMPOUNDS

The Kurt Meyer method is satisfactory for an estimation of the per cent enol in an enolic compound, but it is not satisfactory for a general determination of per cent purity because the rate of enolization of the keto form is not always rapid. There appears to have been no general method in use for this purpose until 1947, when a precipitation method[19] was proposed. This was based on the formation of the insoluble copper(II) salt, but the method required careful control of the pH, to within less than one pH unit in some cases.

Ideally, a functional group method for per cent purity would be based on the fact that both the keto and enol forms are proton donors. Unfortunately, prior to 1948, the only established titration methods for weak acids were based on the use of titrants like aqueous or partly alcoholic sodium hydroxide. Most enolic compounds are too weakly acidic to be titrated by these titrants. (The pK_a values of enolic compounds vary from 4 to as high as 20. The relative rates of ionization of keto and enol tautomers also vary; Eigen, Ilgenfritz and Kruse[5] found that the enol of barbituric acid ionizes more rapidly than the keto form, whereas the keto form of 5,5-dimethylcyclohexan-1,3-dione ionizes more rapidly than the enol form.)

In 1948 the development of nonaqueous titration techniques began, and by 1952 the per cent purity of most enolic compounds could be easily determined by these techniques. Fritz[7] and Beckett and Tinley[1] have reviewed these methods completely; only the pertinent developments will be outlined below.

Most of the titration methods for weak acids were developed on an empirical basis before it was shown that weakly ionized acids (HA) existed in solvents like *tert*-butyl alcohol largely as molecules[14] and ion pairs[14] (and even as ion quadruplets):

$$HA \; \underset{}{\overset{}{\rightleftharpoons}} \; H^+A^- \; \underset{}{\overset{}{\rightleftharpoons}} \; H^+ + A^-$$

molecule   (ionization)   ion pair   (dissociation)   ions

Nevertheless, these methods were excellent for the determination of many compounds. Even though sodium ethoxide and sodium *tert*-butoxide had been used as titrants, the use of sodium amino-ethoxide as titrant by Moss, Elliott, and Hall[17] in 1948 seems to have started intense interest in nonaqueous titration research. They titrated phenols dissolved in ethylenediamine, using a potentiometric end point. Ethylenediamine, however, has to be rendered anhydrous and fumes badly.

In 1951, Fritz and Lisicki[9] reported that sodium methoxide, a more convenient titrant, could be used in connection with dimethylformamide or butylamine. Both of these solvents could be used without purification. The sodium methoxide was dissolved in 1:6 methanol–benzene, which increased the sharpness of the end point because of the low concentration of the methanol. The reason for this is that the methanol hydrogen bonds to the methoxide anion and reduces its basicity. At the end point, the low concentration of methanol permits the establishment of a more favorable equilibrium than is possible with methanol alone:

$$CH_3OH \leftarrow : OCH_3^- + HA \rightleftharpoons 2CH_3OH + A^-$$

Fritz and Lisicki also appear to be the first to propose the use of an indicator, thymol blue, for a convenient visual end point. Using thymol blue, they were able to titrate many carboxylic acids, acid chlorides, and acid anhydrides. They also reported the successful titration of an enolic compound, acetylacetone.

Fritz and Keen[8] next reported the titration of sulfonamides in dimethylformamide or butylamine, using sodium methoxide titrant. They found that azo violet (p-nitrobenzeneazoresorcinol) a weaker indicator than thymol blue, was useful in dimethylformamide, ethylenediamine, and butylamine. Later that same year, 1952, Vespe and Fritz[23] published the successful titration of barbiturates in dimethylformamide, using sodium methoxide titrant. Since barbituric acid is itself an enolic compound (it is only 1.3% enolic[5] however), this demonstrated that enolic compounds could in general be titrated in nonaqueous solvents, and set the stage for a more general investigation.

Later in 1952 Fritz[6] reported the successful titration of many different types of enolic compounds, as well as imides, using the knowledge about solvents, indicators, and titrants developed in earlier papers. Initially, he used sodium methoxide as titrant, but later[7] recommended the use of potassium methoxide. This base required only a $1:10$ methanol–benzene solvent, making possible an even sharper end point than obtained with sodium methoxide. His 1952 paper[6] is reprinted in Part II, Chapter 11.

Fritz found that three different indicators and two or three different solvents were necessary for the titration of the various enolic compounds because their acidities varied so much. Measurements of their pK_a's in water[18] or water–dioxane[22] give some idea of their acidity range although undoubtedly large and inconsistent changes in the pK_a's occur upon changing to a completely nonaqueous solvent. As seen in Table 3, very acidic enolic compounds ($pK_a \leqq 9$) may be titrated readily using thymol blue indicator. Less acidic enolic compounds ($pK_a = 9$ to

11) are best titrated using a weaker indicator like azo violet. Very weakly acidic compounds ($pK_a > 11$) can often be titrated in ethylenediamine using 2-nitroaniline, a very weakly acidic indicator.

Table 3. Titration conditions for some enolic compounds[6]

Enolic compounds (in order of decreasing acidity)	$pK_a(H_2O)$	Indicator	Solvent
$CH_3COCH_2COCH_3$ (Acetylacetone)	8.35[22]	Thymol blue[9]	Butylamine[9]
$C_6H_5COCH_2COC_6H_5$ (Dibenzoylmethane)	9.1[22]a	Thymol blue	Dimethyl-formamide
$C_2H_5O_2CCH_2CN$ (Ethyl cyanoacetate)	>9[18]	Azo violet	Dimethyl-formamide
$NCCH_2CONH_2$ (Cyanoacetamide)	*ca.* 11	2-Nitroaniline	Ethylene-diamine
$H_2NCOCH_2CONH_2$ (Malonamide)	11.0	Not titrable; only slightly acidic to 2-nitroaniline	

a This is extrapolated from values measured in dioxane–water; dibenzoylmethane is insoluble in water.

Fritz was also able to titrate compounds such as diethyl malonate which are essentially 100% ketonic. In 1958 Zaugg and Garven[24] reported the titration of diethyl malonate in the presence of monosubstituted alkyl diethyl malonates using dimethylformamide and azo violet. They also were able to titrate the latter compounds in the presence of the disubstituted alkyl diethyl malonates, using ethylenediamine and 2-nitroaniline.

Cundiff and Markunas[3] later were able to improve this type of titration by using tetralkylammonium hydroxide titrants in pyridine as solvent, with a potentiometric end point. Marple and Fritz[13] improved such potentiometric titrations by developing a calomel reference electrode-salt bridge system. This system gave reproducible potentials to within 2 to 5 mv, compared to discrepancies of up to 50 mv found with calomel electrodes employing methanolic KCl and no salt bridge. Their system consisted of a saturated calomel electrode dipped into a two phase mixture of water and *tert*-butyl alcohol which was saturated with KCl. This solution was connected by a salt bridge of *tert*-butyl alcohol saturated with tetrabutylammonium bromide, to the sample solution containing the indicating electrode.

REFERENCES

 1. BECKETT, A.H., TINLEY, E.H., *Titrations in Non-Aqueous Solvents*, 2nd ed., British Drug Houses Ltd., Poole, England.
 2. COOPER, S.R., BARNES, R.P., *Ind. Engr. Chem., Anal. Ed.* **10**, 379 (1938).
 3. CUNDIFF, R.H., MARKUNAS, P.C., *Anal. Chem.* **28**, 792 (1956).
 4. EIDENOFF, M.L., *J. Amer. Chem. Soc.* **67**, 2073 (1945).
 5. EIGEN, M., ILGENFRITZ, G., KRUSE, W., *Ber.* **98**, 1623 (1965).
 6. FRITZ, J.S., *Anal. Chem.* **24**, 674 (1952).
 7. FRITZ, J.S., *Acid–Base Titrations in Nonaqueous Solvents*, G.F.Smith Chemical Co., Columbus, Ohio, 1952.
 8. FRITZ, J.S., KEEN, R.T., *Anal. Chem.* **24**, 308 (1952).
 9. FRITZ, J.S., LISICKI, N., *Anal. Chem.* **23**, 589 (1951).
10. GERO, A., *J. Org. Chem.* **19**, 469, 1960 (1954).
11. HENECKA, H., *Chemie der β-Dicarbonyl-Verbindungen*, pp. 113–9, Springer-Verlag, Berlin, 1950.
12. JARRETT, H.S., SADLER, M.S., SHOOLERY, J.N., *J. Chem. Phys.* **21**, 2092 (1953).
13. MARPLE, L.W., FRITZ, J.S., *Anal. Chem.* **34**, 796 (1962).
14. MARPLE, L.W., FRITZ, J.S., *Anal. Chem.* **35**, 1223 (1963).
15. MEYER, K.H., *Ann.* **380**, 212 (1911).
16. MEYER, K.H., KAPPELMEIER, P., *Ber.* **44**, 2718 (1911).
17. MOSS, M.L., ELLIOTT, J.H., HALL, R.T., *Anal. Chem.* **20**, 784 (1948).
18. PEARSON, R.G., DILLEN, R.L., *J. Amer. Chem. Soc.* **75**, 2439 (1953).
19. SEAMAN, W., WOODS, J.T., MASSAD, C.A., *Anal. Chem.* **19**, 250 (1947).
20. SCHWARZENBACH, G., FELDER, E., *Helv. Chim. Acta* **27**, 1044 (1944).
21. SCHWARZENBACH, G., WITTWER, C., *Helv. Chim. Acta* **30**, 656 and 669 (1947).
22. VAN UITERT, L.G., HAAS, C.G., FERNELIUS, W.C., DOUGLAS, B.E., *J. Amer. Chem. Soc.* **75**, 455 (1963).
23. VESPE, V., FRITZ, J.S., *J. Amer. Pharm. Assoc.* **41**, 197 (1952).
24. ZAUGG, H.E., GARVEN, F.C., *Anal. Chem.* **30**, 1444 (1958).

CHAPTER 3

Determination of the Hydroxyl and Amino Groups: Base-catalyzed Acylation Methods

ACYLATING agents are convenient reagents for the determination of both alcoholic and phenolic hydroxyl groups as well as amino groups. These reagents can also be used for the determination of mercaptans and hydroperoxides, but they are not used as frequently as other methods. The reactivity of acylating agents follows this order: acid chlorides > acid anhydrides > acids. Acid anhydrides are the reagents of choice, having moderate reactivity with fewer side reactions. This chapter will outline the development of various base-catalyzed acylation methods employing both acid chlorides and anhydrides. Most of these methods employ pyridine as the catalyst and solvent and have definite limitations. In the following chapter, the more powerful acid-catalyzed methods will be discussed.

In general, acid chlorides and anhydrides are attacked by amines and hydroxyl compounds behaving as nucleophiles (N:), to give amides and esters:

Aliphatic amines are by far the best nucleophiles and react rapidly at room temperature with reagents like acetic anhydride acetyl chloride, and 3,5-dinitrobenzoyl chloride, but not with phthalic anhydride. Aromatic amines react less rapidly, requiring a short period of heating or longer reaction times at room temperature with all reagents but 3,5-dinitrobenzoyl chloride. If amines are nucleophilic enough to be determined by acylation, they are also generally basic enough to be titrated with perchloric acid in a nonaqueous solvent. Researchers have thus concentrated on using acylating agents for the determination of less nucleophilic alcohols and phenols.

Mehlenbacher[16] has reviewed acylation methods as recent as 1952, and Mathur[15a] has reviewed methods which have appeared since 1955. Recent books by Siggia[28] and Critchfield[3] have included many methods which have appeared since 1952. Acetylation and phthalation have received the most study. The usual methods involve reaction of the corresponding anhydrides with the hydroxyl compound:

$$\underset{\substack{\| \ \| \\ }}{\overset{\substack{O \ O}}{RCOCR}} + CR_3OH \rightarrow \underset{\|}{\overset{O}{RCOCR_3}} + \underset{\|}{\overset{O}{RCOH}}$$

The unreacted anhydride is hydrolyzed to the corresponding carboxylic acid which is then titrated with standard alcoholic sodium hydroxide. A blank is similarly treated. The difference between the blank and sample titrations is equivalent to the moles of hydroxyl group present.

EARLY ACYLATION METHODS

In 1887 Benedict and Ulzer[1] recorded an acylation method, using acetic anhydride, for hydroxyl groups in fatty acids. Lewkowitsch[13] simplified the method, and his method laid the groundwork for the methods to follow. Neither method appears to have utilized base-catalyzed acetylation although sodium acetate was apparently in use.[18] The first workers to report effective base catalysis were Verley and Bölsing[35] in 1901. Pyridine, in a 1:7 acetic anhydride–pyridine reagent, was used as catalyst for the acetylation of alcohols and phenols at water bath temperatures. This paper is reprinted in Part II.

Twenty years later, pyridine catalysis was again investigated for the acetylation of some sugars and phenols, by Peterson and West.[20] Their 1:2 anhydride–pyridine reagent was too concentrated for accurate work, and was modified to a 1:3 reagent in 1931 by Marks and Morrell[14] for the acetylation of a few phenols in 24 hr at room temperature or 37°C, or in 15 min at 100°. In 1934 West, Hoaglund and Curtis[37] returned to the 1:7 reagent of Verley and Bolsing, but used heat to hydrolyze the anhydride.

In 1935 Smith and Bryant[32] published their acetyl chloride method for alcohols and phenols. The reagent was 1.5 M acetyl chloride in toluene; pyridine was added separately to catalyze the reaction, as it formed a precipitate with acetyl chloride. Quantitative acetylation required 20 min at 60°C. It was shown that acetyl chloride was more reactive than acetic anhydride by comparing their reaction rates with 2,4-dimethylpentan-3-ol. In 20 min, acetylation was quantitative with acetyl chloride but only 23.9% complete with the anhydride. Smith and Bryant did not report quantitative results for amines but appear to indicate that they react to varying degrees with acetyl chloride.

In 1945 Ogg, Porter and Willits[17] proposed both macro and semimicro acetylation methods using a 1:3 anhydride–pyridine reagent[14] with a 2-min heating time for hydrolysis[37] to establish the present standard method. Their paper, including only the macro procedure, is reprinted in Part II, Chapter 13.

Phthalic anhydride, although investigated as early as 1899 by

Stephen,[33] did not undergo the development acetic anhydride did until Sabetay and Naves[22, 23] reported the pyridine catalysis of the phthalation of essential oils in 1939. In 1947 both Verbeck[34] and particularly Elving and Warshowsky[6] reported complete studies of the phthalation of simple alcohols, phenols, and amines. The former procedure, as reported by Siggia, uses a 1 M phthalic anhydride reagent in pyridine. Quantitative phthalation required 30 min to 1 hr of heating at reflux temperature (ca. 100°C) and hydrolysis at reflux temperature also. The latter procedure involved heating samples for 1 hr in a pressure bottle at 100°C, using a 0.66 M anhydride reagent in pyridine. Hydrolysis is performed by adding 50 ml of water to the sample while hot, cooling immediately thereafter, and titrating as soon as possible. The author has found that phthalic anhydride hydrolyzes quantitatively with as little as 0.5 ml of water in 5 min at room temperature.

Since phthalic anhydride is a milder reagent than acetic anhydride, it can be used to advantage in determining alcohols in the presence of phenols and aldehydes without error. In contrast, acetic anhydride reacts quantitatively with phenols and non-stoichiometrically with aldehydes.

One of the disadvantages of phthalic anhydride is that it does not react stoichiometrically with primary amines. It gives high results with aniline and ethylenediamine, probably because of phthalimide formation. It is therefore not suited for the determination of the total of, or mixtures of, alcohols and amines. Siggia and Kervenski[29] have shown that acetic anhydride can be used for this purpose. The author has also found that phthalic anhydride reacts too slowly to be of use in determining hindered secondary alcohols, such as 2-substituted cyclohexanols. Phthalation of 2-*tert*-butylcyclohexanol is only about 80% complete after 3 hr at reflux; 2-cyclohexylcyclohexanol reacts only some 90% after 2 hr at reflux.

BASE-CATALYZED HYDROLYSIS
OF ACETIC ANHYDRIDE

The titrimetric finish in all early acylation methods depended on the quantitative hydrolysis of unreacted anhydride to acid, which is then titrated with standard base. Most early workers were aware that pyridine catalyzed acetylation in some way, but apparently did not recognize that it also catalyzed the hydrolysis of acetic anhydride to acetic acid also.[9] There was only a difference of opinion about whether to hydrolyze acetic anhydride at room temperature or by heating. Verley and Bölsing [35]preferred room temperature, and Peterson and West[20] and Marks and Morrell[14] added ice water to the apparently hot reaction mixture. Ogg, Porter, and Willits[17] adopted the 2-min heating period of West and Hoaglund.[37] This is really only necessary if fatty acids are present, as mixed acid anhydrides, which hydrolyze more slowly than acetic anhydride, form. If only acetic anhydride is present, heating is not necessary because pyridine is such an excellent catalyst. Even if water (5 ml) is added to pyridine–anhydride at room temperature, the heat of hydrolysis of the anhydride is so large that the temperature rises to 40–50°C. The author has found that acetic anhydride hydrolyzes quantitatively with as little as 0.5 ml of water in 5 min at room temperature, compared to the 10 ml of water and heating used by Ogg, Porter, and Willits.

The definitive study of pyridine catalysis was published in 1953 by Gold and Jefferson.[9] They demonstrated that pyridine and other unhindered tertiary aromatic amines were remarkably efficient catalysts for the hydrolysis of acetic anhydride. Their paper is reprinted in Part II, Chapter 14. They found that the rate constant, k_p, for tertiary amine-catalyzed hydrolysis was 30,000 times greater than that for acetate ion-catalyzed hydrolysis in 50% acetone–water. Steric hindrance, not basicity, proved to be the important factor. Even though the ionization constant, K_p, of 2-methylpyridine (2-picoline) is six times larger than that of pyridine, k_p for pyridine was found to be almost 1.3 times larger than k_p was 2-methylpyridine. To compare various tertiary amines on a basis independent of their basicities, Gold and Jefferson formulated a corrected type of rate constant; R:

$$R = k_p \frac{K_w}{K_p \sqrt{[K_a(\text{HOAc})]}}$$

On this basis, R for pyridine was calculated to be 28 and R for 2-methylpyridine was found to be 3 (cf. their Table 2).

On the basis of their kinetic measurements, Gold and Jefferson proposed a two step mechanism for the hydrolysis of acetic anhydride. The first step was the fast formation of an intermediate, the pyridine–acetylium ion:

$$\overset{\text{O}\ \ \ \text{O}}{\underset{C_5H_5N: \ + \ CH_3COCCH_3}{\parallel\ \ \parallel}} \rightleftharpoons \overset{+\ \ \text{O}}{\underset{C_5H_5N:CCH_3 \ + \ CH_3CO_2^-}{\parallel}}$$

The second step was postulated to be a slow attack of water on the intermediate:

$$\overset{+\ \ \text{O}}{\underset{C_5H_5N:CCH_3 \ + \ H_2O}{\parallel}} \rightarrow C_5H_5N:H^+ \ + \ CH_3CO_2H$$

The net result is the formation of 2 molecules of acetic acid. It is very probable that the mechanism of acetylation, and also phthalation, involves the same steps except that the second step is likely to be slower.

Gold and Jefferson looked for physical evidence of a neutral association complex of the anhydride and pyridine, or the ionic intermediate, but were unable to find any. Schenk, Wines, and Mojzis[25] later found evidence for a neutral complex between triethylenediamine and the anhydride.

MODERN ACYLATION METHODS

Pyridine-catalyzed acetylation[17] and phthalation[8, 34] remained the standard acylation methods until 1959–60 when Fritz and Schenk, and Schenk and Fritz,[24] published the perchloric acid-catalyzed acetylation methods discussed in the next chapter. These papers inaugurated a burst of publications of interesting new approaches to base-catalyzed acylation. The best of these methods, the pyromellitic dianhydride method[31] and the 3,5-dinitrobenzoyl chloride method,[21] were published nearly simultaneously, in June and July of 1961.

The better, more convenient, reagent of the two was Siggia, Hanna, and Culmo's[31] pyromellitic dianhydride (PMDA). Its reactivity is more reproducible, it has less interferences, and it utilizes a visual end point with a convenient titrant, standard sodium hydroxide. This paper is reprinted in Part II, Chapter 15.

The reaction between PMDA and alcohols probably involves just one of the two anhydride groups of PMDA:

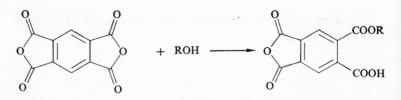

Pyridine catalyzes the reaction but PMDA is unfortunately insoluble in it. The original procedure called for 0.5 M PMDA in tetrahydrofuran, pyridine being added to the reaction flask after the 0.5 M PMDA. During the heating period, the tetrahydrofuran evaporated, resulting in a precipitate and vigorous bumping. In 1965, Harper, Siggia, and Hanna[10] reported that this could be avoided by using PMDA dissolved in a 55% dimethylsulfoxide-45% pyridine solvent. Reaction times were 15–20 min at steam bath temperatures for most alcohols. This modified procedure is also included in Part II, Chapter 15.

The advantages of PMDA over phthalic anhydride are that it is more reactive and that it reacts stoichiometrically with both primary and secondary amines. It can also be used to determine alcohols in the presence of phenols or aldehydes. Using the original method,[31] the author has found that PMDA, like phthalic anhydride, gives incomplete acylation of hindered secondary alcohols such as 2-cyclohexylcyclohexanol. It does not appear to react at all with 2-nitroaniline, but does appear to acylate 4-tert-butylcyclohexanol quantitatively. Using the modified procedure,[10] it is possible to acylate 2-tert-butylcyclohexanol in 1 hr and 2-cyclohexylcyclohexanol in 40 min. However, heating the sample and blank solutions longer than 30 min appears to cause dark brown colors which make the end point difficult to observe.

The other reagent, 3,5-dinitrobenzoyl chloride, has received limited study by Berezein,[2] who has shown in 1954 that some primary and secondary alcohols reacted quantitatively with it in pyridine. In 1960, Johnson and Critchfield[11] have also reported the colorimetric determination of alcohols using this reagent. They used an excess of the reagent in pyridine, hydrolyzed the chloride to the acid and neutralized the pyridine in one step by adding aqueous hydrochloric acid, and extracted the neutral benzoate esters away from the ionic material into hexane. They developed a color (peak at 575 mμ) by adding sodium hydroxide and acetone to the benzoate esters. Because the color reaction involves only the benzene ring, it measures only the mmoles of hydroxyl group. A separate calibration is unnecessary for different alcohols; one curve can be used for all alcohols.

In 1961, Robinson, Cundiff, and Markunas[21] published their titrimetric procedure using 3,5-dinitrobenzoyl chloride. Their method involved reaction of the sample with 4 ml of a 0.2 M solution of the chloride in pyridine at room temperature for 5 to 15 min. After reaction, about 0.5 ml of water and 25–40 ml of pyridine are added, and the solution is heated to boiling to hydrolyze the chloride to 3,5-dinitrobenzoic acid and pyridine hydrochloride. Visual or potentiometric titration, using tetrabutylammonium hydroxide in benzene–methanol, is then performed on a sample and a blank. The difference between the titrations corresponds to the amount of 3,5-dinitrobenzoate ester formed.

This procedure is extremely rapid, and is the only general base-catalyzed acylation method that can be used at room temperature, with the exception of acetylation of amines.[25, 36] Tertiary alcohols, as well as primary and secondary alcohols, react quantitatively although the reaction time may be from 3–24 hr. Aldehydes do not interfere unless present in amounts in excess of 40 mol% of the alcohol. Phenols, amines, most sugars, and two oximes were also determined routinely; no determination of sterically hindered secondary alcohols or phenols was reported.

A serious disadvantage is the difference in the reactivity of different lots of the reagent, particularly if tertiary alcohols are to be determined. The tetrabutylammonium hydroxide titrant may also not be readily available and must then be prepared by an ion exchange procedure. This reagent lacks the selectivity of the PMDA reagent and acid-catalyzed acetylation in pyridine.[24]

Other reagents that have been used for base-catalyzed acylation are p-nitrobenzoyl chloride and 3-nitrophthalic anhydride. In 1964 Scoggins[27] used the former for the determination of traces of primary and secondary alcohols by extraction of the p-nitrobenzoate esters after reaction, and spectrophotomeric measurement at 253 mμ. Floria, Dobratz, and McClure[7] in 1964 used the latter reagent for 10-min room temperature acylation of primary alcohols, especially in polymers. They used triethylamine as catalyst. Unfortunately, secondary alcohols are only partially acylated even after 120 min at room temperature. This

may be the result of a slow reaction between the bulky triethylamine–acylium ion intermediate and the more hindered secondary alcohols.

In 1964, Schenk, Wines, and Mojzis[25] found that triethylenediamine [1,4-diazabicyclo(2,2,2)octane] is a better catalyst
than pyridine for the acetylation of hydroxyl and amino groups.
The bridgehead nitrogens of this amine are almost as free from
steric hindrance in their reactions as the nitrogen of pyridine; in
addition the pK_{b_1} of 5.4 indicates that one nitrogen should be
considerably more nucleophilic than that of pyridine in forming
a triethylenediamine–acetylium ion intermediate:

$$:N\diagdown\diagup N: + CH_3\overset{O}{\overset{\|}{C}}O\overset{O}{\overset{\|}{C}}CH_3 \longrightarrow :N\diagdown\diagup \overset{+}{N}:\overset{O}{\overset{\|}{C}}CH_3 + CH_3COO^-$$

Infrared, NMR, and refractive index studies indicated the formation of an apparently neutral complex between triethylenediamine and pyridine. This may precede formation of the triethylenediamine–acetylium ion intermediate. This paper is reprinted in Part II, Chapter 16.

STERIC HINDRANCE PROBLEMS:
TERTIARY ALCOHOLS
AND ORTHO-SUBSTITUTED PHENOLS

Base-catalyzed acylation of both tertiary alcohols and ortho-
substituted phenols is usually slow, presumably because of
steric hindrance in the reaction of both with the pyridine–acylium ion. Although Verley and Bölsing[35] obtained low results
for the tertiary alcohols linalool and terpineol, it was not recognized until later[18] that this is characteristic of tertiary alcohols. Because the acetylation of tertiary alcohols has not usu-

ally been investigated beyond 1 hr,[18] it has frequently been assumed that dehydration (and polymerization) of most of the tertiary alcohol occurs in that time:

$$(CH_3)_3COH + Ac_2O \rightarrow 2HOAc + CH_2{=}CH(CH_3)_2$$

However, as shown in Table 4 for the case of *tert*-butyl alcohol, acetylation in pyridine reaches an apparent equilibrium value after about 21 hr. Thereafter, decomposition of *tert*-butyl acetate apparently occurs to produce acetic acid so that, after hydrolysis, sodium hydroxide titration indicates an apparent drop in per cent acetylation.

Table 4. Acetylation of tert-butyl alcohol
in 1:3 Ac$_2$O—C$_5$H$_5$N, ca. 90°C[26]

Time (hr)	% Acetylation
1	20
5	44
21	61–69[a]
36	48
48	40

[a] *tert*-Butyl acetate undergoes only 1.5% decomposition after 21 hr.

Elving and Warshowsky[6] reported a similar phenomenon for the phthalation of *tert*-amyl alcohol: 3% reaction after 1 hr, 5.5% reaction after 2 hr, and 10.1% reaction after 4 hr. The only base-catalyzed reagent that can be used for quantitative acylation of tertiary alcohols is apparently 3,5-dinitrobenzoyl chloride.[21] The side reactions are probably minimized because the acylation is conducted at room temperature.

It was not recognized until later that 2- and 2,6-substitution of phenols rendered them difficult to acetylate because of steric hindrance. In 1952 DeWalt and Glenn[5] published an excellent study of the acetylation of such phenols in pyridine. Acetylation of phenols such as 2,6-dimethylphenol or 2-isopropylphenol was fast, acetylation of 2-*tert*-butylphenols was slow, and acetylation of 2,6-di-*tert*-butylphenols was almost negligible. Table 5 lists some results and some of their rate constants. Schenk and Fritz[24] later showed that pyridine-catalyzed acetylation could be used to determine 2-*tert*-butylphenols in the presence of up to a ninefold excess of 2,6-di-*tert*-butylphenols in 45 min time at reflux temperatures. Obviously less hindered phenols can also be determined in the presence of the latter. Schenk and Fritz also showed that a 0.25 M acetic anhydride reagent (pyridine solvent)

Table 5. Acetylation of hindered phenols in pyridine
(Q = Quantitative)

	% Reaction: 2.5 M Ac$_2$O at *ca.* 115°C[17]	1.4–1.6 M Ac$_2$O at 118°C[5]	
		% Reaction	Rate constant
3- or 4-Substituted phenols	Q, <45 min	Q, 1 min	—
2-*tert*-Butyl-5-methylphenol	Q, 45 min[24]	80%, 10 min	1.6 × 10^{-1} M^{-1} min^{-1}
2,4-Di-*tert*-butyl-6-methylphenol[a]	—	10%, 5 min	1.1 × 10^{-2} M^{-1} min^{-1}
2,6-Di-*tert*-butyl-4-methylphenol	1%, 45 min[24]	5%, 118 min	3.9 × 10^{-4} M^{-1} min^{-1}

[a] Rate constant and % reaction determined in 3 M Ac$_2$O.

could be used to determine 3- or 4-substituted phenols in the presence of 2-*tert*-butylphenol and many 2,6-disubstituted phenols.

FUTURE RESEARCH:
APPLICATIONS TO INSTRUMENTAL ANALYSIS

Now that functional group research has provided the conditions and methods for quantitative acylation of hydroxyl and amino compounds, there is a need for instrumental methods utilizing these methods for the analysis of mixtures of these compounds after acylation.

A good example of the use of base-catalyzed acylation in gas chromatography is the work of Croituru and Freedman.[4] Although they were concerned with the separation and measurement of a mixture of o-, m-, and p-thiocresols rather than the methylphenols themselves, the principle involved is still the same: acetylation of the mixture produced acetates having larger differences in retention time than that of the thiocresols themselves. These workers acetylated the thiocresols at room temperature in 30 sec using triethylamine catalyst. After adding water, they extracted the acetates with benzene and injected the extract directly into the gas chromatographic column.

Another problem that needs instrumental study is the determination of primary and secondary hydroxyl groups in mixtures. Siggia and Hanna[30] showed that the differential kinetic method may be used for the determination of primary hydroxyl groups in the presence of secondary hydroxyl groups. Pyridine-catalyzed acetylation at room temperature was the procedure used. However, the method was not general in that large errors resulted when the amount of secondary hydroxyl group was appreciably larger than the amount of primary hydroxyl. A more general approach appears to be the NMR method of Mathias.[15] He employed base-catalyzed acetylation, using either sodium acetate or pyridine, to estimate the relative amount of primary to secondary hydroxyl groups. Acetylation resolved the peaks arising from the —CH_2—O and —CH—O resonances into easily integrated peaks about 1 ppm (δ) apart. This paper is reprinted in Part II, Chapter 17.

Yet another useful approach is infrared spectrophotometry. This has been utilized for the determination of hydroxyl groups, after pyridine-catalyzed acetylation, in oxidized polyethylene.[12] The hydroxyl band at 3300 cm^{-1} is completely lost in the shoulder of the C—H stretching band at 2900 cm^{-1}. After acetylation, the hydroxyl groups can be determined by measurement of the acetate C—O stretching band at 1245 cm^{-1}.

REFERENCES

1. BENEDICT, R., ULZER, F., *Monatsh. Chem.* **8**, 41 (1887).
2. BEREZEIN, I. V., *Doklady, Akad. Nauk S.S.S.R.* **99**, 563 (1954).
3. CRITCHFIELD, F. E., *Organic Functional Group Analysis*, pp. 81–106, Pergamon Press, New York, 1963.
4. CROITURU, P. P., FREEDMAN, R. W., *Anal. Chem.* **34**, 1536 (1962).
5. DEWALT, C. W., GLENN, R. A., *Ibid.* **24**, 1789 (1952).
6. ELVING, P. J., WARSHOWSKY, B., *Ibid.* **19**, 1006 (1947).
7. FLORIA, J. A., DOBRATZ, I. W., MCCLURE, J. H., *Ibid.* **36**, 2053 (1964).
8. FREED, M., WYNNE, A. M., *Ind. Eng. Chem., Anal. Ed.* **8**, 278 (1936).
9. GOLD, V., JEFFERSON, E. G., *J. Chem. Soc.* 409 (1953).
10. HARPER, R., SIGGIA, S., HANNA, J. G., *Anal. Chem.* **37**, 600 (1965).
11. JOHNSON, D. P., CRITCHFIELD, F. E., *Ibid.* **32**, 865 (1960).
12. KRAMM, D. E., LOMONTE, J. N., MOYER, J. P., *Ibid.* **36**, 2170 (1964).
13. LEWKOWITSCH, J., *J. Soc. Chem. Ind.* **16**, 503 (1897).
14. MARKS, S., MORRELL, R. S., *Analyst* **56**, 428 (1931).
15. MATHIAS, A., *Anal. Chim. Acta* **13**, 598 (1964).
15a. MATHUR, N. K., *Talanta* **13**, 1601 (1966).
16. MEHLENBACHER, V. C., *Organic Analysis*, Vol. 1, pp. 1–65, Interscience, New York, 1953.
17. OGG, C. L., PORTER, W. L., WILLITS, C. O., *Ind. Eng. Chem., Anal. Ed.* **17**, 394 (1945).
18. OLLEMAN, E. D., *Anal. Chem.* **24**, 1425 (1952).
19. PETERSON, J. W., HEDBERG, K. W., CHRISTENSEN, B. E., *Ibid.* **15**, 225 (1943).
20. PETERSON, V. L., WEST, E. S., *J. Biol. Chem.* **74**, 379 (1927).
21. ROBINSON, W. T., CUNDIFF, R. H., MARKUNAS, P. C., *Anal. Chem.* **33**, 1030 (1961).
22. SABETAY, S., NAVES, Y. R., *Ann. chim. anal. chim. appl.* **19**, 285 (1937).
23. SABETAY, S., NAVES, Y. R., *Ibid.* **21**, 289 (1939).

24. SCHENK, G.H., FRITZ, J.S., *Anal. Chem.* **32,** 987 (1960).
25. SCHENK, G.H., WINES, P., MOJZIS, *Ibid.* **36,** 914 (1964).
26. SCHENK, G.H., VANCE, P.W., MOJZIS, Unpublished results, Wayne State University, 1964.
27. SCOGGINS, M.W., *Anal. Chem.* **36,** 1152 (1964).
28. SIGGIA, S., *Quantitative Organic Analysis via Functional Groups,* 3rd ed., pp. 8–72, Wiley, New York, 1963.
29. SIGGIA, S., KERVENSKI, I.R., *Anal. Chem.* **23,** 117 (1951).
30. SIGGIA, S., HANNA, J.G., *Ibid.* **33,** 896 (1961).
31. SIGGIA, S., HANNA, J.G., CULMO, R., *Ibid.* **33,** 900 (1961).
32. SMITH, D.M., BRYANT, W.M.D., *J. Amer. Chem. Soc.* **57,** 61 (1935).
33. STEPHEN, K., *J. prakt. Chem.* **60,** 248 (1899).
34. VERBECK, G., talk at Chicago A.C.S. Section, Jan. 24, 1947; from Siggia, S., *Quantitative Organic Analysis via Functional Groups,* p. 7, Wiley, New York, 1949.
35. VERLEY, A., BÖLSING, F., *Ber.* **34,** 3354 (1901).
36. VOGEL, A.I., *Elementary Practical Organic Chemistry,* Part 3, pp. 676 to 697, Longsman, Green, London, 1958.
37. WEST, E.S., HOAGLUND, C.L., CURTIS, G., *J. Biol. Chem.* **104,** 627 (1936).

CHAPTER 4

Determination of Hydroxyl Groups and Alkoxysilanes: Acid-catalyzed Acetylation Methods

THE PREVIOUS chapter discussed base-catalyzed acylation methods and some of the·general considerations involved in using acid chlorides, acid anhydrides, and carboxylic acids as reagents. In all but a few cases, pyridine was the solvent and catalyst for these methods. The use of pyridine limits the scope of these methods to hydroxyl compounds of moderate reactivity; e.g., compounds which are not too hindered to react readily with the bulky pyridine–acylium ion intermediate.

In contrast, acid-catalyzed acetylation has no such limitation because the acetylium ion intermediate is small and very reactive. In addition, a variety of solvents and acid catalysts can be used. The acids that have been used include perchloric acid, sulfuric acid, phosphoric acid, granular zinc metal, boron trifluoride, and p-toluenesulfonic acid. Two important classes of compounds that can be determined by such methods are hydroxyl compounds and alkoxylsilanes. They react as follows:

$$CH_3\overset{O}{\overset{\|}{C}}OC\overset{O}{\overset{\|}{C}}CH_3 + \begin{cases} R_3COH & CH_3COCR_3 + CH_3CO_2H \\ R_3SiOR & \rightarrow CH_3CO_2SiR_3 + CH_3CO_2R \end{cases}$$

The alkoxysilanes produce an acetoxysilane and an acetate ester, as shown. This determination is impossible using base-catalyzed

45

acetylation since no reaction is observed; thus it illustrates the versatility of acid catalysis.

Olleman[24] has reviewed acid-catalyzed methods prior to 1952 and recent books by Siggia[35] and Critchfield[6] have included some evaluation of the perchloric acid-catalyzed acetylation method of Fritz and Schenk.[11] The analytical finish is usually the same for this type of method as for the base-catalyzed methods. Pyridine and water are added to hydrolyze the unreacted anhydride to acetic acid at room temperature, and the acid is titrated with standard sodium hydroxide. A blank is similarly titrated, and the difference between the blank and sample is equivalent to the number of multiequivalents of hydroxyl groups present.

EARLY ACID-CATALYZED ACETYLATION METHODS

Acid-catalyzed acetylation does not appear to have undergone the progressive development that has characterized base-catalyzed acylation. Instead it has developed sporadically. The earliest method employing acid catalysis appears to be that of Franchimont[10] in 1879. He added concentrated sulfuric acid dropwise to a solution of the alcohol in acetic anhydride, chilled the mixture, and isolated the acetate for saponification later. Thereafter no new approaches appeared, but in 1928 a kinetic study[5] of the acetylation of 2-naphthol revealed that perchloric acid was a much better catalyst than sulfuric acid or pyridine. In 1938, hydrogen electrode measurements[28] of the "pH" of 30% acetic anhydride-acetic acid solutions revealed that although sulfuric acid was initially much stronger than perchloric acid in this solvent mixture, it slowly decomposes to the less acidic sulfoacetic acid, $HO_3SCH_2CO_2H$.

In 1934 Sabetay[29] published a phosphoric acid-catalyzed acetylation method for the determination of hydroxyl groups in essential oils. It employed mild conditions: 15 min reaction and a temperature below 50°C. Unfortunately, tertiary alcohols dehydrated under these conditions so that only primary and secondary alcohols could be determined. In 1935 Toennies and Elliot[37] published their first study of acid-catalyzed acetylation using perchloric acid and primarily 2,4-dinitrobenzenesulfonic acid, a strongly ionized acid. Unfortunately, they used such low concentrations of acid (0.002–0.004 M) and such low concentrations of alcohols that they were not able to achieve quantitative results in less than 1 hr in acetonitrile as solvent. They also did not employ base-catalyzed hydrolysis of the unreacted anhydride; acid-catalysis required 80 min for quantitative conversion to acetic acid.

In 1940 Bryant, Smith, and Mitchell[2] reported that boron trifluoride catalyzed esterification of alcohols; they heated alcohols in glacial acetic acid at 67°C for 2 hr:

$$R_3COH + CH_3CO_2H \xrightarrow{BF_3} CH_3CO_2CR_3 + H_2O$$

Pyridine was added to complex the boron trifluoride after reaction, and the water produced was determined by the Karl Fischer titration. Both *tert*-butyl and *tert*-amyl alcohols reacted quantitatively, but terpineol, also a tertiary alcohol, gave 114% reaction. As acetic acid is a less reactive acylating agent than an anhydride or acid chloride, this method might be expected to require the 2 hr long reaction time. In contrast, Valentin[39] used acetic anhydride in dioxane and fluoboric acid catalyst and obtained quantitative results after 5 min heating on the steam bath.

In 1942 Toennies, Kolb, and Sakami[38] reported perchloric acid-catalyzed acetylation in glacial acetic acid of hydroxyl groups on amino acids, but again their conditions were such that the method required 2 hr at room temperature. Thus, the full potential of this catalyst remained unrealized; it was to remain thus for 17 more years.

MECHANISM OF ACID-CATALYZED ACETYLATION

An understanding of the mechanism of any analytical reaction enables the analyst to:

(a) Select optimum conditions for the method.
(b) Broaden the scope of the method to include as many different types of compounds as possible.
(c) Adjust conditions to avoid interferences from other substances.
(d) Predict the effect of solvent, steric hindrance, and different substituents on the rate of the reaction.

Proof for the mechanism of perchloric acid-catalyzed ionization of acetic anhydride appears to have been first reported by Burton and Praill[3] in 1950. They found evidence for the postulated formation of the acetylium ion (Ac^+) from acetic anhydride (Ac_2O) and perchloric acid:

$$Ac_2O + H^+ \rightleftharpoons Ac_2OH^+ \rightleftharpoons Ac^+ + HOAc$$

They added anisole to a mixture of these reagents below room temperature and obtained high yields of p-methoxyacetophenone. They were able to deduce that the above ionization steps were fast compared to the rate-determining acetylation of anisole by either the acetylium ion or the acetic anhydrium ion (Ac_2OH^+):

$$MeOC_6H_5 + \left\{ \begin{array}{l} Ac^+ \\ Ac_2OH^+ \end{array} \right. \rightarrow MeOC_6H_4COCH_3 + \left\{ \begin{array}{l} H^+ \\ H_2OAc^+ \end{array} \right.$$

Later Burton and Praill[4] reported that the mixture of acetic anhydride and perchloric acid slowly turned yellow, then orange, then red, and finally deposited a crystalline perchlorate and some tar. They postulated that a condensation of the acetylium ion with acetic anhydride (enolic form) occurs:

$$CH_3\overset{+}{C}O + CH_2 {=} \overset{HO\ O}{\overset{|\ ||}{COCCH_3}} \longrightarrow CH_3\overset{O}{\overset{||}{C}}CH_2\overset{O}{\overset{||}{C}}O\overset{O}{\overset{||}{C}}CH_3 \xrightarrow{(CH_3\overset{+}{C}O)} tar\ +\ perchlorate$$

They also established that increasing the concentration of acetic acid reduced the formation of side reactions such as this and the rate of acetylation of anisole,[3] as would be predicted from the equation for the ionization of acetic anhydride.

MODERN METHODS: DETERMINATION OF HYDROXYL GROUPS

In 1954, Pesez[25] published the first modern acid-catalyzed method for hydroxyl (and amino) groups. His reagent was 0.15 M p-toluenesulfonic acid catalyst and 1 M proprionic anhydride in glacial acetic acid solvent. This acid is not as strongly ionized in this type of solvent as perchloric or sulfuric acid,[28] and would not be expected to be as effective a catalyst. In addition, the acetic acid probably retards the ionization of the proprionic anhydride. It is not surprising that quantitative acylation of hydroxyl groups required 2 hr at room temperature. However, the reagent can also be safely heated so that quantitative results can also be achieved after 30 min at 100 °C. The unreacted anhydride was determined by adding a measured excess of 0.1 M aniline in benzene, and after 5 min, back titrating the unreacted aniline with 0.1 M perchloric acid in glacial acetic acid:

$$C_6H_5NH_2 + (C_2H_5CO)_2O \rightarrow C_6H_5NH(C_2H_5CO) + C_2H_5CO_2H$$

$$C_6H_5NH_2 + HClO_4 \rightarrow C_6H_5NH_3^+ ClO_4^-$$

A blank was also run, and the difference between the blank and sample titrations gave the milliequivalents of hydroxyl groups.

Most secondary alcohols were determined by heating at 100° rather than by reaction at room temperature. Pesez reported results for three tertiary alcohols: *tert*-butyl alcohol reacted about 90% at 100°, *tert*-amyl alcohol reacted about 97.5% at 100°, and triphenylcarbinol reacted quantitatively at this temperature.

Early in 1959, Mesnard and Bertucat[23] published a phosphoric acid-catalyzed acetylation method which began an era of intense research activity in the field. They used a reagent approximately 0.35 M phosphoric acid and 3 M acetic anhydride in dioxane solvent. Most primary and secondary alcohols were acetylated in 6 hr at room temperature; many tertiary alcohols reacted quantitatively after 24 hr at room temperature. Phenols reacted incompletely. They also found that the addition of pyridine after the reaction permitted rapid room-temperature hydrolysis of the unreacted anhydride. Although this method is not rapid, it illustrates that very mild reagents, as well as very reactive reagents, can be made with acid catalysts. For this reason, this paper is reprinted in Part II, Chapter 18.

Later in 1959 Fritz and Schenk[11] reported two rapid perchloric acid-catalyzed acetylation methods for alcohols. In 1960, Schenk and Fritz[31] extended the methods to the determination of phenols, thiols, and amines. The more reactive reagent consisted of 0.15 M perchloric acid catalyst and 2 M acetic anhydride in ethyl acetate or other aprotic solvents. Quantitative reaction was achieved in 5 min at room temperature. Together with the 5-min hydrolysis of the anhydride to acetic acid at room temperature, this method remains at this time the most rapid and convenient of any base- or acid-catalyzed acylation methods. However, the reagent is quite reactive, has many interferences, and also develops the yellow color which was observed to darken gradually to red by Burton and Praill.[4] Magnuson and Cerri[22] later reported that 1,2-dichloroethane was superior to ethyl acetate was solvent in that the reagent remained colorless or very light yellow, and was stable for at least 2 months. This report is reprinted in Part II, Chapter 20, directly following the first paper of Fritz and Schenk, Chapter 19.

The less reactive reagent of Fritz and Schenk consisted of 0.15 M perchloric acid and 2 M acetic anhydride in pyridine solvent. (Even though pyridine is present, perchloric acid acts as the primary catalyst. A mechanism can be written to rationalize this.[11]) Quantitative reaction was obtained at room temperature, but the reaction time depends on the reactivity and steric bulk of the alcohol among other factors. Although Fritz and Schenk found that some primary alcohols reacted in 5–10 min, Critchfield[6] recommended 30 min at 25°C for many primary alcohols, and 60–120 min for secondary alcohols. Kloucek, Gasparic, and Obruba[17] found that the room temperature is critical for this reagent, and that secondary alcohols could be acetylated in 20 min only at 40°C. Nevertheless, because the reagent employs mild conditions at room temperatures, it is more convenient than most base-catalyzed acylation methods and is therefore widely used. A good example of its utility is the estimation of primary or secondary alcohols in the presence of tertiary alcohols.[11] The former were acetylated in 10–70 min at room temperature with no more than 1% error, even in the presence of a twofold excess of tertiary alcohols. Delahy and Sabetay[7] have previously reported this type of analysis for hydroxyl groups in essential oils using pyridine-catalyzed acetylation at steam bath temperatures. They did not, however, include any experimental data for such mixtures.

A number of acid catalyzed acetylation methods were published in rapid succession after the first two papers of Fritz and Schenk. In 1960, Kyriacou[18] reported that granular zinc metal could be used to catalyze acetylation of polyglycols, using acetyl chloride at room temperature. In 1961, Schenk[30] published a modification of perchloric acid catalyzed acetylation in pyridine that was suitable for ketoximes and vic-dioximes. The reaction produces an oxime acetate:

$$R_2C{=}NO{-}H + Ac_2O \xrightarrow{HClO_4,C_5H_5N} R_2C{=}NO{-}Ac + HOAc$$

This method is superior to acetylating oximes in refluxing pyridine (without perchloric acid) because dark colors are produced which obscure the end point. In addition oxime acetates may hydrolyze in the hot water used to hydrolyze the anhydride. (The author has since found that some ketoximes may be acetylated at room temperature in 30 min or less, using 1:3 pyridine acetic anhydride without perchloric acid catalyst.)

In 1962, Stetzler and Smullin[36] used p-toluenesulfonic acid catalyst for 15-min acetylation of hydroxyl groups in polyoxyalkylene ethers at 50 °C. This avoids the perchloric acid cleavage of the ether groups with accompanying results of 117–129% acetylation. In the same year, Schenk and Santiago[32] devised a micro-acetylation method using a dilute 0.06 M acetic anhydride reagent. The concentration of 0.007 M perchloric acid catalyst was about double that used in 1935 by Toennies and Elliot,[37] but it was effective enough in ethyl acetate to permit determination of 0.05–0.1 meq of hydroxyl group. This paper is reprinted in Part II, Chapter 21. It was a considerable improvement over existing micro-methods because the reagent was dilute enough to be measured with a 5 ml pipet, room temperature conditions being used, and only 20 min reaction time was needed. The micro-method of Peterson, Hedberg, and Christiansen[26] could determine smaller amounts, but the reagent had to be weighed because it was concentrated, and the reaction required 25 hr at room temperature.

In 1964, Jordan[16] applied perchloric acid-catalyzed acetylation to the determination of hydroxyl groups in adducts of propylene oxide and straight chain alcohols. Hexane was used as co-solvent with ethyl acetate. No degradation of ether linkages was observed in 10 min.

MODERN METHODS AND STERICALLY-HINDERED HYDROXYL GROUPS

In Chapter 3, the problem of steric hindrance in pyridine-catalyzed acylation was discussed. Compared to the bulk of any pyridine–acylium ion intermediate, the acetylium ion intermediate generated by acid is quite small, and should react rapidly. An excellent illustration is the difference in the rates of pyridine-catalyzed and acid-catalyzed acetylation of 2-*tert*-butylcyclohexanols. The *cis* isomer exists essentially in the equilibrium conformation having the hydroxyl group in the hindered, less reactive, axial position[13] whereas the hydroxyl group in the *trans* isomer is essentially equatorial:

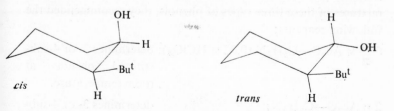

Both of these acetylate slowly in pyridine: no rate constants are reported,[13] but at 0°C the *trans* isomer acetylates in 2 hr whereas the *cis* isomer requires 2 days. (Second order rate constants in acetic anhydride–pyridine have been determined[9] for the corresponding *trans*- and *cis*-4-*tert*-butyl-cyclohexanols; they are $10.65 \times 10^{-5} \text{ M}^{-1} \text{ sec}^{-1}$ and $2.89 \times 10^{-5} \text{ M}^{-1} \text{ sec}^{-1}$ at 25°C, respectively.) In contrast, perchloric acid-catalyzed acetylation of both isomers is complete in 5 min at room temperature.[11] (Even the very reactive pyromellitic dianhydride method discussed in Chapter 3 requires 60 min for quantitative acylation of these isomers.)

Another good example of the greater reactivity of perchloric acid-catalyzed acetylation is the acetylation of hindered phenols. Table 5 in Chapter 3 summarizes the limitations of base-catalyzed acetylation of such phenols. For example, the substitution of two *ortho*-tertiary butyl groups on a phenol almost completely blocks the approach of an intermediate such as the pyridine–acylium ion; yet Schenk and Fritz[31] found that such 2,6-*di-tert*-butylphenols could be quantitatively acetylated in 5 min at room temperature. (Infrared examination of the product indicates the presence of an acetate ester and the absence of a hydroxyl group.)

Schenk and Fritz[31] also found that a dilute 0.25 M acetic anhydride–pyridine reagent (0.02 M perchloric acid) could be used to determine 3- or 4-substituted phenols in the presence of 2-*tert*-butylphenols or 2,6-di-*tert*-butylphenols. For the analysis of mixtures of these three types of phenols, they recommended the following reagents:

0.25 M Ac_2O—C_5H_5N (0.02 M $HClO_4$): determines 3- or 4-substituted phenols at room temperature.

2 M Ac_2O—C_5H_5N: determines 3- or 4-substituted phenols plus 2-*tert*-butylphenols at reflux.

2 M Ac_2—EtOAc (0.15 M $HClO_4$): determines total of above plus 2,6-di-*tert*-butylphenols at room temperature.

Acid-catalyzed acetylation also has the potential to provide a quantitative method for tertiary alcohols. The problem is to select a reagent and reaction times which will minimize side reactions which compete with acetylation of the tertiary hydroxyl group. We[34] have found that a reagent composed of 0.2 M acetic anhydride and dilute perchloric acid in triethyl phosphate solvent permits one to estimate some tertiary alcohols, including *tert*-butyl alcohol. Apparently the phosphoryl oxygen of triethyl phosphate is basic enough to reduce the catalytic activity of the perchloric acid but not so basic as to prevent catalysis of acetylation. Thus the reactivity of perchloric acid in triethyl phosphate is somewhat in between its reactivity in ethyl acetate and its reactivity in pyridine.

During the acetylation of *tert*-butyl alcohol in triethyl phosphate, the principal side reaction appears to the first order acid-catalyzed decomposition of the product *tert*-butyl acetate:

$$\text{Bu}^t\text{OAc} \xrightarrow{\text{[HClO}_4\text{, Ac}_2\text{O, (EtO)}_3\text{PO]}} \text{HOAc} + \text{olefin}$$

At 25°C, this reaction has a first order rate constant of about $4.6 \times 10^{-5} \text{ sec}^{-1}$ in the 0.2 M acetic anhydride–triethyl phosphate reagent.[34] During the 3-min reaction time necessary for *tert*-butyl alcohol, it can be calculated that roughly less than 1 % of the *tert*-butyl acetate will decompose (*assuming* simple first order kinetics). The reaction mixture is then chilled to 0°C during hydrolysis to retard this decomposition even more.

MODERN METHODS: DETERMINATION
OF ALKOXYSILANES

Until 1963, the routine analysis of alkoxysilanes was tedious and complicated. Only the methoxy, ethoxy, and propoxy groups could be determined by the Zeisel–hydriodic acid cleavage method. Alkoxysilanes could be hydrolyzed to alcohols, and the alcohols could then be determined after separation. An understanding and application of the mechanism of acid-catalyzed acetylation led to Magnuson's[20] development of a rapid determination of this functional group in 1963. For a compound such as trimethylethoxysilane, the mechanism predicts:

$$Me_3SiOEt + Ac^+ \rightarrow Me_3Si\overset{+}{\underset{Ac}{OEt}} \xrightarrow{(Ac_2O)} Me_3SiOAc + EtOAc + Ac^+$$

When the pyridine–water hydrolysis reagent is added to hydrolyze acetic anhydride, the trimethylacetoxysilane instantly and quantitatively hydrolyzes also to the corresponding silanol and acetic acid:

$$Me_3SiOAc + H_2O \rightarrow Me_3SiOH + HOAc$$

The usual sodium hydroxide titration then indicates the amount of ethyl acetate formed in the first reaction. This is equivalent to the amount of trimethylethoxysilane present. This paper is reprinted in Part II, Chapter 22. In 1965, Dostal, Cermak, and Novatna[8] independently used the acetylation method for various aroxysilanes and alkoxysilanes.

In 1964, Berger and Magnuson[1] applied this method to the determination of mercaptosilanes as well, and in 1965, Magnuson and Knaub[21] did the same for the determination of alkoxy- and mercaptogermanes. Finally, in 1966, Magnuson and Cerri[22] found that 1,2-dichloroethane was superior to ethyl acetate as solvent for acetylation of alkoxysilanes as well as hydroxyl groups.

APPLICATIONS TO INSTRUMENTAL ANALYSIS AND FUTURE RESEARCH

In contrast to other functional group methods, instrumental applications of acid-catalyzed acetylation appeared very quickly after publication of the original methods. In 1960, a year after the initial publication, acid-catalyzed acetylation in pyridine was utilized by Reynolds, Walker, and Cochran[27] for the photometric titration of aromatic amines with acetic anhydride titrant. Dry hydrogen chloride was absorbed into the pyridine to provide the acid catalyst. The disappearance of the free amine was followed in the ultraviolet region of the spectrum where the amide product did not absorb. In 1961, Kyriacou[19] performed the same sort of titration in the near infrared region, using his granular zinc catalyst and acetyl chloride.

In 1962, Genest and Farmilo[12] reported the infrared spectrophotometric determination of morphine and codeine in opium after extraction of these alkaloids and their conversion to acetates by perchloric acid-catalyzed acetylation in ethyl acetate. The morphine could not be directly analyzed by infrared spectrophotometry because of its poor solubility in suitable solvents such as carbon tetrachloride. Acid-catalyzed acetylation quickly converts the morphine into diacetylmorphine, which is soluble in carbon tetrachloride and can be determined using a wavelength of 1038 cm^{-1}.

In 1962, Gutnikov and Schenk[14] reported a spectrophotometric determination of hydroxyl groups using ferric hydroxamate, after acid-catalyzed acetylation in pyridine at room temperature. After acetylation, the excess acetic anhydride is hydrolyzed with a minimum of water, and the acetate ester is converted to the anion of the corresponding hydroxamic acid with basic hydroxylamine:

$$\underset{\displaystyle CH_3COR}{\overset{\displaystyle O \atop \|}{}} + NH_2OH + OH^- \rightarrow \underset{\displaystyle CH_3CNHO^-}{\overset{\displaystyle O \atop \|}{}} + ROH + H_2O$$

Finally, acidic iron(III) perchloric is added to form the purple-colored chelate of the hydroxamic acid and iron(III):

$$nCH_3CNHOH + Fe^{+3} \rightarrow (CH_3CNHO^-)_nFe^{+3} + nH^+$$

The chelate is measured spectrophotometrically at 524 mμ. The average molar absorptivity is about 1200 M^{-1} cm^{-1} so that it appears a charge transfer transition is involved in the excited state (see Chapter 7).

In 1963, Haken[15] published a gas chromatographic method for the analysis of mixtures containing alcohols. He used p-toluenesulfonic acid-catalyzed acetylation (as well as acetyl chloride instead of the anhydride plus acid) to remove hydroxyl peaks and also measured the resulting ester peaks. That same year, Schenk, Santiago, and Wines[33] reported that perchloric acid-catalyzed acetylation could be used to weaken the π basicity of phenols, aromatic amines, and mercaptans so that tetracyanoethylene might be used to π complex with aromatic hydrocarbons or aryl ethers present in the same solution. (See Chapter 7.) Pyridine-catalyzed acetylation could not be used since pyridine complexes strongly with tetracyanoethylene.

Many other applications undoubtedly have been reported or will be developed in the future with this versatile method. For example, it should be possible to develop a ferric hydroxamate method for alkoxysilanes, based on the acetate ester produced. Many other such possibilities also exist.

REFERENCES

1. BERGER, A., MAGNUSON, J.A., *Anal. Chem.* **36**, 1156 (1964).
2. BRYANT, W.M.D., MITCHELL, J., SMITH, D.M., *J. Amer. Chem. Soc.* **62**, 1 (1940).
3. BURTON, H., PRAILL, P.F.G., *J. Chem. Soc.* 1203 (1950).
4. BURTON, H., PRAILL, P.F.G., *Ibid.* 827 (1953).
5. CONANT, J.B., BRAMANN, G.M., *J. Amer. Chem. Soc.* **50**, 2305 (1928).
6. CRITCHFIELD, F.E., *Organic Functional Group Analysis*, pp. 81–106, Pergamon Press, New York, 1963.
7. DELAHY, R., SABETAY, S., *Bull. Soc. chim. France* 1716 (1935).
8. DOSTAL, P., CERMAK, J., NOVATNA, B., *Coll. Czech. Chem. Comm.* **30**, 34 (1965).
9. ELIEL, E.L., LUKACH, C.A., *J. Amer. Chem. Soc.* **79**, 5986 (1957).
10. FRANCHIMONT, M., *Compt. rend.* **89**, 711 (1879).

11. FRITZ, J.S., SCHENK, G.H., *Anal. Chem.* **31**, 1808 (1959).
12. GENEST, K., FARMILO, C., *Anal. Chem.* **34**, 1464 (1962).
13. GOERING, H.L., REEVES, R.L., ESPY, H.H., *J. Amer. Chem. Soc.* **78**, 4926 (1956).
14. GUTNIKOV, G., SCHENK, G.H., *Anal. Chem.* **34**, 1316 (1962).
15. HAKEN, J.K., *J. Gas Chromatography* **1**, 30 (1963).
16. JORDAN, D.E., *J. Amer. Oil Chem. Soc.* **41**, 500 (1964).
17. KLOUCEK, B., GASPARIC, J., OBRUBA, K., *Coll. Czech. Chem. Comm.* **28**, 1606 (1963).
18. KYRIACOU, D., *Anal. Chem.* **32**, 292 (1960).
19. KYRIACOU, D., *Ibid.* **33**, 153 (1961).
20. MAGNUSON, J.A., *Ibid.* **35**, 1487 (1963).
21. MAGNUSON, J.A., KNAUB, E.W., *Ibid.* **37**, 1607 (1965).
22. MAGNUSON, J.A., CERRI, R.J., *Ibid.* **38**, 1088 (1966).
23. MESNARD, P., BERTUCAT, M., *Bull. soc. chim. France* 307 (1959).
24. OLLEMAN, E.D., *Anal. Chem.* **24**, 1425 (1952).
25. PESEZ, M., *Bull. soc. chim. France* 1237 (1954).
26. PETERSON, J.W., HEDBERG, K.W., CHRISTIANSEN, B.E., *Ind. Eng. Chem., Anal. Ed.* **15**, 225 (1943).
27. REYNOLDS, C.A., WALKER, F.H., COCHRAN, E., *Anal. Chem.* **32**, 983 (1960).
28. RUSSELL, J., CAMERON, A.E., *J. Amer. Chem. Soc.* **60**, 1345 (1938).
29. SABETAY, S., *Compt. rend.* **199**, 1419 (1934).
30. SCHENK, G.H., *Anal. Chem.* **33**, 299 (1961).
31. SCHENK, G.H., FRITZ, J.S., *Ibid.* **32**, 987 (1960).
32. SCHENK, G.H., SANTIAGO, M., *Microchem. J.*, **VI**, 77 (1962).
33. SCHENK, G.H., SANTIAGO, M., WINES, P., *Anal. Chem.* **35**, 167 (1963).
34. SCHENK, G.H., VANCE, P.W., MOJZIS, C., Unpublished results, Wayne State University, 1964.
35. SIGGIA, S., *Quantitative Organic Analysis via Functional Groups*, 3rd ed., p. 8–72, Wiley, New York, 1963.
36. STETZLER, R.S., SMULLIN, C.F., *Anal. Chem.* **34**, 194 (1962).
37. TOENNIES, G., ELLIOT, M., *J. Amer. Chem. Soc.* **57**, 2136 (1935).
38. TOENNIES, G., KOLB, J.J., SAKAMI, W., *J. Biol. Chem.* **144**, 193, 219 (1942).
39. VALENTIN, F.H.H., *J. S. African Chem. Inst.* [*N.S.*] **2**, 59 (1949).

CHAPTER 5

Determination of the Epoxide Group: Quantitative Ring Opening Methods

THREE and four membered rings are inherently unstable and have been found to react quantitatively with many reagents which open the ring to give stable acyclic compounds. Some general types of compounds that can be determined in this manner are the 1,2-epoxide or oxirane (I), the 1,3-epoxide or oxetane (II), and the ethylenimine or aziridine (III):

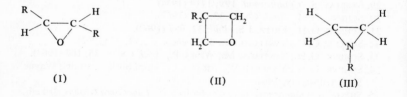

$$(I) \qquad\qquad (II) \qquad\qquad (III)$$

This chapter will outline mainly the development of functional group methods for the 1,2-epoxide function. These methods are not applicable to 1,2-epoxides having a tertiary carbon so that there must be at least one hydrogen on each carbon of the ring, as shown in formula I.

Jungnickel et al.[16] have reviewed 1,2-epoxide methods from the earliest work until 1952, and Critchfield's 1963 monograph[4] contains an evaluation of some of these methods as well as more recent methods. The mechanism for most of these methods involves nucleophilic substitution in either the first or second step of the reaction. Methods conducted in neutral or basic solution involve a slow nucleophilic attack by a good nucleophile (N:) in the first step; in the second step a proton is rapidly transferred to the negatively charged intermediate from the solvent. This will be illustrated later for thiosulfate ion as a nucleophile. An excess of the nucleophile is usually added; the unreacted nucleophile may then be back titrated to determine the per cent reaction.

The first methods used for 1,2-epoxides involved adding a measured excess of a strongly ionized acid (H^+N^-) to the sample. The acid "adds" to the 1,2-epoxide in two steps. The first step is the rapid protonation of the 1,2-epoxide:

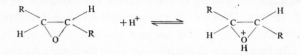

The nucleophilic anion (N^-) then attacks the protonated epoxide in a slower step which opens the ring and completes the "addition" of the acid to the epoxide:

If water or alcohol are present as solvent (ROH), a competing reaction will be:

If the unreacted acid is back titrated with standard base, this side reaction will obviously give low results. Many of the early methods discussed below are subject to this type of error. Frequently a typical impurity in epoxides will be 1,2-diols which result from hydrolysis of the 1,2-epoxide as a result of moisture in the sample.

EARLY ACID ADDITION METHODS

All of the early methods involving the addition of an acid appear to have employed dry hydrogen chloride or aqueous hydrochloric acid to convert the 1,2-epoxide to a *trans*-chlorohydrin. The only variations appear to be the solvent and reaction conditions. The mechanism of the reaction was not understood so that the poor nucleophilicity of the chloride ion could not be appreciated. In fact, Deckert,[5] who appears to have developed the first method, thought that sodium chloride and water reacted with ethylene oxide (epoxide) to give the chlorohydrin plus sodium hydroxide. He believed the function of the hydrochloric acid was to neutralize the sodium hydroxide produced. Furtunately, he used a solution of concentrated sodium chloride (plus dilute acid) so that the high concentration of chloride ion increased the rate of the slow nucleophilic displacement step.

Two years later, in 1932, Lubatti[19] made a careful study of Deckert's aqueous method and found that no reaction occurred, unless hydrochloric acid was present with the sodium chloride. He also found that the heating used by Deckert was unnecessary, the reaction requiring 10 min at room temperature. He further discovered that increasing the concentration of sodium chloride increased the per cent reaction, but that even with nearly saturated sodium chloride, no more than 93.5 % reaction of ethylene oxide could be attained. By substituting saturated magnesium chloride for sodium chloride, Lubatti obtained results as high as 99.7 % ethylene oxide. He was not fully aware of the mechanism either and speculated that the salt might increase the activity of the acid and that it might bind the water of solution and thus hinder the competing side reaction of hydrolysis.

In 1930, Nicolet and Poulter[20] published a method which was the first step in the direction research was later to take. During a fundamental investigation of epoxidation reactions, they evolved a nonaqueous method using a measured excess of 0.1 to 0.2 N dry hydrogen chloride in diethyl ether. The unreacted acid was back titrated with standard base. Their choice of solvent eliminated the side reaction of the protonated epoxide with water, or alcoholic solvent. Unfortunately, this precluded the use of salts to increase the rate of the slow nucleophilic attack of chloride so that 2 hr was required for complete reaction. Selected portions of this paper are reprinted in Part II, Chapter 23. Later Swern et al.[23] developed this method further and showed that 3 hr reaction at room temperature was sufficient for all types of 1,2-epoxides.

A considerable improvement over this approach was reported in 1949 by King[18] who used 0.12–0.18 N hydrochloric acid in dioxane. He found that a strictly anhydrous reagent was unnecessary and simply added concentrated hydrochloric acid to purified dioxane. Only 10 min reaction time at room temperature was needed, and hydrolysis of the epoxide was apparently not a problem. Stenmark[21] later modified King's method by using the Volhard method to determine unreacted hydrochloric acid instead of back titrating with sodium hydroxide.

In 1950 the final development in the hydrogen chloride methods appeared.[4, 16] This was the use of 0.2–0.5 M hydrogen chloride in pyridine; i.e., the pyridinium chloride methods. Pyridine lowers the hydrogen ion concentration so that temperatures of 100 °C or higher for 20–30 min are necessary, but it also decreases the rate of side reactions such as hydrolysis and isomerization to negligible levels. The unreacted acid is routinely titrated with standard base. Isomerization of styrene epoxide (1,2-epoxyethylbenzene) is almost negligible: 93% reaction was obtained. Keen[17] later employed the same system for the determination of 1,3-epoxides (oxetanes):

$$
\begin{array}{c}
R_2C\text{——}CH_2 \\
|\qquad\quad| \\
H_2C\text{——}O
\end{array}
\quad + \quad HCl \quad (C_5H_5N,\ reflux) \quad\longrightarrow\quad
\begin{array}{c}
H_2CCR_2CH_2 \\
|\qquad\quad| \\
OH\qquad Cl
\end{array}
$$

The 1,3-epoxides are less reactive than 1,2-epoxides and require refluxing for as long as 3.5 hr.

MODERN ACID ADDITION METHODS

None of the early hydrogen chloride methods were rapid enough for the direct titration of 1,2-epoxides, primarily because the chloride does not react rapidly enough with the protonated epoxide. In 1956 a breakthrough occurred when Durbetaki[7] found that 0.1 N hydrobromic acid in acetic acid could be used for direct titrations, in glacial acetic acid solvent. The direct titration was obviously possible because the bromide ion is a much better nucleophile than the chloride ion. The titration had to be performed in an almost closed system, but crystal violet, the usual indicator for titrations in acetic acid, could be used as the indicator. This paper is reprinted in Part II, Chapter 24. Durbetaki[9] also applied the procedure to mixtures of amines and epoxides. Critchfield[4] later reported an indirect method involving the addition of a measured excess of 0.5 N hydrogen bromide. This apparently avoided the difficulties involved with the direct titration. Neither of these methods can be used for the determination of acid-sensitive epoxides like styrene epoxide, or cyclopentadiene diepoxide. In acetic acid the latter undergoes acid-catalyzed ring opening on the bicyclic ring:[4]

Jahn *et al.*[13] later reported that 0.2 N hydrobromic acid in dioxane avoided this ring opening, and that both epoxide groups could be determined instead of just one.

The disadvantage of the special handling and frequent restandardization necessary for hydrobromic acid prompted further research. In 1961 Jung and Kleeberg[15] returned to hydrogen chloride, using a 0.3 N solution in methyl ethyl ketone. The real breakthrough came in 1964 when two groups[6, 14] independently published methods consisting of the addition of excess tetraalkylammonium bromide or iodide to the epoxide in a nonaqueous solvent, and titration with 0.1 N perchloric acid in acetic acid. Both papers are reprinted in Part II, Chapters 25 and 26. These methods were convenient in that the perchloric acid titrant was stable and did not require a closed system. The methods were rapid because an excess of bromide or iodide, both good nucleophiles, were present to open the ring as soon as perchloric acid was added to protonate the 1,2-epoxide.

The first paper to appear, that of Jay[14] (Chapter 25), described a method for both 1,2-epoxides and aziridines, using chloroform solvent. He found that tetrabutylammonium iodide was necessary for aziridines but that tetraethylammonium bromide was adequate for most epoxides. He recognized that air oxidation would occur with the iodide reagent but recommended no special provision for avoiding this during the titration. The second paper, that of Dijkstra and Dahmen[6] (Chapter 26) was more fundamental in nature, and emphasized the analytical implications of the mechanism of the reaction which Dahmen had actually published 3 years before. They also investigated various bromide and iodide salts and discovered that light-induced oxidation of the iodides could be avoided by use of a black beaker covered with black paper used in connection with a potentiometric titration. Chlorobenzene or benzene slowed the reaction down relative to acetic acid as solvent.

NUCLEOPHILIC REACTIONS IN NEUTRAL
OR BASIC SOLUTION

Only rather recently have methods been developed in which a powerful nucleophile such as thiosulfate[16] attacks the 1,2-epoxide to open the ring in a slow first step which is then followed by the rapid transfer of a proton from water:

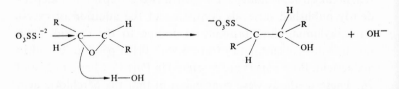

In 1952 Tyler and Beesing[24] adopted this approach for the determination of β-propiolactone in neutral aqueous solution:

$$
\underset{\underset{O-C=O}{|\qquad|}}{H_2C-CH_2} \quad + \quad SSO_3^{-2} \longrightarrow {}^-O_3SSCH_2CH_2CO_2^-
$$

A measured excess of 0.4 M sodium thiosulfate was added, and the unreacted thiosulfate was determined iodometrically. The high concentration was necessary to reduce the error from competing side reaction, as the second order rate constant at 25°C for the main reaction is only 1.9×10^{-1} M^{-1} sec^{-1}. This was especially necessary for cases where acetate buffer had to be used, the rate constant for the thiosulfate–lactone reaction being only 600 times that of the acetate–lactone reaction.

In 1955, Allen and Seaman[2] also reported the use of thiosulfate for the determination of ethylenimines (aziridines). A measured amount of standard hydrochloric acid was added after the reactants were mixed to bring the pH to 4. After a half hour, the amount of acid consumed by the release of hydroxide ion was measured by back titration with standard sodium hydroxide.

A large excess of thiosulfate had to be used in this instance also because of possible error from competing side reactions.[10] Thiosulfate was also used by Sully[22] in 1960 for the determination of styrene epoxide.

In 1960, Gudzinowicz[12] reported the quantitative addition of dodecanethiol, added in measured excess, to 1,2-epoxides in basic solution. The reaction requires 20 min and probably involves nucleophilic attack of the anion (RS^-) of dodecanethiol on the 1,2-epoxide:

Acetic acid is added, and the unreacted dodecanethiol is back titrated with standard iodine. As there is some air oxidation of the dodecanethiol, a blank is run to correct for this. The method can be applied to a number of epoxides including styrene epoxide.

OTHER APPROACHES AND INSTRUMENTAL ANALYSIS

None of the methods discussed above are applicable to the determination of 1,2-epoxides containing a tertiary carbon atom. These compounds will isomerize partially to aldehydes if an acid addition method is used, or will react too slowly because of steric hindrance if a method involving a nucleophilic reagent in neutral solution is used. Durbetaki[8] employed anhydrous zinc bromide in benzene using sealed tubes to isomerize such epoxides quantitatively to aldehydes. The resulting aldehydes can then be determined gravimetrically as the 2,4-dinitrophenylhydrazones. An example of a typical isomerization is the conversion of α-pinene epoxide to campholenic aldehyde:

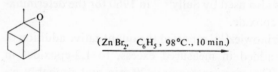

(Zn Br$_2$, C$_6$H$_5$, 98°C., 10 min.)   HC=O

Eastham and Latremouille[11] employed periodate cleavage for the determination of ethylene oxide (epoxide) after perchloric-acid catalyzed hydrolysis to ethylene glycol. The determined the unreacted periodate iodometrically. This reaction is also the basis for one of the few colorimetric methods for epoxides. In 1957 Critchfield and Johnson[3] determined ethylene oxide by the same type of reaction sequence except that the formaldehyde produced in the periodate cleavage was determined by condensation with chromotropic acid. The color of the condensed product was proportional to the amount of ethylene oxide. Their method should also be applicable to the determination of any 1,2-epoxide which will yield formaldehyde after hydrolysis and cleavage.

Other instrumental approaches have been sparse. Some infrared studies have been made,[16] and it also appears that terminal 1,2-epoxides can be determined by measurement in the near infrared at 1.64 and 2.20 μ. Infrared determination of the hydroxyl group in epoxy resins[1] is also possible by clever use of a hydroxyl band at 3.05 μ arising from a pyridine–hydroxyl complex.

REFERENCES

1. ADAMS, M.R., *Anal. Chem.* **36**, 1688 (1964).
2. ALLEN, E., SEAMAN, W., *Ibid.* **27**, 540 (1955).
3. CRITCHFIELD, F.E., JOHNSON, J.B., *Ibid.* **29**, 797 (1957).
4. CRITCHFIELD, F.E., *Organic Functional Group Analysis*, pp. 125–40, Pergamon Press, New York, 1963.

5. DECKERT, W., *Z. anal. Chem.* **82**, 297 (1930) and **109**, 166 (1937).
6. DIJKSTRA, R., DAHMEN, E.A.M.F., *Anal. Chim. Acta* **31**, 38 (1964).
7. DURBETAKI, A.J., *Anal. Chem.* **28**, 2000 (1956).
8. DURBETAKI, A.J., *Ibid.* **29**, 1666 (1957).
9. DURBETAKI, A.J., *Ibid.* **30**, 2024 (1958).
10. EARLEY, J.E., O'ROURKE, C.E., CLAPP, L.B., EDWARDS, J.O., LAWES, B.C., *J. Amer. Chem. Soc.* **80**, 3458 (1958).
11. EASTHAM, A.M., LATREMOUILLE, G.A., *Can. J. Research* B **28**, 264 (1950).
12. GUDZINOWICZ, B.J., *Anal. Chem.* **32**, 1520 (1960).
13. JAHN, H., RAUBACH, H., RODEKRICH, G., TIEGE, W., *Plaste Kautschuh.* **11**, 141 (1964); *CA* **63**, 10689d.
14. JAY, R.R., *Anal. Chem.* **36**, 667 (1964).
15. JUNG, G., KLEEBERG, W., Kunststoffe **51**, 714 (1961); *Ca* **56**, 8912a.
16. JUNGNICKEL, J.L., PETERS, E.D., POLGAR, A., WEISS, F.T., *Organic Analysis*, Vol. 1, pp. 127–54, Interscience, New York, 1953.
17. KEEN, R.T., *Anal. Chem.* **29**, 1041 (1957).
18. KING, G., *Nature* **164**, 705 (1949).
19. LUBATTI, O.F., *J. Soc. Chem. Ind.* **51**, 361T (1932).
20. NICOLET, B.H., POULTER, T.C., *J. Amer. Chem. Soc.* **52**, 1186 (1930).
21. STENMARK, G.A., *Anal. Chem.* **29**, 1367 (1957).
22. SULLY, B.D., *Analyst* **85**, 895 (1960).
23. SWERN, D., FINDLEY, T.W., BILLEN, G.N., and SCANLON, J.T., *Anal. Chem.* **19**, 414 (1947).
24. TYLER, W.P., BEESING, D.W., *Ibid.* **24**, 1511 (1952).

CHAPTER 6

Determination of 1,3-Dienes:
Diels–Alder Addition Methods

As THE determination of 1,3-dienes by the usual functional group methods for olefins is frequently difficult, the Diels–Alder addition reaction has come to be used for a number of 1,3-dienes. In addition to a 1,3-diene, the reaction requires a dienophile; i.e. a compound having a double bond conjugated to one or more electron-withdrawing groups. Maleic anhydride and tetracyanoethylene are two of the most useful of such dienophiles. The Diels–Alder reaction consists of the addition of a dienophile such as maleic anhydride to a 1,3-diene to form a new six-membered unsaturated ring:

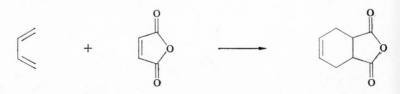

Holmes[5] has reviewed a great many Diels–Alder reactions from the viewpoint of the organic chemist. The mechanism is still not settled but several generalizations and observations are of analytical interest. The stereochemistry of the products has led to the assumption that the reaction occurs preferentially when the reactants are oriented so as to provide for maximum overlap

70

of their unsaturated centers. At some point in this process colored
π complexes are frequently observed. If the reaction is rapid, the
color is transient as is observed for the reaction of anthracene
and tetracyanoethylene.[9] If the reaction is slow, the color may
be quite stable; at room temperature maleic anhydride and anthracene give a stable yellow color.

The rate of the reaction is influenced by many factors. The
more electron-withdrawing groups conjugated to the double
bond of the dienophile, the faster it reacts as long as there is no
appreciable increase in steric hindrance. Thus tetracyanoethylene
is the most reactive common dienophile, and maleic anhydride
is a better dienophile than those with only one electron-withdrawing group. Substitution on carbons two and three of the
diene tend to make the diene more reactive whereas substitution
on the one and four carbons tends to do the opposite. Thus the
order of reactivity is: 2,3-dimethylbutadiene > butadiene > 1,4-
dimethylbutadiene.

The effect of solvent seems to vary somewhat with the reactants. For the maleic anhydride–anthracene system, the order of
solvent reactivity is: chloroform > carbon tetrachloride > acetic acid > acetone. The reaction is also subject to general acid
catalysis.[12] Yates and Eaton[21] have also discovered that aluminum chloride exerts a remarkable catalytic effect at room temperature on reactants such as maleic anhydride and anthracene.

Another analytical difficulty is that, because the reactivity of
most dienophiles is low, side reactions can occur with the 1,3-
dienes. One of these is the Diels–Alder addition of the 1,3-diene
to itself. For example, cyclopentadiene dimerizes readily with itself[19] to give dicyclopentadiene:

Wasserman[20] has studied the kinetics of the second order reactions of cyclopentadiene with various dienophiles at 25°C in benzene. Rate constants for three cyclopentadiene–dienophile reactions were: $0.53 \, M^{-1} \, min^{-1}$ for benzoquinone, $7.7 \times 10^{-3} \, M^{-1} \, min^{-1}$ for acrylaldehyde, and $6 \times 10^{-5} \, M^{-1} \, min^{-1}$ for cyclopentadiene (reacting with itself). Thus very reactive dienophiles must be used for accurate analytical work.

Polgar and Jungnickel[12] have included a summary of Diels–Alder methods appearing as recently as 1952 in their review of methods for olefins. These methods and later methods have not always contributed to a steady, progressive development characteristic of most functional group methods. Instead, research has tended to concentrate on specific areas, such as the determination of 1,3-dienes in certain acyclic compounds such as fats and oil, and on the determination of anthracene and cyclopentadiene.

DETERMINATION OF ACYCLIC COMPOUNDS USING MALEIC ANHYDRIDE

The earliest Diels–Alder method appears to be that of Kaufmann and Baltes[6] in 1936 for the analysis of fats. The method involved heating the 1,3-diene compounds with a measured excess of maleic anhydride in acetone for 20–26 hr at 100°C in a sealed tube. The cooled solution is mixed with water to hydrolyze the unreacted anhydride, the oily layer containing the Diels–Alder adduct is separated by filtration, and the aqueous layer containing the maleic acid is titrated with standard base. This represents double the moles of remaining anhydride. The difference between the moles of anhydride added and the moles remaining gives the moles of 1,3-diene present. Later modifications[7] replaced the sodium hydroxide titration with an iodometric titration of the unreacted maleic anhydride, and reduced the reaction to 4 hr by using toluene and refluxing in open systems.

Ellis and Jones[2] also published a Diels–Alder method in 1936. This involved refluxing with a measured excess of maleic anhydride in toluene under nitrogen for 3 hr. Water is then added and the heating continued for 15 min to hydrolyze the unreacted anhydride. Ether is then added to extract the Diels–Alder adduct away from the aqueous solution containing maleic acid. They also used iodine as a catalyst to reduce the reaction time to 1 hr.

Both of the above methods depend on the separation of unreacted maleic anhydride by hydrolysis to maleic acid, and neutralization of both hydrogens of the acid with standard base:

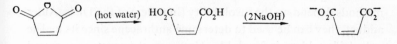

Further research by Bickford, Dollear, and Markley,[1] among others, showed that such maleic anhydride methods gave only the approximate 1,3-diene content of acyclic fatty materials. Work by von Mikusch[10] clarified one of the difficulties. He found that only *trans-trans*-dienes (I) reacted readily; the *cis-trans*-dienes (II), which predominate in natural oils, react slowly, and the *cis-cis*-dienes (III) are apparently unreactive:

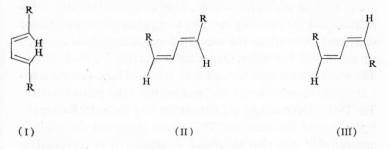

(I)   (II)   (III)

On this basis, von Mikusch[10] developed a method using iodine to catalyze the isomerization of the *cis-trans*-linoleates to the *trans-trans*-isomer at the temperature of the analytical method.

Although all this accomplishes is the rapid equilibration of all possible stereoisomers, the *trans-trans*-isomer will of course be rapidly removed from the equilibrium mixture by reaction with maleic anhydride. This will eventually result in essentially quantitative addition of the two isomers to maleic anhydride.

DETERMINATION OF ANTHRACENE

In contrast to most aromatic hydrocarbons, anthracene behaves as a Diels–Alder active diene, the 1,3-diene group in the middle ring reacting readily with maleic anhydride. As the above methods depend on the insolubility (in water) of the Diels–Alder adduct, they can be used to determine anthracene since its maleic anhydride adduct is insoluble. However, the reaction required 4 hr,[7] which is too long. In 1937, Postovskii and Khmelevskii[13] shortened the reaction time to less than an hour by refluxing the anthracene with a measured excess of maleic anhydride in xylene. They removed the xylene by steam distillation, and titrated the resulting maleic acid with standard base.

In 1949, Ubaldini, Crespi, and Guerrieri[17] reported that a partial hydrolysis of the Diels–Alder adduct occurred in the above method, giving low results. They eliminated the steam distillation and the resulting error by using chlorobenzene (instead of xylene), from which the unreacted maleic anhydride could be extracted with hot water. Quantitative reaction required 30 min. The water layer is then titrated with standard base without separating the chlorobenzene layer, making this a two phase titration. The Diels–Alder adduct did not extract into the water during the hydrolysis or the titration. This paper shortened the analysis considerably and also simplified it greatly. It is reprinted in Part II, Chapter 21.

In 1953, Funakubo, Matsumoto, and Hiroike[3] further modified the method by performing a two phase titration directly, using water at 55°C as the upper phase, and chloroform as the lower phase.

Anthracene can also be determined titrimetrically using the tetracyanoethylene method[11] discussed in a later section. This method and the other methods above can be used to determine anthracene in the presence of aromatic hydrocarbons such as naphthalene, phenanthrene, etc.

DETERMINATION OF CYCLOPENTADIENE

None of the above maleic anhydride methods can be applied to the determination of cyclopentadiene, as its Diels–Alder adduct is not insoluble in water or basic solution. In 1940 Kirsanov, Polyakova, and Kuznetsova[8] devised a somewhat lengthy maleic anhydride to avoid this difficulty. In 1955 Unger[19] published a much simpler method involving the reaction of an excess of maleic anhydride with cyclopentadiene in benzene at 35°C for 10 min:

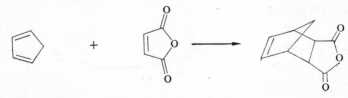

The adduct is extracted away from any dicyclopentadiene that may be present with 2% potassium hydroxide. The solution is acidified and titrated with standard 0.1 N potassium bromate–bromide until a slight yellow color from free bromine is observed. The excess bromine is then determined iodometrically. The bromine reacts rapidly with the double bond of the adduct, but only very slowly with the electron-deficient double bond of maleic acid (maleic anhydride is extracted as maleic acid into the aqueous layer). Bromine does not react stoichiometrically with cyclopentadiene; otherwise it could be used for the direct titration of cyclopentadiene, as long as dicyclopentadiene is absent. Cyclopentadiene can also be determined by either of the general methods discussed below.

GENERAL METHODS FOR 1,3-DIENES

Although the earlier methods[6, 7] for acyclic dienes can be used for a large number of compounds, they are limited to 1,3-dienes forming adducts which are insoluble in water, and are not general in this sense. In 1946, Putnam, Moss and Hall[14] employed chloromaleic anhydride for the determination of dienes such as butadiene, isoprene, and cyclopentadiene. Because of the steric bulk of the chloro group at the reaction site, chloromaleic anhydride is not as reactive as maleic anhydride. It is therefore added by weight, without solvent, to the sample, and the mixture is heated for 2 hr at 55 °C in a pressure bottle. The reaction (using butadiene as an example) produces an adduct having a tertiary chloride group:

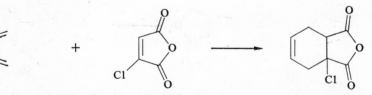

The tertiary chloride of the adduct undergoes β-elimination quite rapidly with refluxing aqueous silver nitrate, whereas the vinyl chloride of the unreacted anhydride is quite unreactive. The Volhard method is used to determine the per cent reaction.

The other general method is the 1961 tetracyanoethylene (TCNE) method of Ozolins and Schenk.[11] This was based on the observations of Middleton et al.[9] that TCNE reacts rapidly and quantitatively with many 1,3-dienes on a preparative scale.

This method is probably the most convenient; it is based entirely on the Diels–Alder reaction and depends on the purity of TCNE being 99 + %. A weighed quantity of excess pure TCNE is added to methylene chloride, heated to dissolve, and the 1,3-diene is added after cooling. Quantitative reaction requires 10 min or more at room temperature. The unreacted TCNE is back titrated with a standard 0.05 M cyclopentadiene solution as follows:

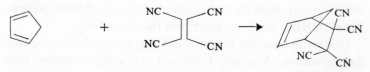

The presence of TCNE is indicated by red colored π complexes of phenanthrene and pentamethylbenzene. The indicator action is explained in detail in the paper, which is reprinted in Part II, Chapter 28. A photometric titration can be used instead of a visual end point.

INSTRUMENTAL ANALYSIS AND SEPARATIONS

Because of the nature of the Diels–Alder reaction, it has great potential for developing selective analytical method and for improving separations. A good example is the use of maleic anhydride and chloromaleic anhydride in the gas chromatographic determination of 1,3-dienes.[4] To analyze impure butadiene, maleic anhydride is added to the column packing to remove butadiene (and other Diels–Alder active dienes). The impurities pass through the column and can be measured without being hidden in a large butadiene peak. Chloromaleic anhydride was used to differentiate *cis*- and *trans*-dienes in mixtures by a differential reaction rate technique.

The Diels–Alder reaction of anthracene with TCNE was also used for its indirect colorimetric determination.[15] The anthracene sample is added to a standard amount of excess TCNE complexed with naphthalene. The destruction of the red color is measured at 550 mμ, and a plot of absorbance vs. molarity of anthracene yields an inverse Beer's law plot. Anthracene can be determined in the presence of cyclopentadiene by first adding an excess of maleic anhydride to react with the cyclopentadiene at room temperature. The anhydride does not react with anthracene under these conditions but does form a weak yellow π complex which serves to indicate that an excess of the anhydride is present. Then TCNE is added to determine the anthracene.

This method has the potential to be applied to the colorimetric determination of acyclic 1,3-dienes and cylopentadiene, thus supplementing the standard method for cyclopentadiene involving formation of the yellow phenylfulvene by base-catalyzed condensation with benzaldehyde.[18] Photochemical reactions appear to prevent application of the method to the determination of naphthacene or 1,2-benzanthracene.

The Diels–Alder reaction has the potential to eliminate interference of anthracene and similar aromatic hydrocarbons in ultraviolet spectrophotometry or fluorometry. Its value is that it destroys the conjugation of aromatic rings, converting anthracene to essentially two benzene rings. Until TCNE was synthesized in 1958, no dienophile was reactive enough for practical application of this principle at the dilute concentrations involved. Unfortunately, TCNE does not quench the fluorescence of anthracene, as the adduct is photodecomposed by the excitation light.[16] Further research is necessary to discover ways of using the Diels–Alder reaction for selectivity in fluorescence analysis.

REFERENCES

1. BICKFORD, W.G., DOLLEAR, F.G., MARKLEY, K.S., *J. Amer. Chem. Soc.* **59**, 2744 (1937).
2. ELLIS, B.A., JONES, R.A., *Analyst* **61**, 812 (1936).
3. FUNAKUBO, E., MATSUMOTO, Y., HIROIKE, S., *J. Chem. Soc. Japan, Ind. Chem. Sect.* **56**, 798 (1953).
4. GIL-AV, E., HERZBERG-MINZLY, Y., *J. Chromatog.* **13**, 1 (1964).
5. HOLMES, H.L., *Organic Reactions*, Vol. 4, pp. 1–173, Wiley, New York, 1948.
6. KAUFMANN, H.P., BALTES, J., *Fette u. Seifen* **43**, 93 (1936).
7. KAUFMANN, H.P., BALTES, J., BUTER, H., *Ber.* **70**, 903 and 905 (1937).
8. KIRSANOV, A.V., POLYAKOVA, I.M., KUZNETSOVA, Z.I., *J. Appl. Chem. U.S.S.R.* **13**, 1406 (1940).
9. MIDDLETON, W.J., HECKERT, R.E., LITTLE, E.L., KRESPAN, C.G., *J. Amer. Chem. Soc.* **80**, 2783 (1958).
10. MIKUSCH, J.D.VON, *Angew. Chem.* **62**, 475 (1950), and *J. Amer. Oil Chem. Soc.* **28**, 133 (1951).
11. OZOLINS, M., SCHENK, G.H., *Anal. Chem.* **33**, 1035 (1961).
12. POLGAR, A., JUNGNICKEL, J.L., *Organic Analysis*, Vol. 3, pp. 310–15, Interscience, New York, 1956.
13. POSTOVSKII, I.Y.Y., KHMELEVSKII, V.I., *Chem. Zentr.* **II**, 2042 (1937).
14. PUTNAM, S.T., MOSS, M.L., HALL, R.T., *Ind. Eng. Chem., Anal. Ed.* **18**, 628 (1946).
15. SCHENK, G.H., OZOLINS, M., *Talanta* **8**, 109 (1961).
16. SCHENK, G.H., RADKE, N., *Anal. Chem.* **37**, 910 (1965).
17. UBALDINI, I., CRESPI, V., GUERRIERI, F., *Ann. Chim. appl.* **39**, 77 (1949).
18. UHRIG, K., LYNCH, E.L., BECKER, H.C., *Ind. Eng. Chem., Anal. Ed.* **18**, 550 (1946).
19. UNGER, P., *Analyst* **80**, 820 (1955).
20. WASSERMAN, A., *J. Chem. Soc.* **1936**, 1028.
21. YATES, P., EATON, P., *J. Amer. Chem. Soc.* **82**, 4436 (1960).

CHAPTER 7

Determination of Electron-rich Compounds: Electron–Donor–Acceptor Complexes and Charge Transfer Spectra

ELECTRON-RICH compounds might be considered to possess a "functional group" consisting of electrons readily available for complexation. Indeed, a number of methods have recently been developed on this basis for characterization and determination of such compounds. These compounds are usually described as electron donors, or Lewis bases, and are classed as either π donors (bases) or n donors (bases), depending on whether π orbitals or nonbonding orbitals are involved. Examples of π donors are aromatic hydrocarbons, aryl ethers, phenols, and in some cases aromatic amines. Examples of n donors are aliphatic amines, halide ions, organic halides, aliphatic ethers, and aromatic amines.

These classes of compounds are characterized or determined by complexation with electron acceptors (Lewis acids). The latter are either π acceptors (acids) or inorganic acceptors (acids). The most useful π acceptors are tetracyanoethylene (TCNE), 1,3,5-trinitrobenzene (TNB), and 2,4,7-trinitrofluorenone (TNF):

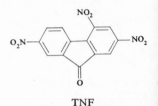

TCNE   TNB   TNF

Common inorganic acceptors are iodine, silver (I), and mercury (II).

Briegleb[5] has chosen to describe such complexes in general as electron–donor–acceptor complexes. Complexes involving only the interaction of π orbitals are called π complexes, although this description is also used in a slightly different sense for complexes of metal ions and π donors. Complexes involving the interaction of both n and π orbitals would be called n, π complexes.

The bonding between donor and acceptor cannot be covalent because X-ray diffraction studies of solid complexes have shown that the distance between the two components is much greater than normal covalent bond lengths. The bonding has been described in valence bond terms as a hybrid between a "no-bond" form and a charge transfer form.[1, 9] Dewar and Lepley[9] do not favor this picture, since very little charge is transferred from the donor to the acceptor in the ground state. A molecular orbital treatment[9, 10, 17] describes the bonding as an interaction of filled orbitals of the donor with empty antibonding orbitals of the acceptor. An appreciable part of complex stability may be the result of back coordination involving interaction between filled orbitals of the acceptor and empty orbitals of the donor.[9] Recently, an electrostatic model involving a quadrupole electric field has been invoked by Hanna[14] to explain the bonding of benzene–halogen complexes. The interaction of the quadrupole electric field above and below the plane of the benzene ring with polarizable halogen molecules was postulated to provide the energy of stabilization of these complexes. Hanna suggests it may be unnecessary to include charge transfer in a description of the ground state of the complexes.

STABILITY OF THE COMPLEXES

The stability or formation constant, K, of a given donor–acceptor complex is usually determined using spectrophotometric methods such as the Benesi–Hildebrand method[1, 5, 31], assuming that essentially only 1:1 complexes are present. Recently this has been seriously questioned as regards complexes of aromatic hydrocarbons and TNB or other nitrobenzenes at high concentration in carbon tetrachloride.[16] The value of K was shown to vary with the wavelength, indicating simultaneous formation of 2:1 and 1:1 complexes as well as isomeric 1:1 complexes. Nevertheless, the constants determined by such spectrophotometric methods can be used for a number of analytically useful calculations. Table 6 lists some values of K for various π

Table 6. Formation constants of π complexes
of tetracyanoethylene in CH_2Cl_2[20]

Aromatic hydrocarbon	K	$\varepsilon(\lambda_{max})$	
Benzene	2.00	3570 (384 mμ)	
Toluene	3.70	3330 (406 mμ)	
Naphthalene	11.7	1240 (550 mμ),	1120 (429 mμ)
Pyrene	29.5	1137 (724 mμ),	856 (495 mμ)
Durene	54.2	2075 (480 mμ)	
Pentamethylbenzene	123	3270 (520 mμ)	
Hexamethylbenzene	263	4390 (545 mμ)	

complexes of TCNE and also includes their molar absorptivities. The analytical use of these constants will follow the convention of Merrifield and Phillips[20] for TCNE π complexes, except that the π donor (base), symbolized as B, will not be used at concentrations higher than that of the π acceptor (acid), symbolized as T. Instead, the acceptor will always be at higher concentrations since the analyst will use TCNE, TNB, or TNF to determine traces of the donor.

The equation for the formation of a π complex, c, is written:

$$T + B \rightleftharpoons C$$

The formation constant expression for the analytical situation were the π acceptor is at concentrations appreciably higher than the π donor is:[24, 26]

$$K = \frac{(C)}{\{(B) - (C)\}\{[T] - [C]\}}$$

in which (C) is the equilibrium molarity of the complex, (B) is the initial molarity of the π donor (base), $[T]$ is the initial mole fraction of acceptors such as TCNE, TNB, or TNF, and $[C]$ is the equilibrium mole fraction of the complex. The $[C]$ term is usually negligible compared to the $[T]$ term. Neglecting $[C]$ and rearranging the above equation gives:

$$\frac{(C)}{(B) - (C)} = K[T]$$

This equation permits the calculation of the ratio of complexed donor to uncomplexed donor in the ground state once a mole fraction is chosen for the acceptor. For the convenient 0.05 M TCNE solution in methylene chloride, $[T]$ is 0.0032. For the TCNE-hexamethylbenzene π complex, the strongest known TCNE complex, the above ratio is:

$$\frac{(C)}{(B) - (C)} = 263 \, [0.0032] = \frac{0.842}{1}$$

Thus, even in the strongest TCNE complex, less than half of the donor is complexed under suitable analytical conditions. For very weak π complexes like TCNE–benzene, less than 1 % of the donor is complexed in the ground state.

As seen in Table 6, substitution of methyl groups on benzene markedly increases the stability of TCNE complexes. Substitution of ethyl groups introduces steric hindrance to the approach of TCNE; K for hexaethylbenzene is 5.11 (CH_2Cl_2) compared to 263 for hexamethylbenzene in the same solvent.[20] Another pertinent observation is that complexes of TCNE with larger aromatic hydrocarbons than benzene are not as stable; larger π acceptors such as TNB and TNF enjoy larger π overlap with naphthalene, pyrene, etc.[1, 26] The value of K for TNF–pyrene is 73[26] in methylene chloride compared to 29.5 for TCNE–pyrene.

In spite of these difficulties, a number of analytical methods have been developed for homogeneous solution. Precipitation of the complexes or evaporation on paper have been frequently employed because much higher stabilities are obtained than in solution.

CHARGE TRANSFER SPECTRA

In solution, electron–donor–acceptor complexes exhibit intense light absorption bands which are different from that of either the donors or acceptors. Such spectral bands have been attributed to charge transfer transitions and are called charge transfer bands. Like the charge transfer transitions of inorganic complex ions, these transitions in organic complexes have molar absorptivities of at least 1000 M^{-1} cm^{-1} or greater. Unlike most inorganic charge transfer bands which possess sharp peaks, organic charge transfer bands are fairly broad because of the many possible transitions. This makes it difficult for the analyst if two different charge transfer peaks must be resolved on the spectrophotometer.

Also of analytical interest is the fact that the longest wavelength charge transfer bands of a number of organic donor–acceptor complexes occur in the visible region at appreciably longer wavelengths than the locally excited π–π^* transitions of the individual donors and acceptors in the ultraviolet region. (This contrasts to the many charge transfer bands of inorganic complex ions found in the ultraviolet region. Well known exceptions of course are the charge transfer transitions of $FeNCS^{+2}$ and $Fe(1,10\text{-phen})_3^+$.) This is of value in the characterization and determination of aromatic π donors. The complexed donors can be measured in the visible region rather than in the ultraviolet region where most organic compounds are liable to interfere.

Figure 1 illustrates all of the above items. It represents the spectrum of a methylene chloride solution of benzene complexed with TCNE. Since relatively few ground state molecules are promoted to the excited state at any given time, both the localized π–π^* transitions of benzene and the charge transfer transitions of the π complex will always be observed in the spectrum. As shown in the figure, the TCNE–benzene charge transfer band (384 mμ) is broad with considerable absorption above 400 mμ, making the complex appear yellow. This band is some distance from the longest wavelength peak of benzene, beginning just beyond the benzene cutoff wavelength of 280 mμ. This separation is more pronounced with the TCNE complex of benzene than with the TNB or TNF complexes of benzene. The TNB–benzene charge transfer band occurs at 284 mμ.[9]

Also of analytical interest is the separation of the absorption bands of the different TCNE complexes, as seen from Table 6. For example, the TCNE–naphthalene absorption band at 550 mμ occurs at a considerably longer wavelength than the TCNE–benzene band. This is readily understood in terms of an energy diagram and molecular orbitals, as shown in Fig. 2. Dewar and his co-workers[9, 10, 17] have interpreted charge transfer spectra as involving an electronic transition from the highest energy occupied orbital of the donor to the lowest energy unoccupied orbital of the acceptor. Since the energy $(\alpha + \beta)$ of the occupied benzene orbitals[15] is the largest of any aromatic hydrocarbons, the TCNE–benzene charge transfer transition will be of the highest energy. The TCNE–benzene charge transfer band will

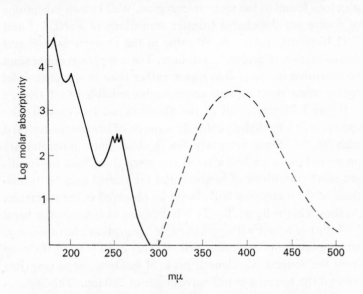

FIG. 1. Hypothetical absorption spectra of benzene complexed with TCNE in methylene chloride solvent. The solid line represents the ultraviolet spectrum of benzene with sharp peaks at 184, 200, and 254 mμ. The dotted line represents the charge transfer spectrum of the yellow TCNE–benzene complex with a broad band at 384 mμ. The ultraviolet spectrum of TCNE has been omitted for clarity.

therefore be located at the shortest wavelength of any TCNE–aromatic complex. The energy of the corresponding naphthalene orbitals[10] is considerably less $(\alpha + 0.618\beta)$ and the TCNE–naphthalene charge transfer band will thus occur at longer wavelengths.[30a]

The type of diagram shown in Fig. 2 also can be used to account for the shorter wavelength, higher energy, charge transfer bands reported in Table 6 for naphthalene and pyrene. These arise from transitions from lower energy occupied orbitals of naphthalene and pyrene.[17a]

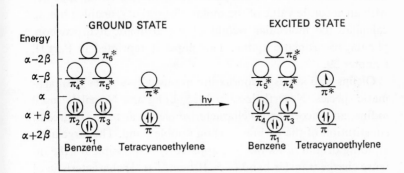

FIG. 2. An energy diagram giving a molecular orbital picture[9,10] for the most likely charge transfer transition of the TCNE–benzene π complex at 384 mμ. At the left, energy is plotted in terms of α, the coulomb integral of carbon, and β, the carbon–carbon resonance integral.[15] The diagram indicates that the charge transfer from the μ_3 orbital of benzene to the π^* orbital of TCNE is of lower energy (longer wavelength) than the localized transitions. Since the energy of the π^* orbital of TCNE is $\alpha - 0.11\beta$, the energy of the c.t. band is 1.11β. (Using $\beta = 24{,}600$ cm^{-1}, this predicts a c.t. band at 27,300 cm^{-1} or 370 mμ.[30a]

CHARACTERIZATION OF ELECTRON DONORS

The earliest use of electron acceptors (acids) involved the characterization of electron donor molecules. Picric acid was the classic reagent. In 1951, Cunningham, Dawson, and Spring[8] reported a spectrophotometric method for the determination of the molecular weight of picric acid complexes to within 1 %. Because of the fact that it is a strong acid and of the fact that trinitrobenzene (TNB) forms many more complexes, Godfrey[12] developed a more general spectrophotometric method using TNB. After precipitation of the complex from absolute ethanol and recrystallization, he added an excess of potassium hydroxide to develop an intense absorption band at 502 mμ. Spectrophotometric measurement of the absorption of this band, together with an accurate value of the molar absorptivity, enabled him to calculate the molecular weight of the aromatic hydrocarbon, phenol, or aromatic amine. This paper is reprinted in Part II, Chapter 29.

Olefins also act as π donors but are usually weaker than aromatic species. Nevertheless, in 1955, Long and Neuzil[18] used iodine, an n acceptor, to characterize olefins as to the degree of substitution of the carbon–carbon double bond. The large antibonding orbital of iodine[1] is apparently responsible for the intense charge transfer band ($\varepsilon > 10^4$ cm^{-1} M^{-1}) characteristic of complexed iodine. The location of the charge transfer band was found to be characteristic of the degree of substitution. However, the wavelength variation with substitution was only about 62 mμ. In addition, photochemical-catalyzed addition of iodine to the olefins had to be avoided by keeping the solutions in the dark. In 1962, Bauer[3] found that tetracyanoethylene (TCNE) was superior to iodine in that the wavelength variation with sub-

Table 7. Maxima of charge transfer spectra of TCNE and iodine complexes of substituted olefins

Olefin type	λ_{max}, Iodine complexes[18]	λ_{max}, TCNE complexes[3]
$RCH{=}CH_2$	275 mμ	340–360 mμ
$R_2C{=}CH_2$	290–295 mμ	392–410 mμ
$RCH{=}CHR$	295–300 mμ	405–422 mμ
$R_2C{=}CHR$	317 mμ	466–482 mμ
$R_2C{=}CR_2$	337 mμ	537–552 mμ

stitution was about 200 mμ. Table 7 compares the location of charge transfer bands of both acceptors.

In 1959, Gordon and Huraux[13] reported the use of 2,4,7-trinitrofluoreneone (TNF) for the characterization of phenols, aromatic amines, and aromatic hydrocarbons by the color and fluorescence of their complexes on filter paper. Four years later, Cundiff and Markunas[7] used the nonaqueous titration of TNF complexes in pyridine to obtain the neutralization equivalent of the complexes, thus indirectly measuring the molecular weight of the donor. As the titrant (Bu_4NOH) reacts with both the TNF and the complexed TNF, the TNF complexes had to be carefully purified.

DETERMINATION OF ELECTRON DONORS

Peurifoy and Nager[22] were the first to use a π acceptor to determine electron donors. In 1960, they reported the estimation of nitrogen compounds such as aliphatic and aromatic amines in petroleum fraction by spraying spots on paper with a solution of TCNE. Heating at 110°C for 5 min produced colored spots which could be compared with similar spots from known amounts at the 100 ppm level.

Not long afterwards, it was reported that TCNE could be utilized for the spectrophotometric determination of anthracene,[23] for the direct photometric titration of selected aromatic hydrocarbons,[24] and for the direct spectrophotometric determination of aromatic hydrocarbons, phenols, and aryl ethers by measurement of the charge transfer bands.[25] Although there has been some question as to whether Beer's law is valid for such complexes,[32] it was found[25] that plots of A, the absorbance, versus (B), the initial molarity of the electron donor, did not deviate seriously from Beer's law.

It was also found[25] that the lower limit of (B) which could be measured accurately ($A = 0.10$) by complexation with TCNE, could be calculated by a simple equation. This equation is obtained by combining Beer's law for 1 cm cells, $A = \varepsilon(C)$, with the formation constant expression where $[C]$ is neglected:

$$(B) = \frac{A\{1 + K[T]\}}{\varepsilon K[T]}$$

This equation gave reasonable agreement with experimental values of (B) at $A = 0.10$, as shown in Table 5 of this paper. The paper is reprinted in Part II, Chapter 30.

In 1965, a similar study[26] of the π complexes of TNF established that it could also be used for the spectrophotometric determination of donors such as aromatic hydrocarbons, aromatic amines, and phenols. Because maximum overlap of the π orbitals of TNF and donors having the equivalent of three fused rings can be attained, TNF can complex more strongly with TCNE than with donors of this size.

In 1966, Schenk, Warner, and Bazzelle[28] devised a spectrophotometric method for the determination of tertiary aromatic amines in the presence of primary and secondary amines by complexation with TCNE after acetylation of the primary and secondary amines. Tetralkylammonium bromides and iodides form n, π complexes readily with TNB,[6] and these compounds can also be determined spectrophotometrically in a number of solvents.[30]

OXIDATION WITH ELECTRON ACCEPTORS

As electron acceptors actually function as oxidizing agents in the charge transfer process during light absorption, it might be predicted that the more powerful acceptors would function as oxidizing agents in the ground state also. This has been observed for acceptors such as TCNE, which oxidizes inorganic reagents like iodide ion to iodine, forming the tetracyanoethylene ion radical in the process[34] However, no analytical applications involving TCNE appear to have been published. A very weak acceptor which has been used for analysis is the stable purple free radical, 2,2-diphenyl-picrylhydrazyl (DPPH·), which has this structure:

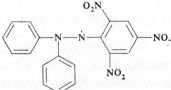

DPPH· has two strong absorption maxima ($\varepsilon > 10^4\,\mathrm{M}^{-1}\,\mathrm{cm}^{-1}$) at 515 m$\mu$ and 325 mμ; it is reduced to a yellow hydrazine, DPPH:H, which has just one maxima at 325 mμ. Thus absorbance measurements at 515 mμ are a direct measurement of the reduction of DPPH·. Blois[4] was the first to use this free radical for the indirect spectrophotometric determination of hydroquinone and selected mercaptane in 95% ethanol. His calibration curve was a plot of the absorbance of unreacted DPPH· (added in measured excess) versus the concentration of the hydroquinone or mercaptan. An inverse Beer's law plot was obtained.

Eight years later, in 1966, Papariello and Janish[21] published a rather complete study of the determination of phenols by oxidation with DPPH· in an acetate buffered 90% methanol solution. They subtracted the absorbance of the sample after reaction, from the absorbance of a buffered solution of a DPPH· blank to obtain a ΔA. Their calibration curve was a plot of ΔA versus the concentration of the phenol to give a normal Beer's law plot. Their paper is reprinted in Part II, Chapter 31.

Neither Blois nor Papariello and Janish investigated these reactions in dry organic solvents, and it was found[29] that

hydroquinone, pyrocatechol (o-dihydroxybenzene), and particularly resorcinol reacted more slowly in dried absolute ethanol.
This made it possible to use DPPH· for spectrophotometric
determination of either pyrocatechol or hydroquinone in the
presence of much larger amounts of resorcinol in dry ethanol.[29]

INSTRUMENTAL ANALYSIS AND SEPARATIONS

The complexation of electron donors and acceptors has great
potential for developing more selective instrumental methods
and for improving separations. However, ignorance of possible
charge transfer bands can cause errors in spectrophotometric
measurements. Fritz and Hammond[11] point out that measurement of 10^{-2} M nitrobenzene at 350 mμ in the presence of 1 M
aniline will be in error because of the charge transfer band of the
very weak aniline–nitrobenzene complex. Weimer and Prausnitz[35] have also shown that weak complexes are formed between aromatic hydrocarbons and common polar organic solvents such as aliphatic ketones, nitroalkanes, and propionitrile.

Electron acceptors are also known to quench the fluorescence
of aromatic hydrocarbons and other donors. McCartin[19] has
pointed put that this is a result, not of complexation in the
ground state of the aromatic donor, but of complexation of the
excited singlet of the donor by the acceptor in its ground state.
Acceptors that form the strongest ground state complexes with
a given aromatic donor also appear to be the most effective
quenchers of the donor fluorescence. Thus, Schenk and Radke[27]
found that TNF and TCNE are better quenching agents than
maleic anhydride or tetrachlorobenzoquinone.

Electron acceptors have also been mixed with chromatographic
materials for more effective separations. In 1964, Tye and Bell[33]
reported that TNB could be mixed with alumina using polyethylene glycol as a liquid phase for such separations. They dem-

onstrated that pyrene and fluoranthene, two aromatic hydro-carbons which are difficult to separate on alumina alone, could be separated readily by column chromatography. They extracted TNB with aqueous base before ultraviolet measurement of the aromatic hydrocarbons. Ayres and Mann[2] used nitrated poly-styrene resin for the same type of column separations. TCNE apparently decomposes on alumina and cannot be used for this type of separation.

REFERENCES

1. ANDREWS, L.J., KEEFER, R.M., *Molecular Complexes in Organic Che-mistry*, Holden-Day, San Francisco, 1964.
2. AYRES, J.T., MANN, C.K., *Anal. Chem.* **38,** 859, 861 (1966).
3. BAUER, R.H., *Ibid.* **35,** 107 (1963).
4. BLOIS, M.S., *Nature* **181,** 199 (1958).
5. BRIEGLEB, G., *Elektronen-Donator-Acceptor Komplexe*, Springer-Ver-lag, Berlin, 1961.
6. BRIEGLEB, G., LIPTAY, W., FICK, R., *Z. Elektrochem. Ber. Bunsenges physik. Chem.* **66,** 851 (1962).
7. CUNDIFF, R.H., MARKUNAS, P.C., *Anal. Chem.* **35,** 1323 (1963).
8. CUNNINGHAM, K.G., DAWSON, W., SPRING, F.S., *J. Chem. Soc.* 2305 (1951).
9. DEWAR, M.J.S., LEPLEY, A.R., *J. Amer. Chem. Soc.* **83,** 4560 (1961).
10. DEWAR, M.J.S., ROGERS, H., *Ibid.* **84,** 395 (1962).
11. FRITZ, J.S., HAMMOND, G.S., *Quantitative Organic Analysis*, p. 177, Wi-ley, New York, 1957.
12. GODFREY, J.C., *Anal. Chem.* **31,** 1087 (1959).
13. GORDON, H.T., HURAUX, M.J., *Ibid.* **31,** 302 (1959).
14. HANNA, M.W., 151st American Chemical Society Meeting, Division of Physical Chemistry, Pittsburgh, 1966.
15. JAFFE, H.H., ORCHIN, M., *Theory and Application of Ultraviolet Spec-troscopy*, pp. 242–250, Wiley, New York, 1962.
16. JURINSKI, N.B., DE MAINE, P.A.D., *J. Amer. Chem. Soc.* **86,** 3217 (1964)
17. LEPLEY, A.R., *Ibid.* **84,** 3577 (1962).
17a. LEPLEY, A.R., THOMPSON C.C., *Ibid.* **89,** 5523 (1967).
18. LONG, D.R., NEUZIL, R.W., *Anal. Chem.* **27,** 1110 (1955).
19. McCARTIN, P.J., *J. Amer. Chem. Soc.* **85,** 2021 (1963).
20. MERRIFIELD, R.E., PHILLIPS, W.D., *Ibid.* **80,** 2778 (1958).
21. PAPARIELLO, G.J., JANISH, M.A.M., *Anal. Chem.* **38,** 211 (1966).
22. PEURIFOY, P.V., NAGER, M., *Ibid.* **32,** 1135 (1960).

23. SCHENK, G.H., OZOLINS, M., *Talanta* **8,** 109 (1961).
24. SCHENK, G.H., OZOLINS, M., *Anal. Chem.* **33,** 1562 (1961).
25. SCHENK, G.H., SANTIAGO, M., WINES, P., *Ibid.* **35,** 167 (1963).
26. SCHENK, G.H., VANCE, P.W., PIETRANDREA, J., MOJZIS, C., *Ibid.* **37,** 372 (1965).
27. SCHENK, G.H., RADKE, N., *Ibid.* **37,** 910 (1965).
28. SCHENK, G.H., WARNER, P., BAZZELLE, W., *Ibid.* **38,** 907 (1966).
29. SCHENK, G.H., BROWN, D.J., *Talanta* **14,** 257 (1967).
30. SCHENK, G.H., TRIFF, D., Unpublished results, Wayne State University, 1966.
30a. SCHENK, G.H., *Rec. Chem. Prog.* **28,** 135 (1967).
31. TAMRES, M., *J. Phys. Chem.* **65,** 654 (1961).
32. THOMPSON, C.C., DEMAINE, P.A.D., *J. Amer. Chem. Soc.* **85,** 3096 (1963).
33. TYE, R., BELL, Z., *Anal. Chem.* **36,** 1612 (1964).
34. WEBSTER, O.W., MAHLER, W., BENSON, R.E., *J. Amer. Chem. Soc.* **84,** 3678 (1962).
35. WEIMER, R.F., PRAUSNITZ, J.M., *Spectrochimica Acta* **22,** 77 (1966).

PART II

Author's note: In order to include more papers than would be ordinarily possible, many of the details have been omitted from each paper. In general, tables of analytical results and most illustrations have been omitted to provide space. The reader should consult the original literature for the omitted material.

CHAPTER 1

The Determination of Aldehydes
in Oil of Lemon†

ALEX. H. BENNETT

THE ESTIMATION of citral in lemon oil is a subject which has at-
tracted a good deal of attention, and a number of methods have
been suggested for the purpose, none of which, however, have
hitherto obtained general acceptance. The process at present to
be described is a slight modification of one originally put forward by Walther (*Pharm. Centralb.*, 1899, **40**, 621), and depending on the reaction between the aldehyde and hydroxylamine. In
this process the lemon oil was heated in alcoholic solution under
a reflux condenser with a sufficient excess of a 5 per cent. solution of hydroxylamine hydrochloride in alcohol, with the addition of 0·5–1·0 gram of sodium bicarbonate, which serves to
neutralise the hydrochloric acid liberated by the action. The excess of hydroxylamine remaining at the end of the reaction is titrated, and comparison with a blank experiment gives the amount
which has entered into combination with the citral.

Messrs. Schimmel and Co. (*Semi-Annual Reports*, April, 1900)
criticised this method on the ground that the carbon dioxide
evolved carries off hydroxylamine, which thus appears as if it
had entered into combination with citral, giving rise, therefore,

† Reprinted from *Analyst* **34**, 14 (1909). Reprinted by permission of the
Society for Analytical Chemistry.

to results which are too high, and which vary according to the excess of bicarbonate, the time and rate of boiling, and other conditions.

To overcome this objection I have, instead of using bicarbonate, proceeded by the addition, to the solution of the hydrochloride, of alcoholic soda or potash, in quantity sufficient to liberate an amount of hydroxylamine in excess of that which would be required to combine with the citral present, but not to complete neutralisation of the acid of the hydrochloride. Such a partially neutralised solution can be boiled under a reflux condenser without any loss of the base, as is shown by the following experiments:

Twenty c.c. of a solution of hydroxylamine hydrochloride in 80 per cent. alcohol, exactly neutralised to phenolphthalein with sodium hydrate, required for retitration (after diluting with water, and using methyl orange as the indicator) 19·9 c.c. of $\frac{N}{2}$ sulphuric acid.

Two similar quantities were each treated with 8 c.c. $\frac{N}{1}$ sodium hydrate and heated under a reflux condenser for half an hour, and an hour and a half respectively. After cooling, diluting with water, and completing the neutralisation to phenolphthalein, each required 19·9 c.c. of $\frac{N}{2}$ sulphuric acid for the retitration.

The actual analysis is conducted as follows:

Twenty c.c. of lemon oil are mixed with 20 c.c. of a $\frac{N}{2}$ solution of hydroxylamine hydrochloride in 80 per cent. alcohol, and to the mixture is added about 8 c.c. of $\frac{N}{1}$ alcoholic potash and 20 c.c. of strong alcohol (which is sufficient to procure complete solution when hot). The mixture is boiled gently under a reflux condenser for half an hour, and then allowed to cool. The condenser is washed down, and the contents of the flask diluted with about 250 c.c. of water, and neutralised to phenolphthalein. The liquid is then titrated with $\frac{N}{2}$ sulphuric acid, using methyl orange as indicator. The number of c.c.'s of acid required, subtracted from the number used in a blank experiment, in which no lemon oil is present, gives the amount of hydroxylamine which has entered into reaction with the citral, and multiplied by 0·076 gives the weight of citral.

When the titration to methyl orange is performed in the usual way with addition of a drop of the indicator to the solution, the end point is often not very satisfactory. I find that much sharper results are obtained by making use of drops of a very dilute aqueous solution of methyl orange scattered on a white plate. When drops of the solution which is being titrated are brought into contact with these the change of colour when neutralisation is complete is well marked.

CHAPTER 2

The Estimation of Aldehydes and Ketones by Means of Hydroxylamine†

ALEX. H. BENNETT and F. K. DONOVAN

THE FOLLOWING experiments were undertaken with the object of ascertaining whether the method described by one of us (*Analyst*, 1909, **34,** 14) for the estimation of citral in lemon oil could be applied to other commonly occurring aldehydes and ketones. The process is fully described in the paper just cited, but an extended experience of its working has shown the necessity for certain precautions which may here be briefly indicated.

Commercial hydroxylamine hydrochloride frequently contains impurities which render the end point of the titration (with phenolphthalein) obscure and uncertain. To render it satisfactory for this purpose it has generally been found necessary to recrystallise it from water. Recrystallisation from hot alcohol, which is much less wasteful, does not effect a satisfactory purification.

In neutralising to phenolphthalein the sodium hydroxide should be added cautiously, any great local excess being avoided, and it is especially necessary that the liquid should not be vio-

† Reprinted from *Analyst* **37,** 146 (1922). Only the introduction to this paper is included since this method is the same as that given in Paper 1. Reprinted by permission of the Society for Analytical Chemistry.

lently agitated or allowed to stand for any length of time in presence of even a slight excess of alkali, as, in this case, a loss of hydroxylamine readily occurs (more marked in the blank experiment than in the presence of, for instance, lemon oil).

In the estimation of citral, benzaldehyde, citronellal, etc., the reaction mixture is boiled gently for half an hour under a reflux condenser. We use a roundbottomed flask of about 200 c.c. capacity, connected by a ground joint with a 25 cm. Liebig condenser fitted throughout with a Young's "rod and disc" in the manner described by Schidrowitz and Kaye (*Analyst*, 1905, **30**, 190). In this way all risk of loss is avoided.

In the case of formaldehyde and acetone the reaction is carried out by leaving the mixture for two hours in stoppered bottles at the temperature of the air, and good results can also be obtained for lemon oil in this way by using double the usual amount of alcohol in order to keep the oil in solution. The results in general are within 0·1 per cent. of those found after boiling the mixture.

We have made some tests with brom-phenol blue as an indicator, but, in our opinion, the end point with methyl orange is decidedly sharper. It is, however, quite possible that some workers may find the colour change of brom-phenol blue more easy to follow. As already described, the methyl orange must be used in very dilute solution, and the tests made by spotting on a plate.

CHAPTER 3

Improved Hydroxylamine Method for the Determination of Aldehydes and Ketones Displacement of Oxime Equilibria by Means of Pyridine†

W. M. D. BRYANT and DONALD MILTON SMITH

THE VALUE of hydroxylamine and its salts as quantitative reagents for aldehydes and ketones has long been recognized. Brochet and Cambier[1] used hydroxylamine hydrochloride for the volumetric analysis of formaldehyde solutions. They titrated the hydrochloric acid liberated in the reaction $HCHO + HONH_3Cl = CH_2=NOH + H_2O + HCl$ and used this as a measure of the formaldehyde present. Bennett[2] and his collaborators modified the analytical procedure and investigated the behavior of several aldehydes and ketones. The most generally applicable procedure in this group is that of Bennett and Donovan, in which most of the hydroxylamine base is first liberated from the hydrochloride by the addition of alcoholic sodium hydroxide and then allowed to react with the carbonyl compound. At the completion of the reaction the remaining unused hydroxylamine is determined alkalimetrically. Schultes[3] has quite recently ad-

† Reprinted from *Journal of the American Chemical Society* **57**, 57 (1935). Reprinted by permission of the copyright owner.

ded some additional carbonyl compounds to the list of substances that can be analyzed by the hydroxylamine method.

The present research arose from the need of an analytical method that would be applicable to a large number of aldehydes and ketones of widely varied constitution. The procedures of Brochet and Cambier, and of Bennett and Donovan were both tried and found to be unsatisfactory in their original form. In the former procedure, equilibrium conditions were often such that complete reaction could not be attained, while the latter was characterized by a slow rate of reaction and erratic losses of hydroxylamine probably resulting from spontaneous decomposition.

In evolving the improved procedure, a special effort was made to extend the scope of the method without adding to its complexity. It was consequently retained in its original form† as an acidimetric method employing hydroxylamine hydrochloride. The principal improving feature resulted from the use of pyridine for the double purpose of forcing oxime formation to completion and of rendering the initial reaction mixture neutral to bromphenol blue, thus eliminating the need of a blank titration. Although pyridine exerts a slight buffer action which makes the indicator color change less sensitive, its value in displacing unfavorable oxime equilibria compensates for the diminished sensitivity. The reaction environment of 90–95 % alcohol, suggested by Bennett's work, is valuable as a solvent for water insoluble samples. Over thirty aldehydes and ketones were analyzed by the new procedure and results close to the theoretical obtained.

The method is applicable to aldehydes and ketones of aliphatic, alicyclic and aromatic character. A great many substituted aldehydes and ketones can be estimated although this does not apply to the carboxyl or amide type of carbonyl group. Struc-

† *Journal of the American Chemical Society* **57**, 57 (1935).

tural peculiarities of carbonyl compounds have a marked effect upon the rate of reaction with hydroxylamine hydrochloride, although this factor alone is seldom sufficient to render the method inapplicable.

In order to determine the most satisfactory analytical conditions for individual ketones of the less reactive class, the relative rates of reaction were measured at room temperature. These experiments show the effect of chemical constitution upon the reactivity of carbonyl compounds, and lead to some interesting qualitative generalizations regarding steric hindrance of the —CO— group by other organic radicals.

The average precision of the new hydroxylamine method is about ± 1%, and the results are stoichiometric within the experimental error in practically all cases.

ANALYTICAL RESULTS

Table I shows the results obtained with the above quantitative procedure for aldehydes and ketones as applied to over thirty pure carbonyl compounds. With the exception of the solids all samples were measured volumetrically in pipets. The temperatures of the liquid samples were noted and the weights calculated from the densities and volumes of the respective materials. The accuracy of these measurements was found to be consistent with that of the analytical procedure.

Time Requirements and Structure

Inspection of Table I discloses that twelve of the thirteen aldehydes reacted practically to completion in thirty minutes in the cold. The exception was glucose which required two hours of heating. All of the substances listed except benzophenone and camphor had finished reacting after two hours at 100°. A few other materials required additional time in the cold because of unfavorable equilibrium conditions at 100°. Camphor required five hours' heating with a 0.5-g. sample; benzophenone reacted completely after three hours of heating using a 1-g. sample.

As an aid in selecting the most favorable analytical conditions for some of the less reactive ketones, groups of experiments with each of these materials were started in the cold and analyzed individually at successive intervals, time being the only variable. Curves of percentage reaction *versus* time were constructed from these numerical data and when plotted on the same scale (Fig. 1)

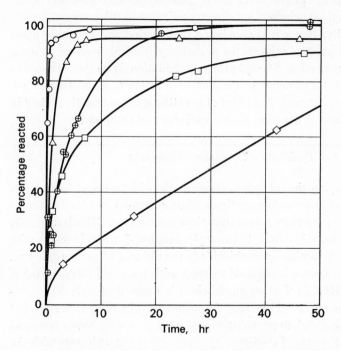

FIG. 1. Relative reaction velocities of various ketones with hydroxylamine hydrochloride and pyridine: ○, 2-methylpentanone-3; ⊕, 2,4-dimethylpentanone-3; □, 2,4-dimethylhexanone-3, △, carvone; ◇, d,l-camphor.

show some interesting qualitative relationships between reactivity and chemical constitution. Steric hindrance of the —CO— group by adjacent substituent groups is a likely explanation for the slow rate of certain ketones.

Pentanone-3, for example, reacts almost instantaneously with hydroxylamine hydrochloride and pyridine. 2-Methylpentanone-3 with a methyl group adjacent to the carbonyl is definitely less reactive, and 2,4-dimethylpentanone-3 and 2,4-dimethylhexanone-3 with a methyl group adjacent on each side are both very sluggish. On the other hand, 2-methylpentanone-4, where the methyl side chain is not directly adjacent to the carbonyl, reacts rapidly. Hence it is concluded that methyl and probably other alkyl groups adjacent to a carbonyl radical produce a steric blocking effect. Phenyl groups linked directly to the carbonyl in ketones also decrease the rate of reaction (*e.g.*, acetophenone, benzophenone). The effect of constitution upon rate is evident in the case of benzoin, benzil, carbone and camphor.

Effect of Pyridine on the Oxime Equilibria

The reaction of hydroxylamine salts with carbonyl compounds to form oximes is sometimes incomplete as a result of unfavorable equilibrium rather than slow reaction rate. This is definitely the case with the 2,4-dimethylpentanone-3 when it reacts with hydroxylamine hydrochloride in the absence of pyridine. If 1 cc. of the ketone is allowed to react with the usual 30 cc. of 0.5 N $HONH_3Cl$ solution, equilibrium is reached at only 50.1 % reaction in the cold or 38.5 % hot (hot samples reacted at 100°, but the equilibrium probably represents a somewhat lower temperature because of cooling). By repeating the experiments with the same amounts of ketone and reagent but adding also the usual 100 cc. of pyridine solution, the equilibrium conversion of 2,4-dimethylpentanone-3 becomes 99.9 % cold or 95.3 % hot.

REFERENCES

1. BROCHET, A., CAMBIER, R., *Compt. rend.* **120,** 449 (1895).
2. BENNETT, A.H., *Analyst* **34,** 14 (1909); BENNETT, A.H., DONOVAN, F.K., *Ibid.*, **47,** 146 (1922); BENNETT, A.H., SALAMON, M.S., *Ibid.*, **52,** 693 (1927); BENNETT, A.H., COCKING, T.T., *Ibid.*, **56,** 79 (1931).
3. SCHULTES, H., *Z. angew. Chem.* **47,** 258 (1934).

CHAPTER 4

Determination of Carbonyl Compounds†

JAMES S. FRITZ, STANLEY S. YAMAMURA,
and EVELIN CARLSTON BRADFORD

DETERMINATION of aldehydes and ketones by oximation is probably the most satisfactory general method. Early work by Walther,[14] Bennett,[1] Bennett and Donovan,[2] Stillman and Reed,[12] Schultes,[11] Bryant and Smith,[3] Montes and Grandolini,[9] Trozzolo and Lieber,[13] and Knight and Swern[7] is significant. The Bryant and Smith method has been widely used for many years, although Higuchi and Barnstein[5] have recently pointed out that the end point is very poor.

Metcalfe and Schmitz[8] used a hydroxylamine solution, prepared *in situ* by mixing approximately equal molar proportions of hydroxylammonium chloride and octadecenylamine, for the analysis of high molecular weight ketones. Fowler, Kline, and Mitchell[4] determined vanillin in the presence of acetovanillone by controlling the reaction time. Higuchi and Barnstein[5] investigated hydroxylammonium acetate as a reagent for aldehydes and ketones. The oximation was performed in glacial acetic acid and the excess reagent was titrated potentiometrically with perchloric acid.

† Reprinted from *Analytical Chemistry* 31, 260 (1959). Copyright 1959 by the American Chemical Society and reprinted by permission of the copyright owner.

REAGENTS

2-Dimethylaminoethanol, 0.25 *M*. Dissolve approximately 22.5 grams of freshly distilled 2-dimethylaminoethanol (Eastman Chemical Products, Inc., white label or equivalent) in 2-propanol to make 1 liter of solution.

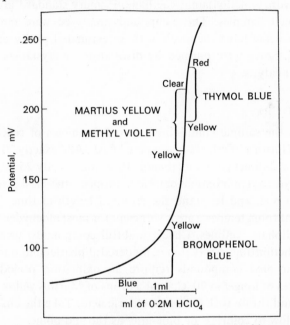

Fig. 1. Titration of blank showing indicator transition ranges.

Hydroxylammonium Chloride, 0.4 *M*. Dissolve 27.8 grams of the pure salt in 300 ml. of absolute methanol and dilute to 1 liter with 2-propanol.

2-Propanol. Reagent grade, absolute. Martius Yellow. Dissolve 0.0667 gram of Martius yellow (Harleco, Hartman-Teddon Co.) and 0.004 gram of methyl violet in ethanol and dilute to 50 ml. with ethanol.

Methyl Cellosolve. Merck & Co., Inc., reagent grade or Union Carbide Chemicals Co.

Perchloric Acid, 0.2 M. Pipet 17.0 ml. of 70% perchloric acid and dilute to 1 liter with methyl Cellosolve. Standardize by titration of tris (hydroxymethyl) aminomethane.

Tris(hydroxymethyl)aminomethane. Primary standard grade.

Carbonyl Samples. The compounds analyzed were mostly Eastman white label chemicals with an estimated purity of 98 to 100%. Some were purified by distillation or crystallization prior to analysis.

PROCEDURE

Weigh the sample containing 1.5 to 2.5 mmoles of reactive carbonyl into a 150-ml. glass-stoppered flask. Add exactly 20 ml. of 0.25 M 2-dimethylaminoethanol, then add exactly 25 ml. of 0.4 M hydroxylammonium chloride. Stopper the flask, swirl gently to mix, and let stand the required length of time. Ten minutes at room temperature is sufficient for most aldehydes and simple aliphatic ketones. Check doubtful compounds, using a longer reaction time. Aryl ketones, hindered aliphatic compounds, and dicarbonyl compounds require an oximation period of 45 minutes or longer at 70°C. Add 5 drops of Martius yellow indicator and titrate with 0.2 M perchloric acid. Take the change from yellow to colorless or blue-gray as the end point.

Determine the blank by titrating a similar mixture of 2-dimethylaminoethanol and hydroxylammonium chloride that has stood for the same period of time as the sample. Use the difference between the blank, V_b, and the sample titration, V_s, to calculate the percentage of the carbonyl compound in the sample.

% carbonyl compound

$$= \frac{(V_b - V_s) \text{ (moles of HClO}_4) \text{ (mol. wt.)}}{10 \text{ (sample wt., grams)}}$$

DEVELOPMENT OF METHOD

In developing a quantitative method involving oximation with a hydroxylammonium salt, several principles should be considered.

The solution should be buffered at a neutral or slightly acidic pH during oximation. If this is not done, the acid liberated may reduce the ratio of (NH_2OH) to $(NH_3OH)^+$ to a low value and result in incomplete or very slow oximation. A basic solution is generally avoided because of the instability of hydroxylamine in basic solution and condensations or other side reactions of carbonyl compounds.

Because oximation is subject to general acid catalysis, a high concentration of protonated species in the buffer will increase the rate of oximation.

Reaction in a solvent containing little or no water should favor the oximation equilibrium.

The buffer and solvent must be such that the excess hydroxylamine (or some other appropriate reactant or product) can be titrated accurately after the oximation is complete.

The reactions involved in the present method are as follows:

$$(NH_3OH)^+Cl^- + B \rightarrow BH^+Cl^- + NH_2OH \tag{1}$$

$$NH_2OH + {>}C{=}O \rightleftharpoons {>}C{=}NOH + H_2O \tag{2}$$

$$(Excess)NH_2OH + H^+ \rightarrow (NH_3OH)^+ \tag{3}$$

A solution of hydroxylammonium chloride in methanol–2-propanol is approximately half neutralized by a measured aliquot of a strong base, B, in 2-propanol. After the oximation is complete, the excess base (now present as NH_2OH) is titrated with standard acid. The difference between this titration and a blank permits calculation of the amount of carbonyl present.

Choice of Organic Base

The organic base used to neutralize the hydroxylammonium chloride should be sufficiently basic to force the equilibrium in Reaction 1 to the right. A tertiary amine should be used to avoid Schiff base formation or other side reactions with carbonyl. The hydrochloride of the base should be soluble in 2-propanol, because extensive precipitation may lead to occlusion or coprecipitation of the sample. Finally the base should be stable over extended storage.

Triethanolamine was sufficiently stable and basic, but copious precipitation of triethanolammonium chloride resulted. 2-Dimethylaminoethanol and 2-diethylaminoethanol fulfilled the requirements and a solution of 2-dimethylaminoethanol in 2-propanol was adopted.

Choice of Solvent

Alcohols are good solvents for the reagents involved, and permit a much sharper final titration of the hydroxylamine than is possible in water or in wateralcohol mixtures. Even 5 or 10% water in the solvent mixture significantly reduces the sharpness of the end point. 2-Propanol permits a sharper end point than does methanol. Some methanol is necessary to dissolve the hydroxylammonium chloride.

Order of Adding Reagents

Because acetal or ketal formation is an acid-catalyzed process, it is minimized by adding the base to the sample prior to the addition of hydroxylammonium chloride. Metcalfe and Schmitz[8] suggested a similar sequence. The ease of formation of acetals or ketals is also dependent upon the nature of the alcohol. Primary alcohols form acetals and ketals the most readily, secondary alcohols less readily, and tertiary alcohols the least of all. Johnston[6] proposed 2-methyl-2-propanol as the solvent to minimize these interferences. 2-Propanol is satisfactory.

Choice of Titrant

Both 0.2 M hydrochloric acid and perchloric acid in 2-propanol give sharp end points and accurate results if the final titration is performed very rapidly. However, with titrations carried out at a slower rate, results several per cent low were invariably obtained for the analysis of carbonyl compounds.

The reason was finally traced to the reaction of carbonyl impurity in the reagent grade 2-propanol during the titration. Although carbonyl in the solvents present during the oximation reaction is accurately accounted for by the blank, it is difficult to correct exactly for any carbonyl in the solvent used for the acid titrant, because more titrant is used to titrate the blank than the actual sample. This introduces an error that can be avoided only by titrating so rapidly that none of the titrant carbonyl has time to react with hydroxylamine, or by making up the titrant in a solvent free of carbonyl.

Methyl Cellosolve, unlike 2-propanol, exhibited no carbonyl band in the infrared spectra, and was satisfactory in actual practice. A methyl Cellosolve solution of either hydrochloric or perchloric acid is a satisfactory titrant, but perchloric acid keeps its titer on storage much better than hydrochloric acid.

Detection of End Point. The end point in the titration of a sample or blank may be detected either potentiometrically or by a visual indicator. Martius yellow mixed with a little methyl violet gives an excellent color change (yellow to colorless) that corresponds exactly with the potentiometric end point (Fig. 1). Thymol blue can also be used, but is less satisfactory because the color change occurs a little late. Bromophenol blue changes too early and is unsatisfactory.

Reaction Time and Temperature. The choice of reaction time and temperature depends on the reactivity of the carbonyl compound with hydroxylamine. Simple aldehydes and ketones oximate completely in 5 to 30 minutes at room temperature. Aryl ketones, hindered ketones, etc., require a longer reaction period and may also require an elevated temperature for quantitative oximation.

Hydroxylamine should not decompose excessively during the oximation period. The data in Table I show that the reagent blank is perfectly constant for at least 2 hours at room temperature. For blanks immersed in a 70°C. circulating water bath there is some initial decrease, but the blank is constant between 15 minutes and 2 hours. The initial decrease in the blank may be caused by oxidation of hydroxylamine by dissolved oxygen.

REFERENCES

1. BENNETT, A.H., *Analyst* **34**, 14 (1909).
2. BENNETT, A.H., DONOVAN, F.K., *Ibid.*, **47**, 146 (1922).
3. BRYANT, W.M.D., SMITH, D.M., *J. Am. Chem. Soc.* **57**, 57 (1935).
4. FOWLER, LEWIS, KLINE, H.R., MITCHELL, R.S., *Anal. Chem.* **27**, 1688 (1955).
5. HIGUCHI, TAKERU, BARNSTEIN, C.H., *Ibid.*, **28**, 1022 (1956).
6. JOHNSTON, V.D., *Mfg. Chemist* **25**, 337 (1954).
7. KNIGHT, H.B., SWERN, DANIEL, *J. Am. Oil Chemists' Soc.* **26**, 366 (1949).
8. METCALFE, L.D., SCHMITZ, A.A., *Anal. Chem.* **27**, 138 (1955).
9. MONTES, A.L., GRANDOLINI, E.A.C., *Anales direc. nacl. quim. (Buenos Aires)* **4**, 9 (1951).
10. PESEZ, MAURICE, *Bull. soc. chim. France* **1957**, 417.
11. SCHULTES, HERMAN, *Angew. Chem.* **47**, 258 (1934).
12. STILLMAN, R.C., REED, R.M., *Perfumery Essent. Oil Record* **23**, 278 (1932).
13. TROZZOLO, A.M., LIEBER, EUGENE, *Anal. Chem.* **22**, 764 (1950).
14. WALTHER, V.J., *Pharm. Zentralhalle* **40**, 621 (1899).

CHAPTER 5

Macro- and Semimicrodetermination of Aldehydes and Ketones by Reaction with Hydroxylammonium Formate†

JAMES E. RUCH, JAMES B. JOHNSON, and FRANK E. CRITCHFIELD

A NEED frequently arises to determine small amounts of aldehydes and ketones, either for process control or for estimation of product quality. Higuchi and Barnstein[2] reported a hydroxylammonium acetate method which employs an acetic acid solvent and is based on the titration of excess reagent. The reagent is relatively unstable, and the method does not afford sharp end points because the oximes formed (particularly ketoximes) are sufficiently basic to interfere.

Fritz, Yamamura, and Bradford[1] have devised a nonaqueous hydroxylamine oximation procedure which uses a titrant of perchloric acid in methyl Cellosolve to obtain sharp end points in titrating excess reagent. Purity data by this method are excellent; however, the strong acid induces interferences by acetals, ketals, and vinyl ethers when these compounds are major components of the sample.

† Reprinted from *Analytical Chemistry* **33**, 1566 (1961). Copyright 1961 by the American Chemical Society and reprinted by permission of the copyright owner.

115

Pesez[3] described an oximation procedure in methanol using hydroxylammonium formate as the reagent (which is adequately stable), perchloric acid in dioxane as the titrant, and thymol blue as the indicator. In methanolic medium, formic acid is neutral to thymol blue indicator; therefore, the course of this reaction can be followed by the direct titration of unreacted hydroxylammonium formate.

However, purity determinations by this method on some compounds (e.g., acetone) were 1 to 2% low. Presumably, most of these difficulties encountered with the Pesez method are due to the formation of peroxides and carbonyl compounds in the perchloric acid–dioxane titrant. Large amounts of acetals and ketals also interfered with the method. Finally, the use of methanol as the medium is not desirable because of its relatively poor differentiating powers in the presence of large amounts of reagent and reaction product.

The hydroxylammonium formate method is attractive because it is simple to apply and because the reaction proceeds rapidly. Modifications of the basic procedure of Pesez have produced a macro method which is reliable for purity determinations and which does not suffer from interferences by acetals, ketals, and vinyl ethers. From these studies, a semimicro method was developed for determining milligram quantities of carbonyl compounds. The development and application of these procedures will be discussed.

MODIFIED MACRO METHOD

The composition of both the reagent and the titrant have been altered so that quantitative results can be obtained by the procedure and former interferences are eliminated. The titration medium was changed to a 2 to 1 mixture of methyl Cellosolve and methanol. Methyl Cellosolve is an excellent differentiating solvent and is neutral to thymol blue indicator. Methanol is added because it brightens the indicator color transition.

Methyl Cellosolve is also used as a titrant medium because large quantities of this solvent have no effect on the titration, whereas large quantities of methanol tend to shift the indicator end point. Perchloric acid has been replaced by nitric acid after consideration of the properties desired. Of the many acids tried, hydrochloric, perchloric, and nitric acids are the only ones which produced satisfactory titrations of the reagent. The first two were rejected because they are so strong that they readily hydrolyze acetals. Although nitric acid does not provide the sharpest end point, its methyl Cellosolve solution is stable, and the specificity of the method is increased because of the diminished acid strength of this titrant. Urea is added to destroy any nitrous acid and p-diethoxybenzene may be used to retard peroxide formation.

The method of titrant standardization is important. In time, weak acids accumulate which could affect the standardization. Tris(hydroxymethyl)-aminomethane is an excellent primary standard for this use, but it is a stronger base than hydroxylamine; hence, in methyl Cellosolve medium, the equivalence point lies in a region below the thymol blue transition point and subject to interference from weak acids. Both difficulties have been averted by using a propylene glycol–methanol medium wherein the equivalence point and the indicator change coincide and are unaffected by relatively large amounts of organic acids (up to 2 ml. of acetic acid).

Reagents. Hydroxylammonium formate, approximately 0.5 N in methyl Cellosolve. Place 32 grams of reagent grade potassium hydroxide pellets in 350 ml. of methyl Cellosolve. Add 20 ml. of concentrated (90%) formic acid to help effect solution and stir. Neutralize the solution to a phenolphthalein end point by addition of more formic acid, then add 2 or 3 more pellets of potassium hydroxide and stir until dissolved. The result is a solution of potassium formate containing a small excess of potassium hydroxide, as shown by the color of the phenolphthalein indicator in the solution.

Prepare a second solution by dissolving 34 grams of hydroxylamine hydrochloride in 650 ml. of methyl Cellosolve. Mix the two solutions, chill to 15°C., and filter to remove precipitated potassium chloride. (The reagent is chilled to remove as much potassium chloride as possible and prevent later deposition of this salt as a solid material.) The reagent is stable for at least 2 weeks, but should be discarded when the blank titration becomes less than 35 ml.

Nitric acid, 0.5 N in methyl Cellosolve. Add 33 ml. of concentrated nitric acid to 500 ml. of methyl Cellosolve. Add and dissolve 1.0 gram of urea and 0.1 gram of p-diethoxybenzene (Eastman Chemical Products Co.), dilute to 1 liter with additional methyl Cellosolve, and mix thoroughly.

To standardize, dissolve 1.5 gram of tris(hydroxymethyl)-aminomethane (primary standard grade) in 50 ml. of hot methanol. Add 100 ml. of propylene glycol and titrate to thymol blue indicator until the color changes from yellow to a definite orange. Run a blank on the solvents.

Thymol blue indicator, 0.3 % solution in dimethylformamide.

Macro Procedure. Pipet exactly 50 ml. of the 0.5 N hydroxylammonium formate reagent into each of two 250-ml. flasks and reserve one flask for a blank determination. Into the other flask, introduce an amount of sample containing no more than 15 meq. of reactive carbonyl compound. Allow blank and sample to stand at room temperature for the length of time specified in Table I.

To each flask add 50 ml. of methanol, 75 ml. of methyl Cellosolve, and 5 or 6 drops of thymol blue indicator. Titrate the blank with standard 0.5 N nitric acid in methyl Cellosolve until the color changes from yellow to a definite orange. Titrate the sample until the color matches that of the blank, approaching the end point dropwise. The difference between blank and sample titrations is a measure of the carbonyl content.

REFERENCES

1. FRITZ, J.S., YAMAMURA, S.S., BRADFORD, E.C., *Anal. Chem.* **31,** 260 (1959).
2. HIGUCHI, T., BARNSTEIN, C.H., *Ibid.* **28,** 1022 (1956).
3. PESEZ, M., *Bull. soc. chim. France* **1957,** 417.

CHAPTER 6

Studies on the Mechanism of Oxime and Semicarbazone Formation[1]†

WILLIAM P. JENCKS

THE CLASSICAL experiments of Barrett and Lapworth,[2] Olander,[3] Conant and Bartlett,[4] and Westheimer[5] demonstrated that the reactions of carbonyl compounds with such nitrogen bases as hydroxylamine and semicarbazide exhibit striking maxima in their pH-rate profiles. These pH optima have been attributed to the opposing effects of general acid catalysis and the decrease in the concentration of attacking free nitrogen base due to conversion to the conjugate acid at low pH.[4, 6]

The observation that hydroxylamine reacts rapidly with p-nitrophenyl esters at neutral pH without significant acid catalysis (to give a mixture of O- and N-substituted products)[7] suggested that in the relatively slow, acid-catalyzed reaction of hydroxylamine with aldehydes and ketones the addition of nitrogen base to the carbonyl group might not be the rate-limiting step. The kinetics of oxime and semicarbazone formation have accordingly been studied by following the changes in the ultraviolet absorption of a number of carbonyl compounds in aqueous solution after the addition of the appropriate nitrogen base. It has been found that at neutral pH the attack of nitrogen base on

† Reprinted from *Journal of the American Chemical Society* **81,** 475 (1959). Reprinted by permission of the copyright owner.

the carbonyl compound is fast, so that the over-all rate is dependent on the equilibrium concentration of a non-absorbing addition compound and on the rate of its acid-catalyzed dehydration. The pH-rate maxima for oxime formation appear to be the result of a transition to a rate-limiting attack of free nitrogen base on the carbonyl-compound at acid pH and are not dependent on general acid catalysis.

$$> C{=}O + H_2NR \underset{k_{-1}}{\overset{k_1}{\rightleftarrows}} > C \underset{NHR}{\overset{OH}{\diagdown}} \overset{H^+}{\underset{k_{-2}}{\overset{k_2}{\rightleftarrows}}} > C{=}NR + HOH$$

RESULTS

In the neutral pH range the rate of dehydration of addition compound to form oxime or semicarbazone is proportional to the amount of complex present and to the concentration of hydrogen ion (Fig. 2). The data for the reactions of acetone and furfural with hydroxylamine cover the range of pH in which hydroxylamine is converted to its conjugate acid, so that the fraction of the carbonyl compound present as the addition compound, which is proportional to the concentration of free hydroxylamine, varied from 0.00066 to 0.016 and from 0.0077 to 0.41 for acetone and furfural, respectively. Some deviation from linearity is noted in the case of furfural as the pH is lowered below 5 (see below). Although individual experiments were carried out at constant pH and with a large excess of nitrogen base so that pseudo first-order kinetics were obtained, the first-order rate constants in dilute solution increase with the concentration of nitrogen base and of hydrogen ion so that the over-all reaction is third order. However, at a higher concentration of base, in which most of the carbonyl compound is present as the addition compound, the rate at a given pH becomes independent of the concentration of nitrogen base and approaches over-all first-order kinetics; this is the case, for example, for pyruvate which is 74–95% in the form of the addition compound in 0.05 to 0.30 M hydroxylamine (Fig. 2, solid triangles). The rate constants for oxime formation from the addition compound, summarized in Table I, increase in the order furfural < pyruvate < benzaldehyde < acetone < cyclohexanone. The rate constants for dehydration of the semicarbazide addition compounds of pyruvate and furfural are almost identical to those of the corresponding hydroxylamine compounds.

The rate of oxime formation from pyruvate, furfural and acetone in the neutral pH region is increased by phosphate buffer (Fig. 3). This acceleration is greater at pH 6.7 than at pH 7.6, suggesting that in this pH region these reactions are subject to general acid catalysis by $H_2PO_4^-$ ion as well as to specific acid catalysis. Acceleration by buffer of the rate of oxime formation from d-carvone has been shown previously by Stempel and Schaffel.[11]

As the pH is lowered to a point at which the rate of acid-catalyzed dehydration of addition compound is fast and the concentration of nitrogen base becomes small because of conversion to its conjugate acid, the rates of oxime and semicarbazone formation no longer follow the above relationships. For the reactions of hydroxylamine with acetone and furfural (Fig. 4) the rate begins to fall off below pH 5 and at low pH appears to approach a small and constant value; this represents the pH-independent reaction observed by Barrett and Lapworth even in strong acid[2] which may be due to a specific acid-catalyzed addition of free hydroxylamine. In the same figure are shown the calculated rates for a rate-limiting acid-catalyzed dehydration of addition compound and for a rate-limiting attack of hydroxylamine as the free base on the carbonyl group. The former curve agrees closely with the experimental results in the region near neutrality and, although some deviation is observed because of the pH-independent reaction, the latter predicts the decrease in rate observed at more acid pH.[12] Although individual runs followed pseudo first-order kinetics in the presence of excess hydroxylamine, the increase of the first-order rate constants with increasing free hydroxylamine concentration indicates that the over-all reaction in this pH region is second order. These data and the known equilibrium constant for acetoxime formation[3,4] permit an approximate calculation of the rate and equilibrium constants for all of the steps of the acetone–hydroxylamine reaction except the base-catalyzed reaction[2] (Table II).

Table II. Apparent rate and equilibrium constants for the reaction of acetone and hydroxylamine[b]

$K_{overall}$	$= [A]/[B][C]$	1.06×10^{6a}
K_1	$= [D]/[B][C]$	1.0
K_2	$= [A]/[D] = K/K_1$	1.06×10^6
k_1;	$v_1 = k_1[C][B]$	6×10^4
k_{1a};	$v_{1a} = k_{1a}[C][B][H^+]$	1×10^7
k_{-1}	$= k_1/K_1$	6×10^4
k_{-1}	$= k_{1a}/K_1$	1×10^7
k_2;	$v_2 = k_2[D][H^+]$	0.91×10^8
k_{-2}	$= k_2/K_2$	86

[a] See references 3 and 4.
[b] $A = (CH_3)_2C{=}NOH$, $B = CH_3)_2C{=}O$, $C = NH_2OH$, $D = (CH_3)_2C(OH)NHOH$.

In contrast to its effect at neutral pH, variation of the phosphate buffer concentration at acid pH does not significantly alter the rate (Fig. 4). This indicates that general acid catalysis by buffer is not responsible for the pH-rate maxima and provides further support for a change in the rate-limiting step of the reaction at acid pH. General acid catalysis by hydroxylammonium ion also does not account for the rate maxima, since such catalysis would lead to a maximum at the pK_a of hydroxylamine[6] and to a rate which would be more than first-order in respect to hydroxylamine.

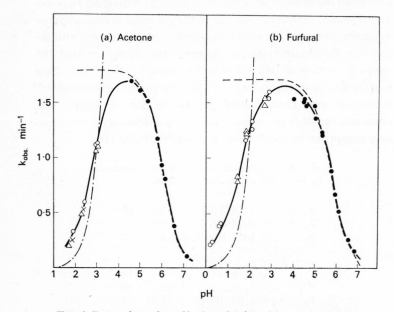

FIG. 4. Rates of reaction of hydroxylamine with acetone and furfural as a function of pH: ●, no added buffer; σ, $\times$, $\triangle$, 0.025, 0.05, 0.10 M potassium phosphate buffer, respectively; ◓, in dilute HCl; ---, calculated for rate-limiting acid-catalyzed dehydration of addition complex; -·-·-, calculated for rate-limiting addition of free hydroxylamine to the carbonyl group. (a) Acetone–hydroxylamine: total hydroxylamine 0.0176 M, acetone 0.0005 M, ionic strength maintained at 0.32 with NaCl, measured at 220 mμ; calculated curves from $k_{obs.} = (1.08 \times 10^8)$ [H⁺] (fraction as complex) and from $k_{obs.} = 6.8 \times 10^4$ [NH₂OH]; concentration of addition compound calculated from the equilibrium constant and the concentration of free hydroxylamine. (b) Furfural-hydroxylamine: total hydroxylamine 0.134 M, furfural 0.000055 M, ionic strength maintained at 0.67 with NaCl, measured at 260 mμ; calculated curves from $k_{obs.} = 2.2 \times 10^6$ [H⁺] (fraction as addition compound) and from $k_{obs.} = 9 \times 10^4$ [NH₂OH].

The reaction of semicarbazide with furfural shows a similar decrease from the predicted rate at acid pH, but in this case the reaction is complicated by both general[4] and specific acid catalysis. Second-order rate constants for semicarbazone formation, obtained by dividing the observed pseudo first-order rate constant by the concentration of free semicarbazide, are plotted logarithmically in Fig. 5 as a function of pH. From pH 5.7 to 7.1 the rate is directly proportional to hydrogen ion concentration and the second-order rate constant does not depend on the concentration of semicarbazide.[13] Below this pH the rate falls below that expected from extrapolation of the results at higher pH. The second-order rate constants become increasingly dependent on the semicarbazide concentration with decreasing pH, indicating general acid catalysis by the conjugate acid of semicarbazide, and after extrapolation to zero semicarbazide concentration the rates still increase with the hydrogen ion concentration, indicating that the reaction is also subject to specific acid catalysis.

DISCUSSION

Since the rate-limiting step of oxime and semicarbazone formation at neutral pH is the acid-catalyzed dehydration of the carbinolamine addition compound, the over-all rate of these reactions at low reactant concentration is dependent on the equilibrium concentration of addition compound and on the rate of its dehydration, while at high reactant concentration, with most of the carbonyl compound in the form of the addition compound the rate at a given pH is first-order and dependent only on the rate of dehydration. Thus the more rapid rate of oxime formation from pyruvate than from furfural in dilute solution is due principally to the more favorable equilibrium constant for formation of the pyruvate–hydroxylamine addition compound, while the rapid formation of acetoxime is a consequence of a rapid dehydration which more than compensates for the low equilibrium concentration of addition compound. Under these circumstances it is not surprising that the over-all rates of semicarbazone formation in a series of aldehydes and ketones show no correlation with the equilibrium constants for formation of other addition compounds.[14] The equilibrium constants given in Table I for formation of hydroxylamine addition compounds, although obtained under somewhat different conditions, increase in the order acetone < cyclohexanone ~ furfural ~ benzaldehyde < pyruvate, which generally parallels the equilibrium constants for the addition of cyanide[15] and bisulfite[16] and the rate constants for the addition of hydride ion to these compounds.[17] The relatively favorable equilibrium constant for the cyclohexanone addition compound compared to acetone is presumably due to the transition from an sp_2 to a less strained sp_3 hybridization of the carbonyl carbon atom in the former compound on addition compound formation[17, 18] and the low equilibrium constants for the addition compounds of the aldehydes, furfural and benzaldehyde, which are only slightly greater than for simple ketones are presumably the result of the loss of conjugation of the carbonyl group with the aromatic ring of these compounds on addition compound formation.[15, 19] It should be noted that the oxime reaction is not symmetrical with respect to the rates of formation of addition compound from carbonyl compound and from oxime since only the latter step is significantly acid-catalyzed. Thus, although the equilibrium constants are not favored, the relatively rapid dehydration of the acetone and cyclohexanone addition compounds may be ascribed to stabilization by the electron-donating alkyl groups of a transition state which resembles the immediate product of the reaction

$$>C=N-,$$ and not the final product, $>C=N-$.

Price and Hammett have shown that the differences in the rates of semicarbazone formation from a group of carbonyl compounds in phosphate buffer at pH 7 are due largely to differences in the entropy of activation, and suggested that these differences were due to differences in restriction of free movement in the transition state.[20] As they pointed out, these differences include the effect of phosphate catalysis, and it now appears that they can be further divided into effects on the equilibrium constant for addition compound formation and on the rate of acid-catalyzed dehydration; exact interpretation of these effects and of similar data from other laboratories[21] must therefore await the determination of the differences in the energy and entropy of the individual reaction steps. Similarly, the recently described lack of correlation of the rates of semicarbazone[22] and Schiff base[23] formation in a series of substituted benzaldehydes with Hammett's substituent constants, σ, may be accounted for, as was already suggested as a possibility by these workers,[22, 23] by the two-step course of these reactions.

The alkali-catalyzed reaction of hydroxylamine with acetone described by Barrett and Lapworth[2] has generally been attributed to a reaction of the H_2NO^- anion, but it has not been clear how the attack of this anion should lead to oxime formation. It now appears that hydroxide ion catalysis of this reaction represents a base-catalyzed dehydration of addition compound, or, in the reverse reaction, an attack of hydroxide ion on acetoxime.

The over-all rates of reaction of hydroxylamine and semicarbazide with the same carbonyl compound are very similar, although the basicity of hydroxylamine is 300 times greater than that of semicarbazide and its nucleophilic strength would be expected to be greater by a similar factor. The nucleophilic strength however, governs only the *rate* of attack of these compounds on the carbonyl group, while the over-all rate of reaction at neutral pH depends on the rate dehydration, which is similar in both cases, and on the equilibrium constant for the formation of addition compound, which depends on the relative affinities of the nitrogen atom for hydrogen and for the carbonyl carbon atom. From the equilibrium constants for the formation of pyruvate addition compounds, this relative affinity appears to vary over only a sixfold range from semicarbazide (pK_a 3.7)[4] to methoxyamine (pK_a 4.6)[24] to hydroxylamine (pK_a 6.0)[24] to hydrazine (pK_a 7.9).[25] Not all nitrogen bases with a replaceable hydrogen atom will form addition compounds, however, since no decrease in the absorption of pyruvate at 320 mμ was found in $2M$ piperidine or $1M$ imidazole, suggesting that the affinity of the nitrogen atom of these compounds for the carbonyl group is much less. The affinity of the oxygen atom of water for the carbonyl carbon atom is also small since all of the compounds examined exist in the carbonyl form rather than as the hydrate in aqueous solution. A possible explanation for the abnormal affinity of semicarbazide, hydrazine and hydroxylamine for the carbonyl group is that the addition compounds may be stabilized by hydrogen bonding of the hydroxyl hydrogen to the α-nitrogen or oxygen atom of the base in a manner similar to that postulated for stabilization of the transition state in the unusually rapid attack of hydroxylamine on the carbonyl group of activated acyl compounds.[7]

The unfavorable equilibrium constants for the addition of water to acetoxime (Table II) and to furfural and pyruvate semicarbazones, calculated from the known equilibrium constants of the over-all reaction and of addition compound formation (Table III), also reflect the relatively low affinity of the water oxygen for carbon as well as the relatively low susceptibility of the weakly electronegative $>C=N-$ group to addition reactions.

*Table III. Apparent rate and equilibrium constants
for the reactions of furfural and pyruvate with semicarbazide*

	$K_{overall}{}^a$	K_1	$K_2{}^b$	$k_2{}^c$
Furfural	1.32×10^5	1.1	1.2×10^5	16.7
Pyruvate	1.96×10^5	10	1.96×10^4	245

^{a} $[>C{=}NR]/[>C{=}O] [H_2NR]$ from ref. 4.
^{b} $[>C{=}NR]/[>C(OH)NHR]$; from $K_{overall}/K_1$.
^{c} $v_{-2}{=}k_{-2} [>C{=}NR] [H^+]$ from k_2/K_2.

At acid pH the rates of oxime and semicarbazone formation
are less than those calculated for a ratelimiting acid-catalyzed
dehydration of addition compound. This is interpreted as a
transition to a rate-limiting addition of free nitrogen base to the
carbonyl group under conditions in which the rate of acid-catalyzed dehydration is very fast and, in the case of hydroxylamine,
the concentration of nitrogen base is lowered by conversion to its
conjugate acid. With the weakly basic semicarbazide molecule,
which would be expected to react relatively slowly with carbonyl
compounds, this transition occurs at a higher pH than with the
more basic hydroxylamine. Moreover, the addition of semicarbazide is subject to both general and specific acid catalysis, as
might be expected for a weak nucleophile,[26] while acid catalysis
is of minor importance for the addition of the stronger base, hydroxylamine.

REFERENCES

1. Publication 14 of the Graduate Department of Biochemistry, Brandeis
   University.
2. BARRETT, E., LAPWORTH, A., *J. Chem. Soc.* **93**, 85 (1908); *cf.* also ACREE,
   S. F., JOHNSON, J.M., *Am. Chem. J.* **38**, 308 (1907); KNORRE, D.G.,
   EMANUEL, N.M., *Doklady Aka. Sci. S.S.S.R.* **91**, 1163 (1953).
3. OLANDER, A., *Z. physik. Chem.* **129**, 1 (1927).
4. CONANT, J.B., BARTLETT, *J. Amer. Chem. Soc.* **54**, 2881 (1932).

5. WESTHEIMER, *Ibid.* **56,** 1962 (1934).
6. HAMMETT, L.P., *Physical Organic Chemistry*, McGraw-Hill, New York, 1940, p. 331.
7. JENCKS, W.P., *J. Amer. Chem. Soc.* **80,** 4581 (1958); **80,** 4585 (1958).
11. STEMPEL, G.H., SCHAFFEL, *Ibid.* **66,** 1158 (1944).
12. Complete conversion of the addition product to its conjugate acid would lead to a constant rate and not to the observed decrease in rate at more acid pH.
13. Experiments in this pH range were carried out in 0.01 M phosphate buffer; consequently the rates shown are approximately 4% greater than the uncatalyzed rates because of buffer catalysis.
14. Cf. ref. 6, p. 211.
15. LAPWORTH, A., MANSKE, *J. Chem. Soc.* 2533 (1928); 1976 (1930).
16. GUBAREVA, M.A., *J. Gen. Chem. U.S.S.S.R.* **17,** 2259 (1947).
17. BROWN, H.C., WHEELER, O.H., ICHIKAWA, K., *Tetrahedron* **1,** 214 (1957); Brown, H.C., Ichikawa, K., *Ibid.* **1,** 221 (1957).
18. BROWN, H.C., FLETCHER, R.S., JOHANNESEN, R.B., *J. Amer. Chem. Soc.* **73,** 212 (1951).
19. Cf. also Baker, J.W., *J. Chem. Soc.* **191** (1942); 1089 (1949); 2831 (1952), for further discussion of the effects of structure.
20. PRICE, F.P., HAMMETT, L.P., *J. Amer. Chem. Soc.* **63,** 2387 (1941).
21. CROSS, R.P., FUGASSI, P., *Ibid.* **71,** 223 (1949); MARIELLA, R.P., STEMPEL, G.H., *Bol. Col. Quim. Puerto Rico* **10,** 12 (1953).
22. NOYCE, D.S., BOTTINI, A.T., SMITH, S.G., *J. Org. Chem.* **23,** 752 (1958).
23. SANTERRE, G.M., HANSROTE, C.J., CROWELL, T.I., *J. Amer. Chem. Soc.* **80,** 1254 (1958).
24. BISSOT, T.C., PARRY, R.W., CAMPBELL, D.H., *Ibid.* **79,** 796 (1957).
25. SCHWARZENBACH, G., *Helv. Chim. Acta* **19,** 178 (1936).
26. Acid catalysis of the addition of a free nitrogen base to the carbonyl group is kinetically indistinguishable from an uncatalyzed addition of the conjugate acid of the base (*cf.* ref. 3); the latter mechanism is very unlikely on chemical grounds because of the inability of the RNH_3^+ group to act as a nucleophilic reagent.

CHAPTER 7

O-Methyloximes as Carbonyl Derivatives in Gas Chromatography, Mass Spectrometry, and Nuclear Magnetic Resonance†

HENRY M. FALES and TAPANI LUUKKAINEN[1]

Laboratory of Metabolism, National Heart Institute, Bethesda, Md.

THE KETO group presents relatively few problems in terms of tailing and decomposition in the gas chromatography of high molecular weight substances. Still, there is a demand for adducts which will allow the full characterization of ketonic compounds through a characteristic shift in retention time as seen on a variety of liquid phases. For this purpose, the adduct should be formed rapidly and quantitatively and it ought to be relatively stable to heat, light, and moisture. This is especially true if analyses are to be attempted in the submicrogram range. N,N-Dimethylhydrazine has been recommended for this purpose[12] since the reagent combines with ketones easily and adds little to their molecular weight. The N,N-dimethylhydrazones are stable enough when pure and crystalline, but impurities frequently found in biological samples appear to accelerate decomposition

† Reprinted from *Analytical Chemistry*, **37**, 955 (1965). Copyright 1965 by the American Chemical Society and reprinted by permission of the copyright owner.

of the derivatives in solutions in the presence of light and air. As a result, aged samples may exhibit spurious peaks and testosterone dimethylhydrazone, even when pure, exhibited peaks on both sides of the main peak at 180° on an SE-30 column. Wiley and Chang[14] report that a series of steroid dimethylhydrazones undergo decomposition on melting.

Simple oximes of low molecular weight compounds have been analyzed directly[2] but aldoximes are reported to dehydrate to their corresponding nitriles under similar conditions.[9] O-Methylhydroxylamine[3, 4] (methoxyamine) adds even less to the molecular weight of the carbonyl component than N,N-dimethylhydrazine and does not show the sensitivity of the latter to its environment. The O-methyloximes (MO's) are stable, easily crystallized derivatives, that survive operations such as treatment with acetic anhydride or trimethylsilyl chloride and hexamethyldisilazane.[8, 10, 11]

EXPERIMENTAL

The ketones are converted to O-methyloximes at room temperature by allowing an excess of methoxyamine hydrochloride (available from Eastman Organic Chemicals, Rochester, N.Y.) in pyridine to stand with the ketone overnight at room temperature. Evaporation of the excess pyridine under a nitrogen stream left the crude adduct which was taken up in benzene, centrifuged away from the excess pyridine hydrochloride, and chromatographed directly. For preparative purposes the adduct was recrystallized from aqueous ethanol or heptane–benzene.

RESULTS AND DISCUSSION

The retention times of a variety of ketosteroids (Table I, Fig. 1), on an nonpolar SE-30 column show that conversion to the O-methyloximes adds a definite increment to the retention time which varies only slightly with its location on the steroid skeleton. O-Methyloxime formation in the 3, 6, 16, and 17 positions all cause nearly the same retention time increase relative to the original ketones.

Since the 3 and 17 positions can be labeled separately by varying the reagent, the utility of this substance in mass spectrometric fragmentation studies of steroids was considered. The fact that N^{15} hydroxylamine hydrochloride is available (Volk Radiochemical Co., Chicago, Ill.) is particularly interesting in this respect since the ordinary oximes, formed in the usual manner, may be converted to their O-methyl ethers with methylating agents.[4] Introduction of the O-methyloxime function considerably alters the fragmentation of the steroid nucleus. Relatively small peaks are seen at high masses compared to the parent ketones.

Finally, in the course of this work it became apparent that the methoxime group is also useful as a means of counting carbonyl groups by n.m.r. spectrometry since the $NOCH_3$ group of protons is an easily integrated singlet at $\delta = 3.81$.

REFERENCES

1. BUDZIKIEWICZ, H., DJERASSI, C., *J. Am. Chem. Soc.* **84**, 1438 (1962).
2. CASON, J., HARRIS, E.R., *J. Org. Chem.* **24**, 676 (1959).
3. DONARUMA, L.G., *Ibid.* **22**, 1024 (1957).
4. HUDLICKY, M., HOKI, J., *Collection Czech. Chem. Commun.* **14**, 561 (1949).
5. JONES, L.W., MAJOR, R.T., *J. Am. Chem. Soc.* **49**, 1538 (1927).
6. JONES, R.N., SANDORFY, C., *Technique of Organic Chemistry*, W.West ed., Vol. IX, p. 467, Interscience, New York, 1956.
7. KIRSCHNER, M.A., FALES, H.M., *Anal. Chem.* **34**, 1548 (1962).

8. LANGER, S.H., PANTAGES, P., *Nature* **191**, 141 (1961).
9. LOHR, J., WARREN, R.W., *J. Chromatog.* **8**, 127 (1962).
10. LUUKKAINEN, T., VANDEN HEUVEL, W. J. A., HAAHTI, E. O. A., HORNING, E.C., *Biochem. Biophys. Acta* **52**, 599 (1961).
11. VANDEN HEUVEL, W.J.A., CREECH, B.G., HORNING, E.C., *Anal. Biochem.* **4**, 191 (1962).
12. VANDEN HEUVEL, W.J.A., HORNING, E.C., *Biochem. Biophys. Acta* **74**, 560 (1963).
13. VANDEN HEUVEL, W. J .A., HORNING, E. C., *Biochem. Biophys. Res. Commun.* **3**, 356 (1960).
14. WILEY, R.H., CHANG, S.H., *J. Med. Chem.* **6**, 611 (1963).

CHAPTER 8

Quantitative Aspects
of the Base-catalysed Halogenation
# of Aliphatic Ketones.
Part I. Iodination of Methyl Ketones†

C. F. CULLIS and M. H. HASHMI

WHEN methyl ketones react with iodine in alkaline solution the principal reaction occurring is generally represented by the equation (1). This reaction has been much used for the

$$CH_3 \cdot COR + 3I_2 + 4NaOH = CHI_3 + R \cdot CO_2Na + 3NaI + 3H_2O. \quad (1)$$

determination of methyl ketones and related compounds.

Kramer[1] devised a gravimetric procedure which is still occasionally employed,[2] but is in general only suitable for semi-quantitative work. Messinger's volumetric method[3] has been much more widely used. This has been extensively studied and modified in order to yield the most accurate results.[4] Even under optimum conditions, however, it seems that reaction does not occur quantitatively according to equation (1). For example, Hatcher and Mueller[5] found that the reaction never gave theoretical yields of iodoform. The method is also said to give high

† Reprinted from *Journal of the Chemical Society* 2512 (1956). Reprinted by permission of the copyright owner.

results in the determination of acetone[6, 7] and ethyl methyl ketone,[8] and low results with methyl *iso*propyl ketone.[6]

In this paper, the quantitative aspects are discussed of the base-catalysed iodination of a number of methyl ketones. It is established that in no case does the overall reaction proceed strictly according to equation (1), though with acetone the extent of side reactions is small enough not to exclude the use of Messinger's method for the quantitative analysis of this ketone.

RESULTS

Kinetic Measurements

The higher methyl ketones show similar kinetic behaviour to acetone.[12, 13] With the alkali present in large excess, the iodine disappears according to a first-order kinetic law. Plots of $\log_{10} (T_t - T_\infty)$ against t (where T_t and T_∞ are the thiosulphate titres after times t and infinity, respectively) are linear over at least the first half of the reaction, after which the rate tends to fall off less rapidly.

Table 2. Rates of iodination of some methyl ketones
Temp. = 25°; [Ketone] = 0·0025 M;
[Iodine] = 0·01 M; [NaOH] = 0·1 M

Ketone	Vel. const. (k) $(sec^{-1} \times 10^3)$
Acetone	16·80
Ethyl methyl ketone	9·01
Methyl *n*-propyl ketone	8·56
n-Butyl methyl ketone	8·08
Methyl *iso*propyl ketone	7·16
tert.-Butyl methyl ketone	3·41

The rates of halogenation in Table 2 are not, however, proportional to the rates of disappearance of ketone and should, strictly speaking, be multiplied by a "statistical" factor to allow for the different amounts of iodine consumed by the various ketones (Fig. 1). Such a correction is difficult to apply in practice since the conditions obtaining in the rate experiments are not those under which the limiting uptake of halogen is achieved. In any case, multiplication of the observed rates of halogenation by the appropriate factors would not alter qualitatively the order of reactivity of the ketones studied.

DISCUSSION

Nature of the Iodinating Species

The main course of the base-catalysed iodination of acetone is well established and is believed to consist of three stages: (i) conversion of the ketone into an enolate ion, (ii) progressive iodination of this ion to yield tri-iodoacetone, (iii) hydrolytic fission of the iodo-ketone to give iodoform and acetic acid. The principal iodinating species in (ii) is thought to be hypoiodous acid.[14] With higher methyl ketones, as with acetone, the *rate* of halogenation is normally controlled by (i), but the *extent* of iodination appears to depend on the balance between (ii) and a competing process involving disproportionation of hypoiodite to iodate. In order to reduce the rate of disproportionation and hence increase the iodine uptake, it is necessary to effect a high degree of dispersion of the halogenating agent.[14] Thus the iodine should be run into the pre-mixed ketone and alkali, and it should be added slowly. The disproportionation of hypoiodite is retarded by hydroxyl ions and accelerated by iodide ions[15, 16] and consequently the extent of iodine consumption is increased by maintaining a high pH and decreased by addition of iodide ions. The use of a high iodine concentration retards (i) by decreasing the effective hydroxyl-ion concentration; this also slows down (ii) and hence favours the disproportionation process so that the iodine uptake is decreased. This factor is predominant at low alkali concentrations or when (i) is relatively slow, and is thus most in evidence with the least reactive ketones. At high alkali concentrations, an increased concentration of halogen increases the extent to which (ii) can occur by maintaining for a longer period a sufficient supply of hypoiodous acid.

Causes of Abnormal Iodine Consumption

The iodine uptake will inevitably be low if the conditions are such that disproportionation of hypoiodous acid is rapid compared with enolisation of the ketone. Even if a sufficient concentration of hypoiodous acid is maintained, however, the iodine consumption rarely corresponds to that required by equation (1). Two opposing factors appear to be operative.

(a) *Factors responsible for high iodine consumption.* A high iodine consumption results from the formation of iodo-acids in addition to the normal reaction products predicted by equation (1). The experimental evidence shows that the production of such compounds must be considered as part of the main reaction and that the "extra" iodine is taken up by the ketone before fission of the C—C bond.

In order to obtain a fuller insight into the mechanism of formation of iodo-acids, it is necessary to consider in more detail the rate-determining (enolisation) stage of the reaction. The direction of enolisation of an unsymmetrical ketone depends on the nature of the solvent. In alkaline solution, substitution at a carbon atom slows down reactions dependent on the enolate ion (Table 2), and this, together with other evidence,[17, 18, 19] suggests that enolisation occurs away from the most substituted group, *i.e.*, towards the methyl group in methyl ketones. The enolate ion formed initially may immediately react to give a monoiodo-etone, $R \cdot CH_2 \cdot CO \cdot CH_2 I$, which will be further rapidly iodinated at the substituted methyl group.[20] If, however, the enolate ion persists in solution long enough, it may undergo a tautomeric change:

$$\text{(I)} \quad [R \cdot CH_2 \cdot CO : CH_2]^- \rightleftharpoons [R \cdot CH : CO \cdot CH_3]^- \quad \text{(II)}$$

(II) is in general stabilised with respect to (I) by hyperconjugation, and if the experimental conditions are such that equilibrium is set up before iodination occurs, substitution will take place to some extent on the "wrong" carbon atom.[21] If this were to happen, iodoacid would eventually be formed in addition to iodoform. The iodine uptake is, however, the same whether the order of mixing is ketone–alkali–iodine or ketone–iodine–alkali, although under the latter conditions, equilibrium between (I) and (II) is less readily established. Furthermore, if the above tautomeric change were faster than iodination, the corresponding process:

$$\text{(III)} \quad [R \cdot CHI \cdot CO : CH_2]^- \rightleftharpoons [R \cdot CI : CO \cdot CH_3]^- \quad \text{(IV)}$$

would be even more rapid, and both direct enolisation and the position of equilibrium would favour (IV) with respect to (III). In other words, any wrongly mono-iodinated compound should, according to the above mechanism, become di-iodinated. In fact, di-iodo-acids are not found among the reaction products.

A more plausible mechanism for the formation of iodo-acids may be constructed if it is assumed that initial attack occurs exclusively at the methyl group and further subsequent iodination at the same point eventually gives rise to the compound $R \cdot CH_2 \cdot CO \cdot CI_3$. This would undergo hydrolytic fission as the predominant, but not necessarily the sole, reaction. It might also enolise to give the ion $[R \cdot CH : CO \cdot CI_3]^-$, which would rapidly suffer iodination at the non-methyl group before cleavage takes place. An increase in alkali concentration would increase the rate of hydrolytic fission of the tri-iodo-ketone, but would also accelerate its enolisation and further iodination. Since both processes are presumably of the first order with respect to hydroxyl-ion concentration, the ratio of iodo-acids to iodoform would, on this theory, be largely uninfluenced by the alkali concentration, as is indeed found. A mechanism for the formation of iodo-acids, involving iodination at the "wrong" carbon atom *after* rather than before tri-iodination has occurred at the methyl group, therefore seems to be more in accordance with the experimental facts.

With ethyl methyl ketone and methyl *n*-propyl ketone, considerably more iodo-acid is formed than with acetone. This suggests that the tri-iodo-compounds $CH_3 \cdot CH_2 \cdot CO \cdot CI_3$ and $CH_3 \cdot CH_2 \cdot CH_2 \cdot CO \cdot CI_3$ are relatively more stable towards alkali than tri-iodoacetone, so that they can be halogenated to a greater extent before C—C bond fission takes place.

(b) *Factors responsible for low iodine consumption.* Except with acetone and ethyl methyl ketone, a parallelism exists between rate of iodination (Table 2) and extent of halogen consumption, the least reactive ketones, such as methyl *iso*propyl ketone and *tert.*-butyl methyl ketone, taking up the smallest amounts of iodine. With these two compounds in particular, less highly iodinated neutral products are formed in addition to iodoform. These are not iodo-ketones, since carbonyl compounds were previously removed from the reaction mixture. They must therefore be iodo-paraffins formed by hydrolytic fission of intermediate mono- and di-iodo-ketones.[22] A factor which may encourage premature fission is steric hindrance. Poggi[23] has shown that, during iodination of *tert.*-butyl methyl ketone, the compound $(CH_3)_3 C \cdot CO \cdot CHI_2$ can be isolated. Experiments with models confirm that, with the enolate ions $[(CH_3)_3 C \cdot CO : CI_2]^-$ and $[(CH_3)_2 CH \cdot CO : CI_2]^-$, steric hindrance makes the introduction of a third iodine atom difficult, so that hydrolysis of the di-iodo-ketones can compete successfully with further iodination. The analytical results show that premature fission sometimes takes place across the "wrong" C—C bond. With methyl *iso*-propyl ketone, for example, iodoacetic acid is found among the products; after a single iodination on the methyl and *iso*propyl groups, some cleavage must presumably occur according to the equation:

$$(CH_3)_2CI \cdot CO \cdot CH_2I + OH^- = CH_3 \cdot CHI \cdot CH_3 + CH_2I \cdot CO_2^-$$

With ketones of low reactivity, it is difficult to maintain a sufficient supply of hypoiodous acid, since the rate of production of enolate ions is small. Attempts to accelerate enolisation by an increase in hydroxyl-ion concentration will also tend to increase the rate of premature hydrolytic fission, so that it may not be easy in practise to achieve a higher iodine consumption.

REFERENCES

1. KRAMER, *Ber.* **13**, 1000 (1880).
2. HENNION and PILLAR, *J. Amer. Chem. Soc.* **72**, 5317 (1950).
3. MESSINGER, *Ber.* **21**, 3366 (1888).
4. See, *e.g.*, GOODWIN, *J. Amer. Chem. Soc.* **42**, 39 (1920).
5. HATCHER and MUELLER, *Trans. Roy. Soc. Canada* **23**, 35 (1929).
6. DAL NOGARE, NORRIS, and MITCHELL, *Analyt. Chem.*, **23**, 1473 (1951).
7. HAUGHTON, *Ind. Eng. Chem. Anal.*, **9**, 167 (1937).
8. CASSAR, *Ind. Eng. Chem.*, **19**, 1061. 1927.
9. MARASCO, *Ibid.*, **18**, 701 (1926).
10. HASHMI and CULLIS, *Analyt. Chim. Acta*, **14**, 336 (1956).
11. DROGIN and ROSANOFF, *J. Amer. Chem. Soc.*, **38**, 711 (1916).
12. BARTLETT, *Ibid.*, **56**, 967 (1934).
13. BELL and LONGUET-HIGGINS, *J.*, 636 (1946).
14. MORGAN, BRADWELL, and CULLIS, *J.*, 3190 (1950).
15. SKRABAL, *Monatsh.*, **32**, 167, 185 (1911); **33**, 99 (1912).
16. LI and WHITE, *J. Amer. Chem. Soc.*, **65**, 335 (1943).
17. SIMONSEN, *J.*, **121**, 2292 (1922).
18. SEMMLER nad SCHILLER, *Ber.*, **60**, 1591 (1927).
19. LEVINE and HAUSER, *J. Amer. Chem. Soc.*, **66**, 1768 (1944).
20. Cf. BELL and LIDWELL, *Proc. Roy. Soc.*, *A*, **176**, 88 (1940).
21. CARDWELL, *J.*, 2442 (1951).
22. RICHARD and LANGLAIS, *Bull. Soc. chim. France*, **7**, 462 (1910).
23. POGGI, *Atti Soc. ital. Progresso Sci. XXI Riunione*, **2**, 376 (1933).

CHAPTER 9

An Improved Kurt Meyer Titration†

S. R. COOPER and R. P. BARNES

MEYER[1] proposed the direct titration of the enolic form of a tautomeric compound with an alcoholic bromine solution, and also an indirect bromine titration method. In the indirect method the compound was dissolved in 96 per cent alcohol and cooled to 10°C., and an excess of an alcoholic bromine solution was added. This excess was removed by adding a small amount of sodium thiosulfate solution. Then a potassium iodide solution was added, and the liberated iodine was titrated with a solution of sodium thiosulfate. Later Meyer and Kappelmeier[2] proposed the use of 2-naphthol, in place of sodium thiosulfate, to absorb the excess bromine.

The authors have had some experience with this indirect titration method and have attempted to improve upon its accuracy. 2-Naphthol and its alcoholic solutions are usually colored brown even after the compound has been carefully purified. This makes it difficult, in many cases, to ascertain the point at which all the excess bromine has been removed, and also causes an error when the alcoholic solution containing free iodine is titrated with sodium thiosulfate until the yellow color due to iodine has

† Reprinted from *Analytical Chemistry*, **60,** 379 (1938). Copyright 1938 by the American Chemical Society and reprinted by permission of the copyright owner.

been removed. This condition can be remedied by using a compound such as diisobutylene which will absorb bromine by forming a colorless bromide, but will not react with iodine to form a stable compound.

The purpose of this investigation was to ascertain if diisobutylene could be used in place of 2-naphthol in the indirect Kurt Meyer titration.

PREPARATION OF REAGENTS

The dibenzoylmethane was prepared according to the method given by Pond, York, and Moore,[3] and was further purified by repeated recrystallizations from methyl alcohol, yielding a practically colorless substance.

The iodine was sublimed twice. An approximately $0.1 N$ solution of sodium thiosulfate was prepared and allowed to stand for several months, protected from the atmosphere by a tube filled with soda lime. The diisobutylene was the practical grade obtained from the Eastman Kodak Company. All the other reagent were c.p. products.

TITRATIONS

A sample of dibenzoylmethane was weighed, placed in a wide-necked Erlenmeyer flask, and dissolved in 25 ml. of absolute methyl alcohol. The resulting solution was cooled to $-5°C$. and an excess of an approximately $0.1 N$ solution of bromine in absolute methyl alcohol was added. The solution was mixed well, and a slight excess of diisobutylene was added. The time consumed in adding the bromine and absorbing the excess of it was about 15 seconds. Then 5 ml. of a 10 per cent aqueous solution of potassium iodide were added and the mixture was warmed to $30°C$. by dipping the flask in hot water while swirling its contents around. The solution was allowed to stand 5 to 10 minutes

Table I. Titration of dibenzoylmethane
with sodium thiosulfate solution

$C_{15}H_{12}O_2$ (Gram)	0.1 N Bromine solution (Ml.)	Decolorizing agent	Enol $C_{15}H_{12}O_2$ (%)
0.2421	25	C_8H_{16}	95.88
0.2407	25	C_8H_{16}	95.52
0.2114	25	C_8H_{16}	95.79
0.2651	25	C_8H_{16}	95.25
0.1799	25	C_8H_{16}	96.15
0.3489	40	C_8H_{16}	95.16
0.2665	35	C_8H_{16}	95.70
0.4505	52	C_8H_{16}	96.07
0.2795	30	C_8H_{16}	95.43
0.2257	25	C_8H_{16}	96.07
0.2774	30	C_8H_{16}	95.34
0.2035	25	C_8H_{16}	95.88
0.1964	25	C_8H_{16}	95.70
0.2206	25	C_8H_{16}	95.52
0.2076	25	C_8H_{16}	95.43
0.1991	25	C_8H_{16}	95.70
0.2382	30	$C_{10}H_7OH$	93.74
0.2551	30	$C_{10}H_7OH$	90.85
0.2403	35	$C_{10}H_7OH$	92.86
0.2486	30	$C_{10}H_7OH$	94.97
0.2128	30	$C_{10}H_7OH$	95.07
0.1797	30	$C_{10}H_7OH$	98.52

and was titrated with an approximately 0.1 N solution of sodium thiosulfate until the color had become a light yellow. Then 250 ml. of water and 4 ml. of a 0.6 per cent potato starch solution, which had been filtered, were added and the titration was continued to the disappearance of the blue color. Some titrations were made without using water and starch.

These titrations were compared with others which were performed according to the indirect Kurt Meyer method, with the exception that after the potassium iodide solution had been added the titration was carried out as above. The results of these and the first titrations are given in Table I.

The sodium thiosulfate solution was standardized according to the method of Treadwell and Hall[4] using iodine as the primary standard. The mean of these titrations was $0.1003 N$, and the average deviation 1 part per 1000.

DISCUSSION

Solutions of bromine in ethyl alcohol are not very stable, but a solution in methyl alcohol retains its strength for a longer time. Therefore absolute methyl alcohol was employed in preparing all the alcoholic solutions used.

The proposed method gives better agreement of results than the original indirect Kurt Meyer method. Some experiments, not included in the table, which were performed by using the indirect Kurt Meyer method, gave variations of the same magnitude. The end point in the authors' titration is sharper and a blue color is always produced with starch, while gray-blue colors are often obtained when Kurt Meyer titrations which employ 2-naphthol are performed under the same conditions. The amount of precipitate formed upon dilution in the original Kurt Meyer titration is greater than that formed when the proposed method is employed. The authors have found it possible to titrate the liberated iodine without dilution and addition of starch if their procedure is used. The end point is sharp and the brown color due to excess 2-naphthol is not present to cause an error in the results. The excess of diisobutylene does not form a precipitate, but floats on the surface as an oil and gradually evaporates.

The mean of the authors' titrations is 95.66 per cent. This represents the approximate percentage of enol under the conditions of the experiment.

The authors believe that they have improved the Kurt Meyer

titration because their titrations agree within 1 per cent, while the indirect Kurt Meyer titration gives variations as high as 7 per cent.

REFERENCES

1. MEYER, K.H., *Ann.*, 380, 212 (1911).
2. MEYER, K.H., and KAPPELMEIER, PAUL, *Ber.*, **44**, 2718 (1911).
3. POND, F.J., YORK, H.J., and MOORE, B.L., *J. Am. Chem. Soc.*, **23**, 789 (1901).
4. TREADWELL, F.P., and HALL, W.T., *Analytical Chemistry*, 7th ed., Vol. II, p. 552, New York, John Wiley & Sons, 1930.

CHAPTER 10

Nuclear Magnetic Resonance Signals from/a Tautomeric Mixture†

H. S. JARRETT and M. S. SADLER
and J. N. SHOOLERY

THE EXISTENCE of keto-enol equilibria in β diketones and β keto esters was established by Kurt-Meyer's bromine titration experiments.[1] The bromine titration technique has remained the most reliable method for determining the equilibrium ratio of the two forms. Studies of keto-enol equilibria have also been made by analysis of infrared[2] and ultraviolet[3] absorption spectra, and by refractive index measurements;[4] none of these methods has been generally applicable for providing accurate quantitative information on keto-enol equilibria.

We have succeeded in determining keto-enol equilibria in two β diketones by measurement of proton resonance with a high-resolution nuclear magnetic resonance spectrometer in the laboratory of Varian Associates at Palo Alto, California. Since this measurement cannot affect the equilibrium, it appears to be well suited to determination of keto-enol equilibrium constants over a range of temperatures.

Nuclear magnetic resonance signals from the protons in 2,4-

† Reprinted from *Journal of Chemical Physics* **21,** 2092 (1953). Reprinted by permission of the copyright owner.

pentanedione (I) and 3-methyl-2,4-pentanedione (II) were observed with a resolution of a few tenths of a milligauss.

$$CH_3C-CH_2-C-CH_3 \rightleftharpoons CH_3-C=CH-C-CH_3, \qquad (I)$$
$$\overset{\parallel}{O} \qquad \overset{\parallel}{O} \qquad \qquad \overset{|}{OH} \qquad \overset{\parallel}{O}$$

$$\overset{CH_3}{\overset{|}{CH_3C-CH-C-CH_3}} \rightleftharpoons \overset{CH_3}{\overset{|}{CH_3-C=C-C-CH_3.}} \qquad (II)$$
$$\overset{\parallel}{O} \quad \overset{\parallel}{O} \qquad \qquad \overset{|}{OH} \quad \overset{\parallel}{O}$$

In compound I there are four structurally nonequivalent kinds of protons in the equilibrium mixture, which can be identified with the CH_3, CH_2, CH, and OH groups. The peaks in Fig. 1

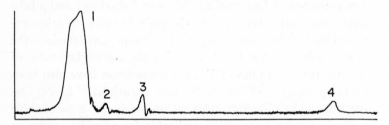

FIG. 1. Proton magnetic resonance from 2,4-pentanedione at 30 mc per sec in a field of 7000 gauss. Total sweep width is about 125 milligauss, the field decreasing linearly from left to right.

have been assigned on the basis of relative areas under the curve. For example, peaks 3 and 4 with approximately equal areas must represent the OH and CH protons of the enol form. The signal occurring at the lowest applied field corresponds to the condition of least diamagnetic shielding and consequently should be the enolic OH proton. Peak 1 represents the CH_3 groups in both forms and peak 2 is the resonance of the CH_2 protons in the keto form.

Figure 2 is the complete spectrum obtained with 3-methyl-2,4-pentanedione (II), while Fig. 3 represents the left-hand portion of that spectrum with higher resolution. Peaks 1 and 2 of these figures have been assigned to the protons of the 3-methyl group

FIG. 2. Proton magnetic resonance from 3-methyl-2,4-pentanedione at 30 mc per sec in a field of 7000 gauss. Total sweep width is about 125 milligauss, the field decreasing linearly from left to right.

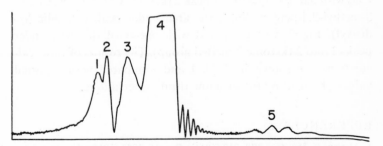

FIG. 3. Proton magnetic resonance from 3-methyl-2,4-pentanedione showing left-hand portion of Fig. 2 with higher resolution.

in the keto form; the resonance absorption is split by spin-spin interaction with the adjacent proton. Peak 3 represents the 3-methyl group in the enol form, whereas peak 4 is identified with proton signals from the terminal CH_3 groups of both forms. Peak 5 is assigned to the CH hydrogen of the keto form, and in Fig. 3 the resonance splitting by spin-spin coupling with the CH_3 hydrogens is apparent. Peak 6 represents the enolic proton.

Table I.

	% Keto		% Enol	
	Proton resonance	Bromine titration[a]	Proton resonance	Bromine titration[a]
2,4-pentanedione	15	24	85	76
3-methyl-2,4-pentanedione	70	68.5	30	31.5

[a] See reference 1.

The relative proportions of keto and enol forms in both samples have been calculated by comparing areas under selected peaks of these spectra. In the case of 2,4-pentanedione, this calculation was made by comparing the area under peak 3 (enolic CH) with half the area under peak 2 (ketonic CH_2). In the case of 3-methyl-2,4-pentanedione, the area under peak 6 (enolic hydroxyl), Fig. 2, was compared with one-third the area under peaks 1 and 2 (ketonic 3-methyl group). The results of these calculations are shown in Table I and compared with reported values obtained by the bromine titration technique.

REFERENCES

1. MEYER, K.H., *Ann.* **380**, 212 (1911); *Ber.* **45**, 2843 (1912); CONANT, J.B., THOMPSON, A.F., *J. Am. Chem. Soc.* **54**, 4039 (1932).
2. LEFEVRE, R., WELSH, M., *J. Chem. Soc.*, 2230 (1949); POWLING, J., BERNSTEIN, H., *J. Am. Chem., Soc.* **73**, 4353 (1951).
3. GROSSMAN, *Z. physik. Chem.* **109**, 305 (1924); BRIEGLEB, G., STROHMEIER, W., *Z. Naturforsch*, **6b**, 6 (1951).
4. MEYER, K.H., WILSON, F.G., *Ber.* **47**, 837 (1914).

CHAPTER 11

Titration of Enols and Imides in Nonaqueous Solvents†

JAMES S. FRITZ

A RECENT paper[3] reported the titration of enols, imides, and several other acidic groups in benzene-methanol and butylamine. Sodium methoxide in benzene-methanol served as the titrant and either a visual (thymol blue) or potentiometric end point was employed. Subsequent papers discussed in more detail the titration of amine salts[1] and sulfonamides[2] as acids and introduced dimethylformamide as the solvent and azo violet (p-nitrobenzeneazoresorcinol) as the indicator for titration of the weaker acids. Moss, Elliott, and Hall[4] introduced the use of ethylenediamine, in reporting the potentiometric titration of phenol and other very weak acids. The purpose of the present study is to show more clearly than has been done in previous work the scope and limitations of nonaqueous acid-base titrations as applied to enols and imides.

REAGENTS AND SOLUTIONS

Benzene, reagent grade.

Benzoic acid, primary standard grade.

Dimethylformamide (DMF), technical grade (Du Pont).

† Reprinted from *Analytical Chemistry*, **24,** 674 (1952). Copyright 1952 by the American Chemical Society and reprinted by permission of the copyright owner.

Enols and imides, commercial samples (98 to 100% purity) analyzed as received.

Ethylenediamine, 95 to 100% (Eastman).

Methanol, reagent grade.

Azo violet, saturated solution of *p*-nitrobenzeneazoresorcinol in benzene.

o-Nitroaniline, 0.15 gram dissolved in 100 ml. of benzene.

Sodium methoxide, a 0.1 to 0.2 N solution in benzenemethanol prepared as described.[3]

Thymol blue, 0.3 gram dissolved in 100 ml. of methanol.

PROCEDURES

A. Two drops of thymol blue or azo violet are added to 10 to 20 ml. of dimethylformamide and the solvent is titrated to a clear blue color to neutralize the acid impurities present. The neutralized solvent is then added to the sample and titrated in a covered beaker to a clear blue color. The titrant is standardized with benzoic acid, using the same procedure but increasing the amount of solvent to about 25 ml. to avoid formation of a gel.

B. Ethylenediamine is employed as the solvent and 2 drops of *o*-nitroaniline as indicator; otherwise the above procedure is followed. The color change of *o*-nitroaniline is from yellow to orange red.

SCOPE

Enols

Compounds of the type A—CH$_2$—A′ are sufficiently acid to permit titration, provided A and A′ are groups possessing suitable electron-withdrawing properties. If A and A′ are $-\overset{\overset{\displaystyle O}{\|}}{C}-R$,

$$
\underset{\|}{\overset{O}{C}}-H, \quad \underset{\|}{\overset{O}{C}}-OR, \quad \underset{\|}{\overset{O}{C}}-NHAr, \quad or \quad -CN,
$$
accurate titration in dimethylformamide is possible using azo violet indicator. The amide group, $\underset{\|}{\overset{O}{C}}-NH_2$, has weaker electron-withdrawing properties. This is shown by the fact that while malononitrile gives a good azo violet end point, cyanoacetamide gives a very

Table I. Titration of enols

Compound	Solvent	Indicator	% Theoretical
Acetoacetanilide	DMF	Azo violet	99.0 99.1
1-Acetyl-2-thiohydrantoin	DMF	Thymol blue	100.0 100.3
Cyanoacetamide	EN[a]	o-Nitroaniline	100.3 99.7
Dibenzoylmethane	DMF	Thymol blue	100.0 100.3
Ethylcyanoacetate	DMF	Azo violet	99.5 99.8
Ethyl malonate	DMF	Azo violet	100.1 99.4
Malononitrile	DMF	Azo violet	98.6 98.7
Methone	DMF	Azo violet	99.8 100.0
1-Phenyl-3-carbethoxy-5-pyrazolone	DMF	Azo violet	98.9 99.1 99.3 99.0
1-Phenyl-3-carboxy-5-pyrazolone	DMF	Azo violet	99.7 99.6

[a] Ethylenediamine

poor end point and malonamide is not at all acid toward azo violet. Cyanoacetamide does give a satisfactory end point in ethylenediamine using *o*-nitroaniline indicator; malonamide is slightly acid to this indicator.

The —C=N— group in conjunction with the carbonyl group in 1-phenyl-3-carbethoxy-5-pyrazolone accounts for the fact that this compound can be titrated as an acid. The $-\overset{\overset{\text{O}}{\|}}{\text{C}}-\text{ONa}$ group has very slight, if any, electron-withdrawing properties. The carboxyl groups in cyanoacetic acid and in malonic acid can be sharply titrated in dimethylformamide, but these compounds apparently have no further acidic properties.

Compounds of the type A—CH$_2$—CH$_2$—A′ were found not to be acid to azo violet even if A and A′ are strong electron-at-tracting groups. Compounds of the type $-\overset{\overset{\text{O}}{\|}}{\text{C}}-\overset{\overset{\text{O}}{\|}}{\text{C}}-\text{CH}_2-$ (example diacetyl) may exhibit some acid properties but are still too weak to be titrated.

Data for the titration of enols are given in Table I.

Imides

Compounds having the configuration A—NH—A′ are in general weaker acids than analogous compounds of the A—CH$_2$—A′ type. Very sharp end points are obtained, however, if A is $-\overset{\overset{\text{O}}{\|}}{\text{C}}-\text{R}$, $-\overset{\overset{\text{O}}{\|}}{\text{C}}-\text{H}$, $-\overset{\overset{\text{O}}{\|}}{\text{C}}-\text{OR}$, or $-\overset{\overset{\text{O}}{\|}}{\text{C}}-\text{NHAr}$ and if A′ is also one of these groups. If either A or A′ is $-\overset{\overset{\text{O}}{\|}}{\text{C}}-\text{NH}_2$ or, $-\overset{\overset{\text{O}}{\|}}{\text{C}}-\text{NHR}$, the success of the titration is uncertain. Acetylurea, for example, gives a very poor end point, yet hydrantoin, which is essentially the cyclic equivalent of acetylurea, gives an excellent azo violet end point.

Although the electron-attracting properties of aryl groups are somewhat less than the above listed groups, a phenyl group in the proper position will noticeably increase the acidity of an imide. Acetylacetanilide ($CH_3COCH_2CONHPh$) will, for example, give a good azo violet end point, while acetylurea ($CH_3CONHCONH_2$) gives a very poor end point. That oxanilide (PhNHCOCONHPh) can be titrated as a monobasic acid while s-diphenylurea (PhNHCONHPh) displays no acid properties, illustrates the interesting fact that a 1,2-dicarbonyl arrangement has greater electron-attracting properties than does a single carbonyl group. The failure of oxamide ($NH_2COCONH_2$) to react acidic to azo violet or o-nitroaniline again demonstrates the electron-withdrawing properties of aryl groups.

Substitution of a carbonyl group with a thiocarbonyl group increases the acidity of imides considerably. Thus while s-diphenylurea is not acid to azo violet, s-diphenylthiourea can be sharply titrated as a monobasic acid. Phenylthiourea gives a premature azo violet end point but can be successfully titrated using o-nitroaniline. Even thiourea is somewhat acid toward o-nitroaniline, although no sharp end point can be obtained. Dithio-oxamide can be titrated as a monobasic acid but its oxygen analog, oxamide, is not acidic. The $—SO_2—$ configuration constitutes another very powerful electron-attracting group. Titration of sulfonamides as acids in nonaqueous solvents has been discussed.[2]

INTERFERENCES

Interfering substances include acids, phenols, amine salts, thiols, and active halogens. Esters do not hydrolyze in dimethylformamide or ethylenediamine under the conditions employed, but in some cases they may undergo condensation to form acidic compounds:

$$2CH_3CO_2Et \xrightarrow{\text{base}} CH_3COCH_2CO_2Et + EtOH$$

Esters which cannot condense do not interfere. Water causes high results in titrations carried out in dimethylformamide, but small amounts do not interfere if ethylenediamine is the solvent.[1]

DISCUSSION

Dimethylformamide readily dissolves most enols and imides. It is not possible to heat dimethylformamide appreciably to aid solution of less soluble compounds, because heat causes partial decomposition of the solvent and high results in the subsequent titration. Although it is somewhat more expensive, ethylenediamine will dissolve many compounds which are difficultly soluble in dimethylformamide. Ethylenediamine is also recommended for titration of the more weakly acidic enols and imides.

Compounds which are not sufficiently acid to give a sharp thymol blue or azo violet end point can often be titrated satisfactorily using o-nitroaniline indicator. Best results are obtained with this indicator if ethylenediamine is used as the solvent and if the sample weight is chosen so that not more than about 4 ml. of titrant will be required.

REFERENCES

1. FRITZ, Anal. Chem., 24, 306 (1952).
2. FRITZ and KEEN, Ibid., 24, 308 (1952).
3. FRITZ and LISICKI, Ibid., 23, 589 (1951).
4. MOSS, ELLIOTT, and HALL, Ibid., 20, 784 (1948).

CHAPTER 12

Quantitative Ester Formation and the Determination of Alcohols and Phenols†

A. VERLEY and FR. BÖLSING

IT IS known that a mixture of alcohols or phenols reacts only slowly in the cold with organic acid anhydrides. We have now found that the addition of *pyridine* immediately causes this mixture to react vigorously so that, with a pronounced rise in temperature, the corresponding esters are produced almost instantaneously and very frequently in quantitative yield:

R·OH + (R'·CO)$_2$O + pyridine = R·O·CO·R' + R'·COOH, pyridine

The half-molecule of the anhydride liberated combines immediately with the pyridine to form a neutral salt; there is therefore no possibility of resaponifying the ester formed.

This reaction, which we have so far investigated only with acetic anhydride, appears to be capable of very wide application. Nevertheless, we do not go so far, where it is a question of the preparation of esters, to recommend it above the well-known methods; rather, we should like to propose it as a quantitative method of determining alcohols or phenols. Particularly in the investigation of the ethereal oils, this method offers the advantage,

† Reprinted from *Berichte der deutschen chemischen Gesellschaft* **34,** 3354 (1901). Reprinted by permission of the copyright owner.

as compared with the method of determining alcohols previously customary (acetylation by means of acetic anhydride and sodium acetate, washing out the ester, and subsequent saponification) that it requires much less time and material.

DESCRIPTION OF THE METHOD

We first prepare an acid solution ("mixture") by mixing *ca.* 120 g of acetic anhydride with *ca.* 880 g of pyridine, which, when anhydrous materials are used, remain completely without mutual interaction. If this mixture is treated with water, the anhydride is saponified immediately with the formation of pyridine acetate which, in turn, is decomposed by alkalis to give alkali-metal acetate and pyridine—both materials which react neutral to phenolphthalein. The acid can therefore be titrated.

In our case, 25 cm^3 of the mixture corresponded to 60 cm^3 of normal alkali, but we later went over to the use of seminormal alkali in order to achieve greater accuracy.

With monohydric alcohols or phenols, each molecule of acetic acid absorbed corresponds to one molecule of alcohol (or phenol).

1–2 g of the alcohol (or phenol) concerned is weighed out into a *ca.* 200 cm^3 flask, 25 cm^3 of the mixture is added, and the flask is heated in the water bath without a condenser for $\frac{1}{4}$ hour; after cooling, *ca.* 25 cm^3 of water is added and the non-bound acetic acid is back-titrated using phenolphthalein as indicator.

The fact that none of the anhydride evaporates on heating in the water bath was determined by an experiment:

25 cm^3 of the mixture heated on the water bath in an open flask for 3 hours consumed 60 cm^3 of normal alkali for saturation.

It is important to bring the mixture and the normal alkali before titration exactly to that temperature at which their mutual equivalence was determined, since when this condition is not observed considerable differences can arise.

Ethyl alcohol, $C_2H_5 \cdot OH = 46$ (an alcohol of sp. gr. at 15° of $0.811 = 94.5$ per cent was used)—1.1445 g of alcohol.

$$25 \text{ cm}^3 \text{ of mixture} = 60.0 \text{ cm}^3 \text{ of normal alkali}$$
$$\text{titrated} \quad \underline{36.6 \text{ cm}^3}$$
$$\text{absorbed} \quad 23.4 \text{ cm}^3 = 94.05 \text{ per cent ethyl}$$
$$\text{alcohol.}$$

Phenol, $C_6H_5 \cdot OH = 94.$—2.2516 g of phenol.

$$25 \text{ cm}^3 \text{ mixture} = 60.0 \text{ cm}^3 \text{ normal alkali}$$
$$\text{titrated} \quad \underline{35.9 \text{ cm}^3}$$
$$\text{absorbed} \quad 24.1 \text{ cm}^3 = 100.6 \text{ per cent of phenol.}$$

Linalool, $C_{10}H_{17} \cdot OH = 154.$

Here, even with various changes in the experimental conditions, we obtained only quite unsatisfactory results, so that we must state that our method unfortunately cannot be used for the determination of linalool.

CHAPTER 13

Determining the Hydroxyl Content of Certain Organic Compounds Macro- and Semimicromethods†

C. L. OGG, W. L. PORTER and C. O. WILLITS

THE WEST, Hoagland, and Curtis[14] modification of the Verley and Bölsing[13] procedure for determining hydroxyl specifies the acetylation of fats and fatlike material with a solution of 1 volume of acetic anhydride in 7 volumes of pyridine, followed by hydrolysis with hot water and titration of the acid formed with alcoholic alkali solution. Peterson and West[10] recommended an acetylating solution of 1 volume of acetic anhydride in 2 volumes of pyridine, and Marks and Morrell[6] adopted the use of a solution of 1 volume of acetic anhydride in 3 volumes of pyridine. In the last two procedures, the excess acetic anhydride is hydrolyzed by adding ice water to the reaction mixture. Malm, Genung and Williams[5] studied the effects of time, temperature, and concentration of the acetic anhydride in the anhydride-pyridine solution on the acetylation of cellulose derivatives. They found that an acetylation period of 24 hours was required to obtain calculated free hydroxyl values when they used a 0.5 molar acetic anhydride reagent (1 part of acetic anhydride to 19 parts of

† Reprinted from *Analytical Chemistry*, **51**, 394 (1945). Copyright 1945 by the American Chemical Society and reprinted by permission of the copyright owner.

pyridine). Titrations were conducted electrometrically in an open beaker.

The methods of West, Hoagland, and Curtis and of Marks and Morrell gave low results with hydroxylated higher fatty acids, certain oxidation products if higher fatty acids, and long-chain alcohols analyzed in this laboratory. However, by combining the acetic anhydride acetylating solution of Marks and Morrell with the hot-water hydrolysis and the homogenization with n-butanol of West, Hoagland, and Curtis, good results were obtained on the types of material mentioned. Since a concentration of 1 part of acetic anhydride in 7 parts of pyridine gave incomplete acetylation, the more dilute solution of Malm, Genung, and Williams was not investigated. Other work[1-4, 8, 9, 11, 12] has been described in which both acetic anhydride and acetyl chloride were used for determining the hydroxyl content of organic compounds.

In each of the methods, except that of Malm *et al.*, an internal indicator is employed, which limits the accuracy of analysis of samples producing dark solutions. For these materials a procedure using potentiometric titrations was developed. When the reaction was carried out in the usual manner in an iodine flask, it was necessary to transfer the reaction mixture to a beaker to make the potentiometric titration. During this transfer, small amounts of acetic acid were inevitably lost, introducing relatively large errors. To eliminate these errors, a modified iodine flask was designed that would permit the electrometric titration to be made in the reaction vessel when a Beckman pH meter equipped with extension electrodes is used.

MACROPROCEDURE

Place a weighed sample containing from 1 to 2.5 milliequivalents of hydroxyl in the modified iodine flask and add exactly 3.00 ml. of the acetic anhydride–pyridine solution (1 to 3) from a reservoir-type 5-ml. microburet with a Drierite protecting tube in the reservoir. Moisten all stoppers of the flask with pyridine and place the two stoppers firmly in the electrode arms. The center, or main stopper, should be loosely seated. Place the flask on a steam bath. After heating for 45 minutes, add 5 to 6 ml. of water to the cup of the flask and loosen the stopper in such a manner as to rinse the stopper and inside walls of the flask. Continue heating for 2 minutes and then cool under the tap with the main stopper partly removed. With 10-ml. of n-butanol rinse the three stoppers and inside walls of both the flask and side arms. Insert the glass and calomel electrodes in the side arms and titrate with $0.5N$ alcoholic alkali to pH 9.8 (volume A). Make a blank determination (volume B) on 3.00 ml. of the acetic anhydride–pyridine solution.

Determine the free acid of the sample by repeating the procedure described above, using pyridine instead of acetic anhydride–pyridine solution and adding 5 ml. of neutral ethanol just prior to the titration to make the solution homogeneous. Shake well and titrate with $0.5N$ alcoholic alkali. Calculate the volume of alkali required to neutralize the acidity of 1 gram of the sample (volume C).

CALCULATION

$$\frac{[B - (A - C \times \text{wt. of sample for —OH determination})] \times N \times \dfrac{OH}{1000} \times 100}{\text{weight of sample for —OH determination}} = \% \, OH$$

Because of the ease of manipulation, it is recommended that for colorless solutions ordinary iodine flasks and the mixed indicator be used with this procedure instead of the special flasks and the potentiometric titration.

DISCUSSION

The titration curve for alcoholic alkali versus acetic acid in a pyridine-water-n-butanol-ethanol solution is shown in Fig. 3. The point of color change for the mixed indicator in this solution was at pH 9.8. Since the vertical portion of the curve extends between 9.2 and 10.3, a pH of 9.8 was selected for the potentiometric end point to make the potentiometric and indicator procedures interchangeable.

As indicated in Table I, both the age and the strength of the acetic anhydride-pyridine acetylating solution are important. The reagent made by mixing 1 volume of acetic anhydride with 3 volumes of pyridine gave theoretical results and remained effective for at least 4 days. A 1 to 7 acetic anhydride-pyridine solution was so dilute that it resulted in incomplete acetylation, as shown by the data for dihydroxystearic acid and oleyl alcohol. As this reagent aged, it became less effective as an acetylating agent, giving still lower results. The 1 to 3 acetic anhydride-pyridine solution permits the use of reagent grade pyridine without its further purification, since a sufficient excess of the acetic anhydride is assured for complete acetylation of the sample, even though some has been consumed by moisture or other impurities in the pyridine.

For colorless solutions, identical values were obtained by the indicator method and the potentiometric method, as shown in Table II. Good precision was obtained with both methods. The cyclohexanol and benzyl alcohol, Eastman Kodak Company White Label reagents, were not further purified. The compounds for which theoretical values are cited were established as pure by such physical and chemical constants as iodine value, neutralization equivalent, saponification equivalent, melting point, and carbon and hydrogen analysis.

Groups such as primary and secondary amines, and sulfhydryl, which contain active hydrogen and form acetylated products not hydrolyzed by hot water, interfere in the analysis. Comparison of the method of Mitchell, Hawkins, and Smith[7] for determining primary and secondary amines with the one herein described indicates that it may be possible to adapt this hydroxyl method to the determination of these amines and other interfering substances of the type noted above. Any compound which undergoes condensation to produce hydroxyl groups, such as aldehydes, interferes in the procedure described.

REFERENCES

1. CHRISTENSEN, B.E., PENNINGTON, L., and DIMICK, P.K., *Ind. Eng. Chem., Anal. Ed.*, **13**, 821 (1941).
2. FREED, M., and WYNNE, A.M., *Ibid.*, **8**, 278 (1936).
3. HAFNER, P.G., SWINNEY, R.H., and WEST, E.S., *J. Biol. Chem.*, **116**, 691 (1936).
4. KLEINZELLER, A., and TRIM, A.R., *Analyst*, **69**, 241 (1944).
5. MALM, C.J., GENUNG, L.B., and WILLIAMS, R.F., Jr., *Ind. Eng. Chem., Anal. Ed.*, **14**, 935 (1942).
6. MARKS, S., and MORRELL, R.S., *Analyst*, **56**, 428 (1931).
7. MITCHELL, J., Jr., HAWKINS, W., and SMITH, D.M., *J. Am. Chem. Soc.*, **66**, 782 (1944).
8. MOORE, J.C., and BLANK, E.W., *Oil and Soap*, **20**, 178 (1943).
9. PETERSEN, J.W., HEDBERG, K.W., and CHRISTENSEN, B.E., *Ind. Eng. Chem. Anal. Ed.*, **15**, 225 (1943).
10. PETERSON, V.L., and WEST, E.S., *J. Biol. Chem.*, **74**, 379 (1927).
11. SMITH, D.M., and BRYANT, W.M.D., *J. Am. Chem. Soc.*, **57**, 61 (1935).
12. STODOLA, F.H., *Mikrochemie*, **21**, 180 (1937).
13. VERLEY, A., and BÖLSING, FR., *Ber.*, **34**, 3354 (1901).
14. WEST, E.S., HOAGLAND, C.L., and CURTIS, G.H., *J. Biol. Chem.*, **104**, 627 (1934).

CHAPTER 14

The Hydrolysis of Acetic Anhydride. Part III.† The Catalytic Efficiency of a Series of Tertiary Amines

V. GOLD and E. G. JEFFERSON

IN VIEW of the remarkable catalysis of the hydrolysis of acetic anhydride by pyridine (Part II†) the effect of other tertiary amines has been examined. The catalytic coefficients were evaluated on the basis of the analysis given in Part II. In order to remove the uncertainties consequent upon the use of a mixed solvent the measurements now reported relate to water at 0° as solvent.

More reliable dissociation constants, at 25°, of several of the amines used have recently been reported (Herington, *Discuss. Faraday Soc.*, 1950, **9,** 26; cf. Gero and Markham, *J. Org. Chem.* 1951, **16,** 1835) and therefore comparative catalytic coefficients may be deduced from the kinetic data. A slight gap remains in the complete evaluation of catalytic coefficients through lack of knowledge of the temperature dependence of basic dissociation constants.

† Reprinted from *Journal of the Chemical Society* 1409 (1953). Part II is the preceding paper on p. 1406. A more recent paper in this same journal (p. 4362 (1961)) finds the second step to be rate-controlling.

EXPERIMENTAL

The evaluation of catalytic coefficients was based on equation (6) of Part II. For each catalyst the dependence of k_{HL} on the stoicheiometric concentration of catalyst ($[P]_0$) was studied for a fixed initial concentration of anhydride ($[Ac_2O]_0$). This dependence was found to be linear only at the lowest concentrations of catalyst. Since equation (6) was derived on the assumption that $[P]_0$ is small, the slope of the initial low-concentration portion of the curve was used in the evaluation of R (Fig. 2). R is related to the catalytic coefficient k_p by equation (7) of Part II, and the following assumptions were made regarding the other factors occurring in that equation: (i) The ratio $f_I^2 : f_{II}$ was evaluated from the Debye–Hückel limiting law for activity coefficients; at the ionic strength of 0·05 M-acetic acid ($\mu \sim 0·001$), this ratio is calculated to have the value 0·96. (ii) The constants K_w and K_{AcOH} are accurately known for water at 0° ($K_w = 1·14 \times 10^{-15}$ mole^{-2} l.$^{-2}$; $K_{AcOH} = 1·66 \times 10^{-5}$ mole l.$^{-1}$). (iii) The recent basic dissociation constants *(locc. cit.)*, at 25°, of some of the amines studied by us differ by a factor of 2–3 from those accepted hitherto. There is, however, no information on the values at 0° or the temperature dependence of the dissociation constants. We preferred not to correct for this temperature variation by some arbitrary procedure based on analogies, but we substituted for K_p in equation (7) the experimental value at 25°. In this way we do not obtain the true catalytic coefficient (k_p) at 0°, but the coefficient k_p' which is related to k_p' by the equation $k_p' = k_p(K_p)^°/(K_p)^{(25)}$, where the superscripts indicate the temperatures to which the dissociation constants refer. For comparisons of the catalytic efficiency of different amines, k_p is probably almost as useful as k_p since the factor $(K_p)^0/(K_p)^{25}$ would not be expected to depend very markedly on the nature of the amine for the particular series considered.

Table 2. Catalytic coefficients for different amines

Catalyst	$10^3 R$ sec.$^{-1}$ (mole l.$^{-1}$)$^{-\frac{1}{2}}$	$10^9 (K)^{25}$ (mole l.$^{-1}$)	$10^{-1} k'_p$ (sec.$^{-1}$ mole^{-1} l.)
Pyridine	$28 \cdot 2$	$1 \cdot 44^a$	14
3-Picoline	$25 \cdot 1$	$4 \cdot 54^a$	39
4-Picoline	$25 \cdot 7$	$10 \cdot 6^a$	93
isoQuinoline	39	$2 \cdot 5^b$	33
2-Picoline	$3 \cdot 4$	$8 \cdot 77^a$	11
2:6-Lutidine	$2 \cdot 3$	$38 \cdot 4^a$	33
Quinoline	$3 \cdot 3$	$0 \cdot 87^c$	1

[a] Herington, *loc. cit.* [b] Golumbic and Orchin, *J. Amer. Chem. Soc.*, 1950, **72**, 4145. [c] Albert and Goldacre, *Nature*, 1944, **153**, 407.

DISCUSSION

The amines examined can be divided into two groups according to their catalytic efficiency. At a given stoicheiometric concentration of amine, pyridine, 3- and 4-picoline, and *iso*quinoline (group *A*) are about ten times more effective catalysts than the members of group *B*, made up of 2-picoline, 2:6-lutidine and quinoline (cf. values of *R* in Table 2). On evaluation of the cata-

Table 4. Test of catalysis law, $\log k'_p = 10 \cdot 36 + 0 \cdot 92_5 \log K_p$

Base	$\log K_p$	$\log k'_p$ (calc.)	$\log k'_p$ (expt.)	Difference
Class A				
Pyridine	$\overline{9} \cdot 16$	$2 \cdot 18$	$2 \cdot 15$	$-0 \cdot 03$
3-Picoline	$\overline{9} \cdot 66$	$2 \cdot 64$	$2 \cdot 59$	$-0 \cdot 05$
4-Picoline	$\overline{8} \cdot 03$	$2 \cdot 99$	$2 \cdot 97$	$-0 \cdot 02$
*iso*Quinoline	$\overline{9} \cdot 40$	$2 \cdot 41$	$2 \cdot 52$	$+0 \cdot 11$
Class B				
2-Picoline	$\overline{9} \cdot 94$	$2 \cdot 90$	$2 \cdot 04$	$-0 \cdot 86$
2:6-Lutidine	$\overline{8} \cdot 58$	$3 \cdot 50$	$2 \cdot 52$	$-0 \cdot 98$
Quinoline	$\overline{10} \cdot 94$	$1 \cdot 98$	$1 \cdot 00$	$-0 \cdot 98$

lytic coefficients k'_p this division seems to disappear but it again comes into evidence if we attempt to relate the catalytic coefficient to the basic dissociation constant of the amine (Table 4). The members of group A follow the Brönsted catalysis law: those of the group B appear to have catalytic coefficients only about one-tenth of those to be expected from their basic strengths. The effect may in reality be still more pronounced. It is not impossible that some of the feeble catalysis found with amines of group B may in fact be due to small amounts of impurities of group A amines.

The division into the two groups may be linked with structural similarities. The less active amines are those having a substituent in one or both of the positions adjacent to the heterocyclic nitrogen atom and this suggests steric influence on the mechanism of catalysis. Chemical considerations already render it unlikely that the catalysis involves a proton transfer from anhydride to base, and the steric effect reinforces this view. Furthermore, the hydrolysis of benzoic anhydride is also catalysed by pyridine and in this case the anhydride molecule has no hydrogen atom that could be transferred to the catalyst.

We may also take into consideration the results of related work. It was found that the catalysis is not confined to the acetylation of water, but that pyridine will catalyse the acetylation of o-chloroaniline and of ethanol, and that quinoline is again inactive, at least in the former of these reactions (Gold and Jefferson, unpublished work). More significantly still the same division of catalytic amines into two groups occurs in the decomposition of acetic formic anhydride in an aprotic solvent (*idem, J.*, 1953, 1416) where the only possible catalytic effect of the amine is by interaction with the anhydride. We therefore suggest that in the hydrolysis too the catalysis is due to an interaction of amine and anhydride, and that it does not take the form of a proton transfer.

Whatever the nature of this interaction, it fairly certainly does not produce an appreciable equilibrium concentration of a new species. All experiments to detect such a product have had negative results: (1) The absorption spectra of pyridine and acetic anhydride in *cyclo*hexane over the range 2300 and 2800 Å (the chief absorption region of pyridine in the near ultra-violet) are strictly additive. (2) In the infra-red absorption spectra of acetic anhydride and an equimolecular mixture of acetic anhydride and pyridine in carbon tetrachloride the intensity and position of the bands due to carbonyl vibrations (at 1769 and 1936 cm^{-1}) and C—O—C skeletal vibrations (at 1124 cm^{-1}) of acetic anhydride are unaffected by the presence of pyridine. (3) The electrical conductivities of mixtures of acetic anhydride and pyridine in dry acetone were not significantly higher than the sum of the conductivities of solutions of acetic anhydride and of pyridine in acetone; the same result was obtained with benzoic anhydride and pyridine in 50% acetone–water at 0°, *i.e.*, under conditions where the hydrolysis is sufficiently slow to permit reliable back-extrapolation of the conductivity measurements to zero time, but otherwise in a solvent and with an anhydride for which the operation of catalysis has been established. (4) Depressions of the freezing point of benzene by acetic anhydride and pyridine are additive. Thus neither an association complex nor an ionic reaction product between an anhydride and pyridine are formed in analytically detectable amounts.

There are two chemically plausible interaction products between acetic anhydride and pyridine, *viz.*, (I) and (II) (the formulae being the classical ones to represent molecules in which the real electron distribution will be such as to minimise the energy), but postulation of the complex (I) does not seem sufficient to explain all the observed catalytic effects. It is difficult to see why the bimolecular reaction of (I) with a water or amine molecule should be easier than that of acetic anhydride alone, and it is even less obvious why a structure such as (I) should be an intermediate in the decomposition of acetic formic anhydride (cf. Ingold, *Trans. Faraday Soc.*, 1941, **37**, 718). If we wish to attribute the higher reactivity of (I) than of acetic anhydride to a greater ease of unimolecular heterolysis, then we are in effect postulating the formation of (II) from (I). A consistent interpretation of the phenomena can be base on the postulate that (II) is the complex between amine and anhydride whose formation is important

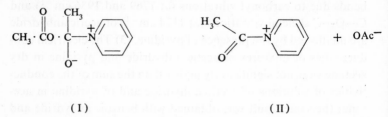

(I)   (II)

in the catalysis. A structure to which the approximate formula (I) can be assigned would, of course, be the transition state in the formation of (II) from acetic anhydride and pyridine. It does not seem very important for our present purposes to decide whether—with a certain set of equilibrium internuclear distances—a structure (I) also corresponds to a minimum in the potential energy profile, *i.e.*, whether it is a reaction intermediate.

The reaction scheme of the hydrolysis may then be formulated

$$Ac_2O + P \underset{-1}{\overset{1}{\rightleftharpoons}} PAc^+ (II) + OAc^-$$

$$PAc^+ + H_2O \xrightarrow{\quad 2 \quad} AcOH + PH^+$$

where steps 1 and 2 may also be composite (involving the transient formation of free acetylium cations), without experimentally significant consequences. Since no detectable amounts of intermediates are formed we may apply the stationary-state hypothesis,

$$v \equiv - \frac{d[Ac_2O]}{dt} = \frac{\varkappa_1 \varkappa_2 [Ac_2O] [P]}{\varkappa_{-1}[OAc^-] + \varkappa_2}$$

where the $\varkappa$'s are the rate coefficients of the individual steps of the scheme. Since the concentration of the reagent water is large and invariant, $\varkappa_2$ is defined to incorporate the function of the concentration of water upon which the velocity of this step depends. If we may set

$$\varkappa_2 \gg \varkappa_{-1}[OAc^-] \quad \text{or} \quad \varkappa_2 \ll \varkappa_{-1}[OAc]^-$$

simplified forms of this equation are obtained, viz.,

$$v = \varkappa_1 [Ac_2O] [P]$$

i.e., a rate-determining acetylium-ion transfer from acetic anhydride to pyridine, or

$$v = \frac{\varkappa_1 \varkappa_2}{\varkappa_{-1}} \cdot \frac{[Ac_2O] [P]}{[OAc^-]}$$

which implies the establishment of a rapid pre-equilibrium made up of reactions 1 and −1.

The activation energy for the unimolecular heterolysis of acetic anhydride appears to be too unfavourable for such a mechanism to operate in the absence of catalyst. On the other hand, the considerable resonance energy to be expected for PAc^+ allows the rate of this step to become comparable with the bimolecular hydrolysis. The amount of resonance energy is reduced by α-substitution which prevents coplanarity of the $C=O$ bond and the aromatic ring of PAc^+. This inhibition of resonance may be responsible for the strict steric requirements for catalytic efficiency in the amine.

It might be thought that hydrolysis of PAc$^+$ should still only proceed at a speed comparable to that of hydrolysis of acetic anhydride itself since the two molecules are combinations of acetylium cations with bases of almost identical strength (acetate ion and pyridine). The postulated higher reactivity of PAc$^+$ is ascribed to a more favourable entropy of activation. The hydrolysis of PAc$^+$ does not involve a change in the total electrical charge of the reagents and would not require significant reorientation of the solvation shell, whereas the bimolecular hydrolysis of acetic anhydride involves an electrical-charge separation (cf. Gold, *loc. cit.*) requiring the creation of order in the solvent and hence a low entropy of activation.

CHAPTER 15

Determination of Hydroxy and Amino Compounds Using Pyromellitic Dianhydride†

Sidney Siggia, J. Gordon Hanna,
and Robert Culmo

The most commonly used methods for the determination of hydroxyl groups involve acetylation, using acetic anhydride,[2, 3] and phthalation, using phthalic anhydride.[1, 5] Acetic anhydride reacts more rapidly than phthalic anhydride, but suffers interference from low molecular weight aldehydes.[4] Phthalic anhydride can be used in the presence of aldehydes. Larger concentrations of phthalic anhydride are necessary for complete reaction. Phthalic anhydride is less volatile than acetic anhydride; therefore, there is less possibility for loss of reagent during heating. Phthalic anhydride can be used to determine alcohols in the presence of phenols. Pyromellitic dianhydride (PMDA) combines the advantages of the two reagents. It can be used in the presence of aldehydes; it is not volatile; it can be used to determine alcohols in the presence of phenols; and its rate of reaction is comparable to that of acetic anhydride. The time involved for

† Reprinted from *Analytical Chemistry* **33,** 900 (1961). Copyright 1961 by the American Chemical Society and reprinted by permission of the copyright owner.

analysis is approximately the same as that for the perchloric acid-catalyzed acetic anhydride reaction,[2] although the PMDA method does require a heating period.

REAGENTS

Pyromellitic dianhydride, 0.5 M in tetrahydrofuran.

The pyromellitic dianhydride can be purchased from E.I.du Pont de Nemours & Co., Inc.

PROCEDURE

A sample containing 0.010 to 0.015 equivalent of alcohol or amine is weighed and placed in a 250-ml. flask. Fifty milliliters of 0.5 M pyromellitic dianhydride solution are pipetted into the flask, along with 10 ml. of pyridine. The flask is placed on a steam bath for 2 minutes and then on an electric hot plate for 5 minutes. Most of the tetrahydrofuran will boil off during the heating. Twenty milliliters more of pyridine are added, and the heating continued for 3 minutes. A 20-ml. portion of water is added, and the mixture again heated for 2 minutes to hydrolyze the excess anhydride. The mixture is cooled to room temperature and is titrated with 1 N sodium hydroxide to the phenolphthalein end point. A blank is run in the same manner, omitting only the sample.

DISCUSSION AND RESULTS

Hydrolyzed pyromellitic dianhydride titrated with standard sodium hydroxide solution showed only one inflection in the plot of volume of titrant *vs.* pH. The mid-point of the maximum slope occurred at pH 9.1 to 9.2, indicating that phenolphthalein is a suitable indicator. Calculated on the basis of alkali consumed up to this point, all four acid groups are neutralized. Tetrahydrofuran was used as the solvent because of the limited solubility of the anhydride in pyridine.

Possible interference from aldehydes was checked by treating 2 to 3 grams each of formaldehyde, acetaldehyde, furfural, and acrolein according to the procedure. No anhydride was consumed in any case. Alcohols to which aldehydes were added were determined. The results show that there is no significant interference from the aldehydes.

Table II contains results obtained for various alcohols and amines. The accurcacy and precision are comparable to that obtained by either the acetic anhydride or the phthalic anhydride methods. The recoveries obtained for methanol and ethanol indicate that no special precautions are necessary to prevent loss by volatilization.

Phenols do not react with the pyromellitic dianhydride under the conditions of the procedure. This was proved by the fact that no significant amount of anhydride was consumed when phenols were tried. Tertiary alcohols do react, but not quantitatively; therefore, they cannot be determined by this method.

REFERENCES

1. ELVING, P.J., WARSHOWSKY, B., *Anal. Chem.* **19**, 1006 (1947).
2. FRITZ, J.S., SCHENK, G.H., *Ibid.*, **31**, 1808 (1959).
3. OGG, C.L., PORTER, W.L., WILLITS, C.O., *Ind. Eng. Chem., Anal. Ed.* **17**, 394–7 (1945).
4. SIGGIA, S., *Quantitative Organic Analysis via Functional Groups*, 2nd ed., p. 9, Wiley, New York, 1954.
5. VERBECK, G., *Determination of Alcohol by Means of Phthalic Anhydride*, Chicago Section, ACS, Jan. 24, 1947.

Modified Procedure†

EXPERIMENTAL

Reagent

Pyromellitic dianhydride, 0.5 *M*. The pyromellitic dianhydride 109 grams, is dissolved in 525 ml. of dimethyl sulfoxide, and then 425 ml. of pyridine are added.

Procedure

Fifty milliliters of 0.5 *M* pyromellitic dianhydride solution are pipetted into a glass-stoppered 250-ml. flask. A sample containing 0.010 to 0.015 equivalent of alcohol or amine is weighed and added to the reagent. The flask is placed on a steam bath and the stopper is wetted with pyridine and loosely seated in the flask. The contents are heated for 15 to 20 minutes (30 minutes for polyglycols). A 20-ml. portion of water is added and the heating is continued for 2 minutes. The mixture is cooled to room temperature and titrated with 1 *N* sodium hydroxide to the phenolphthalein end point. A blank in which only the sample is omitted is treated in the same manner.

DISCUSSION AND RESULTS

The results show that the values obtained using DMSO as the solvent are practically identical to those obtained using the original PMDA method. The reaction proceeds smoothly, and the mixture remains clear. Crystals of pyromellitic acid do appear on cooling after the reaction is complete, but these redissolve on neutralization, and the solution is again clear at the end point of

† *Analytical Chemistry* **37,** 600 (1965).

the titration. The hydroxyl values for polyglycol ethers in Table II demonstrate that results obtained for these materials by the PMDA and phthalation methods are equivalent. The PMDA method has the advantage that it requires significantly less time. The PMDA reaction was complete in 30 minutes, but the phthalation reaction required 2 hours' reflux at the boiling point of pyridine.

CHAPTER 16

A Study of Base-catalyzed
and Salt-catalyzed Acetylation
of Hydroxyl Groups†

GEORGE H. SCHENK, PATRICIA WINES,
and CAROLYN MOJZIS

THE CHOICE of reagents for the determination of organic hydroxyl groups has widened considerably since Mehlenbacher's review[14] of this field. As recently compiled by Siggia,[17] this choice includes, in addition to base-catalyzed acetylation and phthalation, acid-catalyzed acetylation and the base-catalyzed reactions of 3,5-dinitrobenzoyl chloride and pyromellitic dianhydride. Interestingly enough, pyridine still remains the solvent and/or base catalyst for all of these methods. It is not difficult to appreciate why since pyridine is at the same time a good enough nucleophile to catalyze the ionization of acetic anhydride, and a poor enough base to avoid interference at the end point with the basic titrants used to assess the per cent reaction.

If any better nucleophile is to replace pyridine, it obviously must not be used as a solvent, but must be used at a low enough concentration so that it will be conveniently titrated in a titri-

† Reprinted from *Analytical Chemistry*, **37,** 914 (1964). Copyright 1964 by the American Chemical Society and reprinted by permission of the copyright owner.

metric finish such as that below:

$$Ac_2O + PhNH_2 \rightarrow PhNHAc + HOAc \tag{1}$$

$$PhNH_2 + HClO_4 \rightleftharpoons PhNH_3ClO_4 \tag{2}$$

The excess acetic anhydride is removed by reaction with excess aniline and the excess of the aniline is titrated with standard perchloric acid in a nonaqueous medium.

Few strong bases possess the steric requirements necessary for effective catalysis at the low concentrations demanded by reactions 1 and 2. However, triethylenediamine [1,4-diazabicyclo-(2,2,2)octane], a bicyclic bridgehead diamine, is known to be a far superior catalyst than pyridine or triethylamine for the isocyanate-alcohol reaction.[2, 4] Hanna and Siggia[12] have made analytical use of this catalysis. The mechanism[2] of this reaction as shown below closely resembles the chief mechanism of base-catalyzed acetylation given elsewhere.

$$R-N=C=O + :NR_3 \rightleftharpoons R-N=C-O^- \tag{3}$$
$$\underset{\oplus NR_3}{|}$$

$$\underset{\underset{\oplus NR_3}{|}}{R-N=C-O^-} + :OR \rightarrow R-\underset{H}{N}H-CO_2R + :NR_3 \tag{4}$$

The fact that triethylenediamine was found to have seven times the catalytic activity of triethylamine and almost 100 times the catalytic activity of pyridine in the above process,[4] suggested that it would make an excellent catalyst for the acetylation of alcohols.

This led also to a broad investigation of catalysis by sodium acetate and other salts where other mechanisms seemed to predominate. Three methods were studied in detail and are presented below: a macro method employing 2.5 M acetic anhydride–0.19 M triethylenediamine, a semimicro method employing 0.6 M

acetic anhydride–0.28 M triethylenediamine, and a macro method employing 2.5 M acetic anhydride–0.5 M tetraethylammonium bromide. Thereafter the mechanisms are discussed for both base-catalyzed and salt-catalyzed acetylation. Of great importance is the evidence for an intermediate complex of triethylenediamine and acetic anhydride since no such evidence has been found for such an intermediate between pyridine and acetic anhydride.[9]

EXPERIMENTAL

ACETIC ANHYDRIDE (2.5 M)–TRIETHYLENEDIAMINE (0.19 M). Triethylenediamine (1.7 grams) was mixed with 20 ml. of acetic anhydride and 60 ml. of ethyl acetate. The reagent was used immediately but was stable for 2 weeks even though a yellow color slowly developed.

ACETIC ANHYDRIDE (2.5 M)–TETRAETHYLAMMONIUM BROMIDE (0.5 M). Tetraethylammonium bromide (8.1 grams) was mixed with 20 ml. of acetic anhydride and 60 ml. of acetic acid.

ACETIC ANHYDRIDE (0.6 M)–TRIETHYLENEDIAMINE (0.28 M). Triethylenediamine (1.2 grams) was mixed with 2.5 ml. of acetic anhydride and 37.5 ml. of ethyl acetate.

ANILINE (0.6 M and 0.4 M). Baker Analyzed reagent grade aniline was dissolved in reagent grade chlorobenzene. Prepared fresh monthly.

PERCHLORIC ACID (0.2 M and 0.1 M). These titrants were prepared in glacial acetic acid according to Fritz[7] and standardized against primary standard potassium acid phthalate.

Procedures

ACETIC ANHYDRIDE (2.5 M) REAGENTS. Weigh accurately a sample containing 2.5 to 3.5 mmoles of hydroxyl or amino groups into a 125 ml. glass-stoppered (or iodine) flask and pipet in exactly 5 ml. of 2.5 M acetic anhydride reagent. Lubricate the stopper with reagent grade chlorobenzene; do not use ethyl acetate or any solvent that may contain low concentrations of hydroxyl groups or water. For the $0.19M$ triethylenediamine-$2.5M$ anhydride reagent, heat at reflux (80°C.) on a hotplate for 15 to 20 minutes or more for hydroxyl groups; determine amino groups at room temperature after reaction for 15 or more minutes. For the $0.5M$ tetraethylammonium bromide–$2.5M$ anhydride reagent, heat at reflux for 5 minutes for primary and secondary alcohols and 45 to 65 minutes for tertiary alcohols.

Remove from the hotplate and cool; pipet in exactly 25 ml. of the $0.6M$ aniline reagent, and allow to react 10 minutes at room temperature. Add 20 ml. of acetic acid. For either reagent, back titrate the excess aniline potentiometrically with $0.2M$ perchloric acid after inserting the combination electrode into the flask. For the visual titrations, use methyl violet indicator and take the color change found from a potentiometric check of the end point. For the visual titration of the $0.5M$ tetraethylammonium bromide reagent, the correct color change may vary from the usual purple to blue, to blue to green or red to green for the sample. The usual color change for the blank was purple to blue.

Run a reagent blank by pipetting exactly 5 ml. of the acetylating reagent into a 125-ml. flask, and, for the $0.19M$ triethylenediamine reagent, pipetting in exactly 25 ml. of the $0.6M$ aniline reagent. Heat the $0.5M$ tetraethylammonium bromide reagent blank as long as the sample before adding 25 ml. of $0.6M$ aniline reagent. Allow 10 minutes reaction at room temperature for either acetylating reagent and titrate as above for the sample. Use the difference between the sample titration and blank titration ($V_s - V_b$) to calculate the per cent purity of the sample.

ACETIC ANHYDRIDE ($0.6M$) REAGENT. Weigh accurately a polymer or monomer containing about 0.6 mmole of hydroxyl groups into a 125-ml. glass stoppered flask and pipet in exactly 5 ml. of $0.6M$ acetic anhydride reagent. For primary hydroxyl groups, allow to stand at room temperature for 1 hour or more; for secondary hydroxyl groups, lubricate the stopper with chlorobenzene and heat at 60°C. for 40 or more minutes.

Cool if necessary and pipet in exactly 10 ml. of 0.4 M aniline reagent. Allow to react at room temperature for 20 minutes, add 6 drops of methyl violet indicator, and back titrate with 0.1 M perchloric acid, taking the purple to blue color change as the end point. If the precipitate of triethylenediamine perchlorate obscures the end point, titrate potentiometrically as above.

Run a reagent blank by pipetting exactly 5 ml. of the acetylating reagent into a 125-ml. flask and allowing it to stand or heat as long as the sample.

BASE-CATALYZED ACETYLATION

Mechanisms

Three mechanisms that may be followed in the presence of base are given below; a fourth proposed mechanistic comment found in the literature is shown to be incorrect. The bases involved are those normally thought of as bases: tertiary amines such as pyridine and triethylenediamine and acetates such as sodium acetate.

The most important, but perhaps not the exclusive, pathway for base catalysis is suggested by the work of Gold and Jefferson.[9] This is the pyridine-catalyzed ionization of acetic anhydride and the displacement of pyridine from the pyridine-acetylium ion intermediate as shown below:

$$R_3N: + Ac_2O \rightleftharpoons R_3NAc^+ + OAc^- \qquad (5)$$

$$R_3NAc^+ + :OR \rightarrow R_3NH^+ + ROAc \qquad (6)$$
$$H$$

Gold and Jefferson were unable to find physical evidence for an intermediate, but its presence in triethylenediaminecatalyzed acetylation is suggested by the evidence related below.

Fieser and Fieser[5] suggest the following pathway for pyridine catalysis, where B: represents a base such as pyridine:

$$B: + ROH \rightleftharpoons BH^+ + RO:^- \tag{7}$$

$$RO:^- + Ac_2O \rightarrow ROAc + OAc^- \tag{8}$$

Although this pathway is not rigorously excluded by the results of Gold and Jefferson, it cannot be the predominate pathway because 2- and 2,6-substituted pyridines, which are nearly as basic or more basic than pyridine, are much poorer catalysts than pyridine. Although reactions 7 and 8 do not rationalize the rate of pyridine-catalyzed acetylation or acid-catalyzed acetylation in pyridine,[15] they may explain the catalysis of ions like the acetate ion.

Guenther,[10] for example, indicates that 1.2 M sodium acetate in acetic anhydride catalyzes the acetylation of essential oils in 1 hour at reflux.

The third mechanism available for acetylation is the ionization of acetic anhydride into the acetylium ion and the acetate ion, and the reaction of the acetylium ion with an alcohol as shown below.

$$Ac_2O \rightleftharpoons Ac^+ + OAc^- \tag{9}$$

$$Ac^+ + ROH \rightarrow ROAc + H^+ \tag{10}$$

The relatively large specific conductance of pure acetic anhydride was interpreted by Mackenzie and Winters[13] to indicate an ionization of this type. This mechanism may possibly contribute to the acetylation of alcohols at reflux temperatures in ionizing solvents such as dioxane and acetonitrile.

Intermediate Complex

Although Gold and Jefferson[9] postulated the pyridine-acetylium ion intermediate, they were unsuccessful in attempting to prove its existence or the existence of a pyridine–acetic anhydride intermediate complex. Their use of ultraviolet and infrared spectrophotometry, cryoscopy, and conductance methods probably failed because the concentrations of the intermediate or intermediate complex were too low to detect.

Triethylenediamine, however, is over 2000 times stronger a base in aqueous solution than pyridine and is certainly a much better nucleophile. It might predictably yield a detectable concentration of an intermediate complex or perhaps a triethylenediamine-acetylium ion. Ultraviolet spectrophotometry failed to detect any interaction because triethylenediamine appeared to absorb ultraviolet light too strongly for investigation at suitable concentrations. An intermediate complex was detected by infrared, refractive index, and NMR measurements.

An interaction was detected by the appearance of a third peak at 5.82 microns in addition to the usual anhydride carbonyl peaks at 5.45 and 5.65 microns in the infrared region (Fig. 1). This indicates a possible carbonyl nitrogen interaction since an amide carbonyl group absorbs at 5.9 to 6.0 microns. The appearance of this peak with the addition of triethylenediamine to acetic anhydride was also accompanied by a decrease of about 0.5 absorbance units in the C—O—C peak at 8.9 microns. No acetate ion peak was detected in the 6.2- to 6.45- or 7.0- to 7.7-micron regions. This is consistent with the formation of an intermediate complex in the carbon tetrachloride solvent used, but inconsistent with the formation of the triethylenediamine-acetylium ion and acetate ion (reaction 5).

Although acetic anhydride alone in dioxane again showed two carbonyl peaks at 5.45 and 5.68 microns, the addition of triethylenediamine to the anhydride resulted in only one clearly distinguishable peak at 5.82 microns. A shoulder was evident at 5.70 microns.

The ratio of anhydride to triethylenediamine in the intermediate complex was studied by the method of continuous

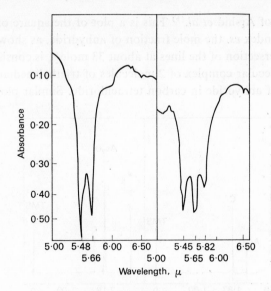

FIG. 1. Infrared spectrum. Left: 0.2 M Ac$_2$O/CCl$_4$; right: 0.2 M
Ac$_2$O + 0.7 M C$_6$H$_{12}$N$_2$ in CCl$_4$

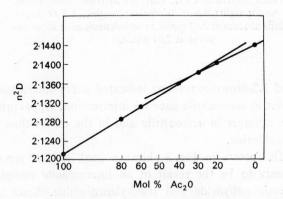

FIG. 2. Plot of the square of the refractive index $vs.$ the mole %
Ac$_2$O in Ac$_2$O-C$_6$H$_{12}$N$_2$ mixtures in CCl$_4$

variations of Arshid *et al.*[1] This is a plot of the square of the refractive index *vs.* the mole fraction of anhydride, as shown in Fig. 2. Intersection of the lines at about 33 mole% is consistent with a molecular complex of 2 molecules of triethylenediamine with one of anhydride in carbon tetrachloride. Similar plots in

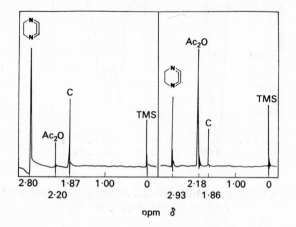

FIG. 3. NMR spectra in CCl_4. Left: 0.6 M triethylenediamine, 0.25 M Ac_2O; right: 0.6 M triethylenediamine, 1.5 M Ac_2O. Ac_2O alone absorbs at 2.17 p.p.m.; triethylenediamine alone absorbs at 2.61 p.p.m.

dioxane and 1,2-dimethoxyethane indicated a 1:1 interaction; the same plot in acetonitrile gave no intersection. Apparently, solvation is stronger in acetonitrile and in the ethers than in carbon tetrachloride.

The NMR spectra in Fig. 3 shows a peak at 1.87 p.p.m. which appears to be the result of an intermediate complex between acetic anhydride and triethylenediamine. Since the CH_3CO- protons of dimethylacetamide were found to absorb at 2.06 p.p.m. relative to tetramethylsilane, the position of the complex peak up-field (1.87 p.p.m.) from the acetic anhydride peak at 2.20 p.p.m. does not appear to be inconsistent with a complex involving a tertiary nitrogen and a carbonyl group.

Another possible indication of complexation in Fig. 3 is that triethylenediamine appears to undergo chemical shifts of 2.61 to 2.80 p.p.m., when present in excess over acetic anhydride, and of 2.61 to 2.93 p.p.m., when the anhydride is in excess. Since the two[11] $(CH_3)_2N-$ peaks of dimethylacetamide were found to occur at 2.96 and 3.11 p.p.m., the down-field direction of the shift again does not appear to be inconsistent with a complex involving a tertiary nitrogen and a carbonyl group. No explanation is offered for the fact that only one peak is observed for triethylenediamine when it is present in excess.

Since no acetate peak was observed at 2.07 p.p.m., the NMR spectra is also inconsistent with the formation of the acetate ion and the triethylenediamine-acetylium ion.

NMR spectra of acetic anhydride in pyridine and carbon tetrachloride indicated only the usual peak for the anhydride at 2.14 p.p.m. and no other peak in that region.

In summary, the physical evidence has established a definite triethylenediamine–acetic anhydride interaction, which appears to be an intermediate complex involving a tertiary nitrogen and a carbonyl group. The evidence is consistent with reactions 5 and 6, but does not establish these reactions to be the reaction mechanism.

Comparison of Catalysts

Various catalysts are compared with triethylenediamine in Table I. Pyridine and 3-methylpyridine were used in the usual 3:1 proportions with acetic anhydride.[8] Pyrazine (20 grams) was dissolved in 10 ml. of ethyl acetate and 10 ml. of acetic anhydride. The analyses were concluded by the usual hydrolysis and sodium hydroxide titration.[8] Perchloric acid titration was used for the analysis of the triethylenediamine, triethylamine, and sodium acetate reagents.

The results indicate that triethylenediamine is as effective a catalyst as pyridine even though present at one-fiftieth the concentration. Actually acetylation was complete with the former in 15 minutes but only 93% complete with the latter in that time. Triethylamine and sodium acetate are poorer catalysts than triethylenediamine at comparable concentrations.

Croitoru and Freedman[3] found that a reagent, consisting of 1 volume of triethylamine ($4M$) and 1.5 volumes of acetic anhydride, acetylates thiocresols 30 seconds prior to gas chromatographic analysis. This reagent could not be employed in connection with any of the present titrimetric finishes.

Reagent Variables

The concentration of triethylenediamine catalyst in the $2.5M$ acetic anhydride reagent was varied from zero to $0.38M$ to explore the effect of concentration on the acetylation of cyclohexanol for 5 minutes at 80°C. From an 8% reaction with no catalyst, the degree of reaction increased to 31% at $0.045M$, 55% at $0.09M$, 75% at $0.19M$, and 86% at 0.285 and $0.38M$. Although $0.285M$ triethylenediamine gives optimum catalysis, the $0.19M$ catalyst gives almost the same reaction rate and keeps the bulk of the precipitated triethylenediammonium perchlorate at a minimum. Hence $0.19M$ catalyst was used in the final reagent.

The effect of solvent was studied by replacing ethyl acetate with other solvents.

Solvents which solvate poorly, such as triethyl phosphate and carbon tetrachloride, seem to favor the rate of reaction. Triethyl phosphate, for instance, is oriented with its dipoles close together, is thus shielded from appreciable interaction with solute ions,[6] and is prevented from appreciable solvation of the positively charged intermediate in reactions 5 and 6. It is possible that appreciable solvation of the intermediate may retard its reaction with an alcohol.

Unfortunately, the potentiometric break at the titration end point in triethyl phosphate, as compared to ethyl acetate, is very poor.

The slower rate of reaction in 1,2-dimethoxyethane may possibly be accounted for by its ability to form a chelation-type hydrogen bonded species at some stage in the rate-determining step. The rate of reaction in acetic acid is similar to that of sodium acetate in acetic acid (Table I), suggesting a substantial equilibration of triethylenediamine to acetate ion, which then catalyzes the reaction.

Table I. Comparison of catalysts
Acetylation of cyclohexanol at 80°C. for 5 minutes

$pK_b(H_2O)$	Catalyst	Molarity	% Reaction
7.5	3-Methylpyridine	8	78
8.7	Pyridine	9.5	75
5.4, 11.0	Triethylenediamine/EtOAc	0.19	75
12.9	Pyrazine	6	41
3.4	Triethylamine/EtOAc	0.19	4
9.3	NaOAc/HOAc	0.19	21
	NaOAc/HOAc	0.5	39
	NaOAc/HOAc	0.7	44

REFERENCES

1. ARSHID, F.M., GILES, C.H., McLURE, E.C., OGILVIE, A., ROSE, T., *J. Chem. Soc.*, 67 (1955).
2. BAKER, J.W., HOLDSWORTH, J.B., *J. Chem. Soc.*, 713 (1947).
3. CROITORU, P.P., FREEDMAN, R.W., *Anal. Chem.* **34,** 1536 (1962).
4. FARKUS, A., *J. Org. Chem.* **26,** 779 (1961).
5. FIESER, L.F., FIESER, M., *Introduction to Organic Chemistry*, pp. 148–9, D.C.Heath & Co., Boston, 1957.

6. FRENCH, C.M., HART, P.B., MUGGLETON, D.F., *J. Chem. Soc.* 3582 (1959).

7. FRITZ, J.S., *Acid-Base Titrations in Nonaqueous Solvents*, p. 13, G.F. Smith Chemical Co., Columbus, Ohio, 1952.

8. FRITZ, J.S., HAMMOND, G.S., *Quantitative Organic Analysis*, p. 261, Wiley, New York, 1957.

9. GOLD, V., JEFFERSON, E.G., *J. Chem. Soc.* 1409 (1953).

10. GUENTHER, E., *The Essential Oils*, Vol. I, p. 275, Van Nostrand, New York, 1948.

11. GUTKOWSKY, H.S., HOLM, C.H., *J. Chem. Phys.* **25,** 1228 (1956).

12. HANNA, J.G., SIGGIA, S., *J. Polymer Sci.* **56,** 297 (1962).

13. MACKENZIE, H.A.E., WINTERS, E.R.S., *Trans. Faraday Soc.* **44,** 159 (1948).

14. MEHLENBACKER, V.C., *Organic Analysis*, Vol. I, pp. 1–38, Interscience, New York, 1953.

15. SCHENK, G.H., FRITZ, J.S., *Anal. Chem.* **32,** 987 (1960).

16. SCHENK, G.H., SANTIAGO, M., *Microchem J.* **VI,** 77 (1962).

17. SIGGIA, S., *Quantitative Analysis via Functional Groups*, 3rd ed., pp. 8–37, Wiley, New York, 1963.

18. STETZLER, R.S., SMULLIN, C.F., *Anal. Chem.* **34,** 194 (1962).

19. STREULI, C.A., *Ibid.*, **30,** 997 (1958).

20. VOGEL, A.I., *Elementary Practical Organic Chemistry*, Part 3, p. 694, Longmans, Green, London, 1958.

21. WINSTEIN, S., SMITH, S., DARWISH, D., *J. Am. Chem. Soc.* **81,** 5511 (1959).

CHAPTER 17

The Detection and Estimation of the Relative Amounts of Primary and Secondary Hydroxyl Groups using N.M.R.†

A. MATHIAS

HYDROXYL groups are usually detected fairly readily in organic compounds by high-resolution proton magnetic resonance spectroscopy. In the 10% solutions normally used, they appear as a single sharp peak that can be moved steadily downfield by successive additions of small amounts of acid to the sample; trifluoroacetic acid is often used for this purpose. This variation in peak position is due to exchange between the hydroxyl group protons of the alcohol and acid, which results in these protons losing their separate identities and appearing as one peak whose position depends upon the concentration of acid added.[1, 2] Alternatively, a hydroxyl peak can be recognised by shaking the sample with D_2O whereupon the peak is reduced in intensity and may even disappear. Exchange of the hydroxyl protons is again responsible for this behaviour.

However, because of similar exchange processes, the various chemically different hydroxyl groups that may be present in a molecule or mixture, again give only a single peak; this is illus-

---

† Reprinted from *Analytica Chimica Acta* **31**, 598 (1964). Reprinted by permission of the copyright owner.

trated in Fig. 1 where the spectrum of 1,3-butanediol is shown. From the area of this peak information can be obtained on the total amount of hydroxyl present, but not on the relative amounts of primary, secondary and tertiary hydroxyl groups. The relative amounts of primary and secondary hydroxyl groups can be obtained in favourable cases from a comparison of the areas of the resonances due to the protons on the carbon atoms carrying the OH groups, *i.e.* —CH$_2$OH and >CHOH, but in most cases, these resonances give overlapping bands between *ca.* 3 δ and 4 δ. (Throughout this paper the Varian system of chemical shift measurement is used, in which positive δ values refer to the chemical shifts, quoted in parts per million, downfield from an internal reference of tetramethylsilane.) This can be seen in Fig. 1

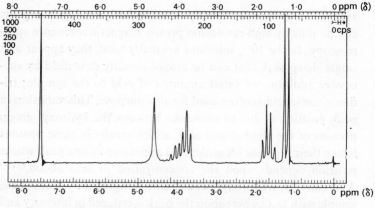

Fig. 1. 1,3-Butanediol in CHCl$_3$ at 60 MC. 1.20 δ due to CH$_3$—, 1.68 δ due to —CH$_2$—, 3.60–4.30 δ due to —CH$_2$OH and > CHOH, 4.70 δ due to OH.

even in the simple case of 1,3-butanediol. In Fig. 2 the spectrum is shown of the reaction mixture after 1,3-butanediol has been acetylated with excess acetic anhydride. Here it can be seen that the resonances due to those protons on the carbon atoms that originally carried the hydroxyl groups have both been moved downfield and are in fact now separated by about 1 p.p.m. The —COOCH$_2$— multiplet is centred at 4.1 δ whilst that due to —COOCH$<$ is centred at 5.0 δ. The areas of these resonances

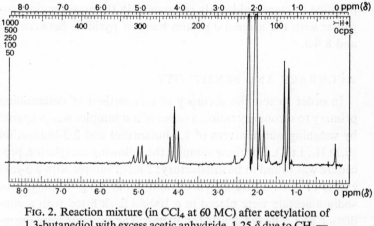

FIG. 2. Reaction mixture (in CCl$_4$ at 60 MC) after acetylation of 1,3-butanediol with excess acetic anhydride. 1.25 δ due to CH$_3$—, 1.65–2.50 δ due to —CH$_2$— and CH$_3$CO, 4.10 δ due to —COOCH$_2$—, 4.95 δ due to —COOCH$<$.

can then be compared. Hence acetylation of a hydroxyl-containing compound or mixture followed by an N.M.R. examination of the product can yield directly the primary to secondary hydroxyl ratio, provided of course that the acetylation is quantitative.

ACETYLATION

Several methods are available for achieving quantitative acetylation.[3] In order that the reaction mixture after acetylation may be examined by N.M.R. immediately, the reagents used in the acetylation must not have any resonances falling in the range of 3.5 δ to 5.5 δ. In fact, this proviso debars none of the usual procedures. Thus excess acetic anhydride either alone or with sodium sulphate or sodium acetate contributes only the resonances of the methyl protons of acetyl groups, which occur between 2 δ and 2.5 δ. Similarly, acetylation with acetic anhydride–pyridine mixtures adds only resonances in the acetyl region, together with the aromatic proton band of pyridine between 7 δ and 8.6 δ.

ACCURACY AND SENSITIVITY

In order to test the accuracy of this method of determining primary to secondary ratios, a series of test samples was prepared by weighing out mixtures of 1,4-butanediol and 2,3-butanediol (B.D.H., Ltd.). For these samples the following acetylation procedure was found to be satisfactory: 2 ml of sample with a 3-fold excess of A.R. acetic anhydride and about 0.5 g of anhydrous sodium acetate were placed in a 100-ml flask fitted with a condenser and refluxed gently for 30 min. The reagents were examined before use by N.M.R. for trace impurities. After cooling, about 0.5 ml of the reaction mixture was withdrawn and mixed with about 0.5 ml of a standard solution of 1 % T.M.S. in CCl_4 and the spectrum recorded using a Varian A-60 N.M.R. spectrometer. The areas of the —COOCH< resonance centred at 4.95 δ (area A) and of the —COOCH$_2$ resonance centred at 4.05 δ (area B) were then obtained using the electronic integrator. A minimum of 4 repeat integrations was performed on each sample. The required ratio was then simply:

$$\frac{\text{(primary OH)}}{\text{(secondary OH)}} = \frac{B}{2A}$$

The factor of two arises since each primary group contributes two protons to B whereas each secondary group only contributes one proton to A.

Table I shows the percentage of primary hydroxyl group calculated from the weighed amounts of diols and the values obtained by acetylation and N.M.R. examination. The agreement between the two, sets of data was quite good. The deviations of

Table I

% Primary OH calculated (X)[a]	% Primary OH measured (Y)	Difference (Y=X)
97.28	96.4	−0.9
93.67	94.3	−0.6
88.50	89.6	+1.1
76.03	75.3	−0.7
62.98	64.7	+1.7
49.92	50.8	+0.9
39.05	39.8	+0.8
25.36	26.0	+0.6
12.29	12.3	0.0
2.93	3.8	+0.8

[a] $\left[\dfrac{(\text{primary OH}) \times 100}{(\text{primary OH}) + (\text{secondary OH})}\right]$.

the experimental values in no case exceeded 1.7%. The average deviation of the experimental values over the whole range of concentration was 0.8%. At first sight it seems possible from the signs of the deviations that the N.M.R. method may have slightly over-estimated the amount of primary hydroxyl. However, a Student *t*-test of significance applied to the data showed that the measured mean value did not differ from zero at the 5% level of significance. The deviations were, in fact, comparable with the limits of accuracy claimed for the electronic integration method of the Varian A-60 spectrometer. The nature of the integration method implies that as the amount of one component becomes smaller with respect to the other, the relative uncertainty in the estimation of this smaller component must increase. In the present work it was found that samples 1 and 10, with only 2.72% secondary OH and 2.93% primary OH respectively, represented the limits of reliable estimation.

The above accuracy tests of the method were performed on butanediol mixtures where hydroxyl made up 38% by weight of the samples. It was necessary to know the lowest level of OH that could be detected in an unknown sample. For this purpose two ethylene oxide–propylene oxide block co-polymers were used. These polymers of molecular weight about 3500, had terminal OH groups and a mixture of $-OCH_2CH_2OH$ and $-OCH_2CH(CH_3)OH$ chain ends was present. The samples contained 1.46 and 1.70% by weight of OH, determined as 48 mg and 56 mg KOH per gram respectively. The samples (2 ml) were heated for 2 h with 0.5 ml of acetic anhydride and 0.25 g of anhydrous sodium acetate. In both cases, after acetylation, the $-COOCH_2-$ and $-COOCH<$ resonances could be observed on the higher sensitivity scales of the A-60 and a comparison of the relative areas could just be made. This gave $25 \pm 5\%$ and $50 \pm 5\%$ primary hydroxyl respectively for the 2 samples. These samples therefore, approached the limit at which the presence of primary and secondary hydroxyl groups could be confirmed, but the quantitative estimation became less accurate.

REFERENCES

1. POPLE, J.A., BERNSTEIN, H.J. and SCHNEIDER, W.G., *High Resolution Nuclear Magnetic Resonance* p. 100, McGraw Hill, New York (1959).
2. JACKMAN, L.M., *Applications of N.M.R. Spectroscopy to Organic Chemistry* p. 28, Pergamon Press, Oxford (1959).
3. MEHLENBACHER, V.C., *Organic Analysis*, Vol. 1, Interscience, New York, (1953); SIGGIA,S., *Quantitative Organic Analysis via Functional Groups*, Wiley, New York (1963).

CHAPTER 18

Phosphoric Acetylation
of the Hydroxyl Group†

PIERRE MESNARD and MICHAEL BERTUCAT

A NEW method of acetylation, phosphoric acetylation has been tested. It is valuable for all three classes of alcohols and can be used in identification. The results are compared with those obtained by pyridine acetylation. The method has been applied, also, to phenols.

Pyridine acetylation is, at the present time, the method most often used for the estimation of the hydroxyl group. First studied by Verley & Boelsing[17, 18] following the work of Einhorn & Hollandt[5] then popularised in France by Sabetay,[4] it presents indisputable advantages with regard to the speed of acetylation, the rapidity of measurement, the absence of secondary reactions. But it also presents the unfortunate inconvenience of not being applicable to tertiary alcohols which react only slightly. Ott,[14] in the meantime, started to acetylate these completely, but with the help of a more lengthy method requiring refluxing for 5 hours as well as the separation and final saponification of the acetyl derivative. The acetylation of tertiary alcohols could be done by two methods: that of Fiore[6] with acetyl chloride and that of Boulez[3] with acetic anhydride in the presence of sodium ace-

† Reprinted from *Bulletin de la Societe Chimique de France*, 307 (1959). Reprinted by permission of the copyright owner.

tate. The method used by Glichitch[7] with acetoformic anhydride is actually a formylation.

We investigated a simple technique approaching in its exe-
cution, the pyridine acetylation, and considered for this purpose
the replacement of pyridine by phosphoric acid. It has been recognised for a long time that it facilitates the acetylation of cellulose and phenols (notably by Landsberg[9] Lederer,[10] Baeyer,[1]
Schwalbe;[16] Sabetay[15] has used it with primary and secondary alcohols and has evolved a method of "acetylation accé-
léréé" which he considers is inapplicable to linalool from the
quantitative standpoint. Naves[13] states that he reacted euca-
lyptol with acetic anhydride. Isoguljanz & Smoljaninova,[8] in
1933, first reported the action of this acid on the acetylation of
the tertiary alcohol, linalool, which is isolated from the essence
of coriander. The yield of linaloyl acetate is of the order of 90 to
95%.

Starting from this data, we have tried to find an easy method
requiring only the minimum of time. We call it "phosphoric
acetylation".[2] We shall describe its technique. We shall show
its application to alcohols, then to phenols; we shall discuss the
comparison of the indices of pyridine acetylation and of phosphoric acetylation.

I. Determination of the Phosphoric Acetylation Index

The work of Isoguljanz & Smoljaninova[8] appertains to the
industrial sphere.

In quantitative analysis the only technique studied is that of
Sabetay[15] repeated by Naves[13] called "acetylation accélérée"
approximating to our phosphoric acetylation, but not suitable
for tertiary alcohols.

SABETAY'S METHOD

7–10 ml of essential oil is treated with 14–20 ml acetic anhydride in the presence of 1–5 ml of a catalyst composed of 10 g of H_3PO_4 for each 90 gm of acetic anhydride. After 15 min contact, it is treated with soda and water. The acetyl derivative is isolated and saponified.

We wished to avoid the final saponification by titrating the excess acetic anhydride directly.

PERSONAL RESEARCH

1. Conditions for the Acetylating Reagent

Phosphoric acid being required in only small proportion, the reagent necessarily requires a solvent conforming to these conditions:

(a) to be miscible with acetic anhydride—phosphoric acid mixture.

(b) to be miscible with water as the excess acetic anhydride is subject to hydrolysis.

(c) to dissolve the substance to be acetylated.

Our choice fell on dioxane.

To establish a quantitative formula, we carried out our tests on alcohols belonging to the three types. The tricky point is to decide on the strength of the phosphoric acid. We started with 10 ml of acetic anhydride and 20 ml of dioxane. We tried out increasing strengths of phosphoric acid up to 80%, that is 55° Beaumé varying between 6 and 20 drops. The optimum is 15 drops. Below, acetylation is incomplete, above, the medium being too acid, certain alcohols are dehydrated and polymerised.

The formula for the reagent is, therefore, as follows:

80% phosphoric acid	15 drops
Acetic anhydride	10 ml
Dioxane	20 ml

It is necessary to point out that the order in which the reactants are mixed is important. To obtain a clear liquid, it is strictly necessary to add in turn (a) phosphoric acid, (b) acetic anhydride (c) dioxane. The mixture of the first two is accompanied by a slight evolution of heat and causes a turbidity which disappears on shaking. If, on the other hand, one or other of the reagents is diluted with dioxane before adding it to the second, a permanent cloudy colloidal suspension appears which spoils the reaction for quantitative determinations.

2. Hydrolysis of Excess Acetic Anhydride

Like the pyridine acetylation, phosphoric acetylation necessitates the use of a large excess of acetic anhydride compared with the quantity of substance to be acetylated. It is therefore necessary to carry out hydrolysis of this at the end of the reaction. Now, Leman[38] has shown the difficulty of this operation without the addition of pyridine. Moreover we have discovered an unexpected effect in the course of the titration of the free acetic acid in the absence of pyridine. Using a 0.5 N sodium hydroxide solution and a 1% alcoholic solution of phenolphthalein, the titration takes place normally until the moment when the neutrality point is approached. When only 0.4 to 0.5 ml of alkali are needed, the red colour obtained when the drop encounters the liquid no longer appears and the indicator only changes colour with an excess of 5 or 6 ml.

Thus, it appears that the phenolphthale forms a complex unstable in a medium sufficiently acid or alkaline, in which case it would be free and would react normally, but stable in the neighbourhood of neutrality, with the result that (the colour change) is marked in a *slightly* alkaline medium. To obviate the difficulty we added an excess of pyridine just before the hydrolysis. Under these conditions, the titration becomes normal and presents no difficulty.

Method of determination. We adopted the following modus operandi:

To a small amount of the substance, varying between 0.25 g to 0.5 g (depending on the moleculae weight of the pure alcohols) in a dry Erlenmeyer flask, 5 ml of the acetylating reagent is added. It is corked and shaken. After sufficient contact at the temperature of the laboratory, 15 ml pyridine is added. The mixture is left for 1 to 2 minutes. Then 50 ml distilled water is added. The mixture is shaken and left for about 5 minutes and then the titration is carried out using a 0.5 N solution of sodium hydroxide. By subtraction the number of millilitres of sodium hydroxide, corresponding to the acetic anhydride used, is obtained and this enables us to calculate the phosphoric acid acetylation index, the definition of which is the same as that of the pyridine acetylation index. It represents the number of milligrams of acetic acid required to esterify the hydroxyl groups contained in one gram of the compound.

Remarks:

(a) The time of contact between the reagent and the hydroxylated compound is 24 h. This time which, to us, seems to be the most satisfactory, has been deduced from a study of the acetylation graphs of the three classes of alcohols.

(b) Except for fatty compounds such as castor oil, it is not advisable to use a water bath, for it causes a troublesome colouration in the medium and the colour change of the indicator is difficult to see.

II. Phosphoric Acetylation of Alcohols

For primary and secondary alcohols the acetylation is complete at the end of about 6 hours. Tertiary alcohols would react more slowly, but they, too, would react completely.

Terpene, a tertiary bialcohol, only slightly acetylated in a pyridine medium (5% at the maximum) is here completely esterified. Two alcohols however are exceptions, linalol and nerolidol. They are only acetylated to about 75%, even after being in contact with the reagent for 48 hours. After several hours, a dark brown colouration of the mixture is observed, which seems to indicate dehydration followed by polymerisation. Possibly it is due to the formation of a diethylenic carbon linkage, linalol and neroidol possessing the same configuration as regards the position of the double bonds the tertiary alcohol group.

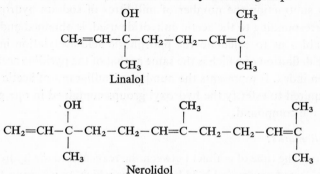

Linalol

Nerolidol

In neither case have we noted the complete acetylation in 15 mins as in Sabetay's method.[15] The results are tabulated as follows:

| | % Acetylation | | | |
	3 hrs.	6 hrs.	18 hrs.	24 hrs.
Methanol	100	—	—	—
Ethanol	88.4	100	—	—
sec-Propanol	70.8	100	—	—
tert-Butyl alcohol	32.5	50.2	92.1	100
tert-Amyl alcohol	32.9	50.6	92	100
Terpineol	35.1	54.7	89.9	99.9
Linalol	23.8	39.2	72.8	77.2
Nerolidol	24.2	39.6	73.1	77.7

III. Phosphoric Acetylation and Pyridine Acetylation

If we compare the indices of phosphoric acetylation with those we have determined for pyridine acetylation, we are led to the following commentary: In pyridine medium, primary alcohols are completely acetylated in about three hours, secondary in 5 hours, whereas tertiary have reacted at the end of that time to an extent of about 10%.

In phosphoric medium, all the alcohols, including tertiary, are completely acetylated having, of course, a different rate for each class:

(a) Primary alcohols would react more slowly in phosphoric medium, the rate of acetylation being about one quarter of that in pyridine medium.

(b) Secondary alcohols behave like primary alcohols and, in consequence, in a different manner from their behaviour in pyridine acetylation.

(c) Tertiary alcohols react a little more slowly than the first two classes but much more rapidly than in the presence of pyridine.

REFERENCES

1. BAEYER and CIE, D.R.P., 107508 (Frdl., 1901, 5, 156).
2. BERTUCAT, Doctoral Thesis, Pharm. État Bordeaux, 1957.
3. BOULEZ, *B.S.C.*, **1097**, 1, 117; 1924, 35, 419, *Schimmels Ber.* **190**, 28; *Proceedings of the Seventh Intern. Congress of Applied Chem.*, London, May 27–June 2, 1909.
4. DELAHY and SABETAY, *B.S.C.* 1716 (1935).
5. EINHORN and HOLLANDT, *Lieb. Ann.* 301, 95 (1898).
6. FIORE, *Givaudanian*, Dec. 1937, p. 5.
7. GLICHITCH, *B.S.C.*, 33, 1284 (1923).
8. ISOGULJANZ and SMOLJANINOVA, *Riechstoffind.* 8, 194 (1933).
9. LANDSBERG, D.R.P., 316500 du 3/12/1901.

10. LEDERER, D.R.P. 124408 (Frdl., 1904, 6, 1119).
11. MESNARD and BERTUCAT, *Bull. Soc. Pharmacie, Bordeaux*, 94, 148 (1955).
12. *Ibid.*, C.R., 2793 (1958); *Bull. Soc. Pharm., Bordeaux*, In Press.
13. NAVES, *Helv. chim. Acta* 1626 (1954); 796, 1613 (1947).
14. OTT, *Helv. chim. Acta* 786 (1954).
15. SABETAY, *C.R.* 390, 1419 (1934).
16. SCHWALBE, *Z. ang. Chem.* 23, 233 (1910).
17. VERLEY and BOELSING, *Ber.* 34, 3354 (1910).
18. VERLEY, *B.S.C.* 43, 1287 (1928).

CHAPTER 19

Acid-catalyzed Acetylation of Organic Hydroxyl Groups†

JAMES S. FRITZ and GEORGE H. SCHENK

ORGANIC hydroxyl groups are commonly determined by acetylation. The sample is heated with an excess of acetic anhydride in pyridine, water is added, and the resulting acetic acid is titrated with alcoholic sodium hydroxide. Most procedures require about 45 minutes on a steam bath for acetylation. A blank containing the same amount of acetic anhydride but without alcohol is treated with water, and the acetic acid formed is titrated. The amount of organic hydroxyl is calculated from the difference of these two titrations.

Mehlenbacher[15] has reviewed the pertinent literature through 1952 on acetylations in pyridine. Conant and Bramann[4] studied the acid- and base-catalyzed acetylation of 2-naphthol with 0.88 M acetic anhydride in glacial acetic acid and found that 0.2 M perchloric acid catalyzed the reaction better than sulfuric or other acids or pyridine. Toennies, Kolb, and Sakami[21] used perchloric acid to catalyze the acetylation of amino acids in glacial acetic acid. Pesez[18] used p-toluenesulfonic acid to catalyze acylation of alcohols with propionic anhydride in glacial acetic

† Reprinted from *Analytical Chemistry*, **31**, 1808 (1959). Copyright 1959 by the American Chemical Society and reprinted by permission of the copyright owner.

acid. Recently, Mesnard and Bertucat[16] used phosphoric acid to catalyze acetylation of alcohols at room temperature in dioxane as solvent. Erdos and Bogati[6] employed chlorosulfonic acid to catalyze acetylation actions in glacial acetic acid. However, even acid-catalyzed acetylations in glacial acetic acid required 30 minutes to 6 hours for complete reaction.

With the present method, primary and secondary alcohols are determined by acetylation in ethyl acetate or pyridine solution using perchloric acid to catalyze the reaction. Soluble alcohols in ethyl acetate are completely acetylated within 5 minutes at room temperature. In pyridine, a somewhat longer reaction period is required for secondary or hindered alcohols.

REAGENTS AND SOLUTIONS

2 M ACETIC ANHYDRIDE IN ETHYL ACETATE. Add 4 grams (2.35 ml.) of 72% perchloric acid to 150 ml. of ACS grade ethyl acetate in a clean 250-ml. glass-stoppered flask. Pipet 8 ml. of ACS grade acetic anhydride into the flask and allow it to stand at room temperature for at least 30 minutes. Cool the contents of the flask to 5°C. and add 42 ml. of cold acetic anhydride. Keep the flask at 5°C. for an hour, then allow the reagent to come to room temperature. Some yellow color will develop, but the color and anhydride content of the reagent remain at satisfactory levels for at least 2 weeks at room temperature.

2 M ACETIC ANHYDRIDE IN PYRIDINE. Cautiously add 0.8 gram (0.47 ml.) of 72% perchloric acid dropwise to 30 ml. of reagent grade pyridine in a 50-ml. flask. Pipet 10 ml. of acetic anhydride into the flask with magnetic stirring. As this reagent discolors and decreases in anhydride content after a few hours, it should be prepared fresh daily. For acetylation of sugars at 50°C., use 1.2 grams of p-toluenesulfonic acid instead of the perchloric acid.

PROCEDURE

Weigh accurately a sample containing from 3 to 4 mmoles of hydroxyl into a 125-ml. glass-stoppered flask and pipet into it exactly 5 ml. of 2 M acetic anhydride in ethyl acetate or pyridine. Stir the solids or immiscible liquids until they are dissolved. Allow the reaction to proceed for at least 5 minutes at room temperature; some alcohols require a somewhat longer reaction period if pyridine is used as the solvent. Add 1 to 2 ml. of water, shake the mixture, then add 10 ml. of 3 to 1 pyridine-water solution and allow the flask to stand for 5 minutes. Titrate with 0.55 M sodium hydroxide using the mixed indicator, and take the change from yellow to violet as the end point. Titrate dark-colored samples to an apparent pH of 9.8 using glass-calomel electrodes and a pH meter.

Run a reagent blank by pipetting exactly 5 ml. of acetylating reagent into a 125-ml. flask containing 1 to 2 ml. of water. Add 10 ml. of 3 to 1 pyridine-water solution, allow to stand 5 minutes, and titrate as above.

CONCENTRATION OF REAGENTS

The anhydride reagent used contained 3 volumes of pyridine or other solvent to 1 volume of acetic anhydride. This is a sufficiently high concentration of anhydride to ensure rapid acetylation, yet dilute enough so that the reagent can be accurately measured with a 5-ml. pipet, and the blank titration with 0.55 M sodium hydroxide will be within the limits of a 50-ml. buret.

In 3 to 1 ratios of solvent to acetic anhydride, 0.15 M perchloric acid is satisfactory. A 0.30 M perchloric acid solution is unsatisfactory, as the results are somewhat erratic and the water in the perchloric acid reduces the anhydride concentration of the reagent.

SOLVENTS

After testing several organic solvents, ethyl acetate was selected as the solvent of choice. Acetylations in this solvent proceed rapidly and quantitatively. Acetic anhydride has reasonably good stability in ethyl acetate.[17] The titration of acetic acid after hydrolysis gives essentially constant values for a period of 2 weeks, and the anhydride content as determined by reaction with aniline decreased only about 5% in 2 weeks. After 2 weeks the yellow color of the reagent darkens to orange, and the end point of the titration is no longer as sharp as it should be. The method of preparing the reagent described previously minimizes color formation.

Solutions of acetic anhydride in pyridine are less stable than in ethyl acetate and must be prepared fresh daily. Also, acetylation of some compounds requires a longer reaction period in pyridine. Nevertheless, pyridine is an important solvent and supplements the use of ethyl acetate for acetylation of alcohols.

Table II. Acetylation of 4 mmoles of alcohols
with 3 to 1 solvent-acetic-anhydride

Alcohol	Reaction, no acid		% Reaction, $0.15\,M$ HClO$_4$	
	Ethyl acetate	Pyridine	Pyridine	Ethyl acetate
Methanol	66	87	100	100
Ethyl alcohol	25	45	100	100
2,2-Dimethyl-1-propanol	17	38	95	100
2-Propanol	5	10	80	100
Diisobutyl carbinol	2	7	64	100
Cyclohexanol	0	0	75	100
2-Methylcyclohexanol	0	0	60	100
2-*tert*-Butylcyclohexanol	0	0	7	100
2-Methyl-2-propanol	0	0	0	70

Chloroform and triethyl phosphate show very good solvent characteristics and may be regarded as possible alternatives to ethyl acetate. Acetylation of 2-*tert*-butyl-cyclohexanol in the latter three solvents is quantitative in 5 minutes.

To show the effect of acid catalysis in different solvents, several alcohols were acetylated for 5 minutes at room temperature (Table II).

These data confirm the fact that acetylation is catalyzed by the presence of a basic solvent such as pyridine. However, the rate of acetylation is much faster when catalyzed by perchloric acid. Acid catalysis occurs to a significant extent even in pyridine where the basic solvent is present in large excess over the perchloric acid added.

MECHANISM OF ACETYLATION

Burton and Praill[1, 2] give the following reaction path for perchloric acid–catalyzed acetylation in acetic acid.

$$Ac_2O + H^+ \rightarrow Ac_2OH^+ \qquad (1)$$

$$Ac_2OH^+ \rightleftharpoons Ac^+ + HOAc \qquad (2)$$

$$Ac^+ + ROH \rightarrow ROAc + H^+ \qquad (3)$$

Perchloric acid–catalyzed acetylations in ethyl acetate also follow this mechanism.

To explain perchloric acid–catalyzed acetylation in pyridine, the reaction of the pyridinium ion (which supplies a proton to the anhydride molecule while another pyridine molecule probably forms the pyridine-acetylium ion) with acetic anhydride to form a pyridine-acetylium ion is postulated.

$$C_5H_5\overset{+}{N}H + Ac_2O \rightleftharpoons (C_5H_5NAc)^+ + AcOH \qquad (4)$$

The pyridine-acetylium ion then reacts with the alcohol to form the ester and regenerate the pyridinium ion.

$$(C_5H_5NAc)^+ + ROH \rightarrow ROAc + C_5H_5\overset{+}{N}H \qquad (5)$$

Gold and Jefferson[13] have suggested the existence of the pyridine-acetylium ion.

Further support of this mechanism is obtained by acetylating alcohols in other basic solvents with perchloric acid for 5 minutes at room temperature (Table III).

Table III. Acetylation of 4 mmoles of alcohols
with 3 to 1 solvent–acetic anhydride

Solvent	% Reaction	
	Ethyl alcohol	Cyclo-hexanol
Pyridine	100	86
2-Methylpyridine	39ₐ	5ᵃ
3-Methylpyridine	93	85
4-Methylpyridine	100	92
2,6-Dimethylpyridine	30ᵇ	...
N,N-Dimethylaniline	26	7
Dimethylacetamide	10	1

ᵃ Temperature 35°C, perchlorate insoluble at room temperature.
ᵇ Temperature 45°C, perchlorate insoluble at room temperature.

The slower acetylation in 2-methyl-pyridine compared to 3- and 4-methylpyridine indicates that steric hindrance makes it appreciably more difficult for the 2-methylpyridine to react with acetic anhydride according to Equation 4. The same argument would be valid for N,N-dimethylaniline and for dimethylacetamide.

OTHER REACTION CONDITIONS

In Table IV the catalytic ability of several monoprotic acids is compared. Acetylation of 4 mmoles of cyclohexanol was run for 5 minutes at room temperature using $0.15 M$ acid in 3 to 1 solvent–acetic anhydride. The results show that perchloric acid is the most effective catalyst, but that *p*-toluenesulfonic acid is also very good. If acetylation were to be carried out at elevated temperatures, *p*-toluenesulfonic acid would be safer to use than perchloric acid.

Table IV. Comparison of acid catalysts

Acid	% Reaction	
	Ethyl acetate	Pyridine
Perchloric	100	75
Hydrochloric	100	30
p-Toluenesulfonic	65	60
Trichloroacetic	5	13
Nitric	4	55
None	1	1

The reaction time required for complete acetylation depends on the structure of the alcohol and on the solvent used. However, the acetylation of primary alcohols in ethyl acetate is almost instantaneous. All alcohols and sugars tested were completely acetylated in 5 minutes in ethyl acetate except those that did not dissolve immediately.

Conventional methods employ heating with water in pyridine to hydrolyze acetic anhydride following acetylation of the alcohol. With perchloric acid as catalyst the hydrolysis is complete in 5 minutes at room temperature, provided the pyridine to water ratio is about 3 to 1. When acetylations are carried out in ethyl acetate, pyridine is added along with water to effect complete hydrolysis.

RESULTS

The reaction time for all compounds tested with the ethyl acetate reagent is 5 minutes except for four sugars. Primary alcohols and glycols react in 5 minutes with the pyridine reagent;

hydroperoxides require 10 minutes. As is seen from Table VII, secondary alcohols react more slowly in pyridine. Diluted samples require at least a 5- to 10-minute longer reaction than pure compounds with the pyridine reagent.

Acetylation in ethyl acetate is very advantageous for sterically hindered alcohols such as 2-substituted cyclohexanols. *cis-2-tert*-Butylcyclohexanol has the hydroxyl group in the hindered, less reactive axial position.[12] At 0°C. the trans isomer is said to acetylate in 2 hours but the cis compound requires 2 days for acetylation.[12] This compound contained 72% of the less reactive cis isomer, yet acetylation in ethyl acetate was complete in 5 minutes at room temperature.

Hydroperoxides can be safely and conveniently analyzed at room temperature with the acid-catalyzed pyridine acetylating reagent. Existing methods which require heating in pyridine would decompose some of the hydroperoxide before it was completely acetylated.

Of the sugars, lactose, maltose, and mannose can be determined in 5 minutes with stirring with the ethyl acetate reagent. Glucose and cellobiose are not immediately soluble and require longer reaction times. The ethyl acetate reagent is not recommended for fructose or sucrose, as results are low and a brown color appears which is similar to that occurring with tetrahydrofurfuryl alcohol, where the perchloric acid causes ring opening.

Heating at 50°C. for 5 to 10 minutes with *p*-toluenesulfonic acid in the pyridine reagent is satisfactory for glucose and sucrose. The pyridine reagent with perchloric acid is satisfactory for fructose although only four hydroxyl groups are acetylated. Only Christensen and Clarke[3] have reported analytical acetylations of fructose with acetylation of 4.15 hydroxyl groups. Hudson and Brauns[14] report preparation of a cyclic tetraacetate of fructose at low temperatures in contrast to the open-chain pentaacetate.

Mixtures

The pyridine reagent is a mild enough acetylating reagent at room temperature so that primary and some unhindered secondary alcohols can be acetylated in the presence of tertiary alcohols. *tert*-Butyl alcohol and dimethylbenzyl alcohol do not react appreciably in mixtures of 50 and 66 mole % with primary and secondary alcohols. Delahy and Sabetay[5] have estimated primary and secondary alcohols in the presence of tertiary alcohols.

INTERFERENCES

In ethyl alcohol–water mixtures, perchloric acid catalyzes the acetylation of ethyl alcohol even though more water is present than the amount of anhydride in the acetylating reagent. However, for quantitative reaction of the ethyl alcohol it is necessary to have a definite excess of anhydride over water.

By increasing the concentration of acetic anhydride in the acetylating mixture it should be possible to determine more dilute solutions of ethyl alcohol in water.

In Table X the effect of compounds containing various functional groups on the acetylation of alcohols is studied. The interference of simple ketones, such as acetone, is eliminated by chilling the sample and acetylating the reagent to 0°C., or by using the pyridine reagent at room temperature. Cyclic ketones, which are somewhat enolic, interfere at 0°C. in ethyl acetate, but do not interfere when the acetylation is carried out in pyridine. Aldehydes interfere seriously in both solvents, but this interference has also been noted in existing acetylation methods.[9, 19] The carbonyl group in benzoin does not interfere with the acetylation of the α-hydroxyl group.

The following compounds do not interfere with the acetylation of alcohols: indene (in pyridine), thiourea, urea, and triphenyl-

Table X. Interferences

Added compound, mmoles	% Reaction	
	EtOAc, 5 min.	Pyridine, 10 min.
Benzaldehyde, 4	270 (0°)	93
Formaldehyde, 12	...	129
Formic acid, 8	...	147
Acetone, 2	99.5	...
Acetone, 20	108; 101.0 (0°)	99.0
Diethyl ketone, 4	101.0 (0°)	...
Diethyl ketone, 12	114; 104 (0°)	98.8 (15 Min).
Acetophenone, 12	100.2	...
Cyclohexanone, 4	159; 155 (0°)	98.0
Cyclopentanone, 4	112; 109 (0°)	99.0
Benzene, 16	99.5	...
Anisole, 4	120	...
1,3-Dimethoxy-benzene, 4	146	99.5

methane. Enols are acetylated to varying degrees, as are imides, hydrazides, and oximes. In ethyl acetate, double bonds and furan rings interfere, but triple bonds do not. Amines, phenols, mercaptans, and some oximes are quantitatively acetylated.

REFERENCES

1. BURTON, H., PRAILL, P. F. G., *J. Chem. Soc.* 1203 (1950).
2. *Ibid.*, 522 (1951).
3. CHRISTENSEN, B. E., CLARKE, R. A., *Ind. Eng. Chem., Anal. Ed.* **17**, 265 (1945).
4. CONANT, J. B., BRAMANN, G. M., *J. Am. Chem. Soc.* **50**, 2305 (1928).
5. DELAHY, R., SABETAY, S., *Bull. soc. chim. France* 1716 (1935).
6. ERDOS, J. B., BOGATI, A. G., *Rev. soc. quim. Mex.* **1**, 223 (1957).
7. FRITZ, J. S., *Acid-Base Titrations in Nonaqueous Solvents*, p. 13, G. F. Smith Chemical Co., Columbus, Ohio, 1952.
8. FRITZ, J. S., FULDA, M. O., *Anal. Chem.* **25**, 1837 (1953).

9. Fritz, J.S., Hammond, G.S., *Quantitative Organic Analysis*, p. 261, Wiley, New York, 1957.
10. *Ibid.*, p. 278.
11. Fritz, J.S., Yamamura, S.S., Bradford, E.C., *Anal. Chem.* **31**, 260 (1959).
12. Goering, H.L., Reeves, R.L., Espy, H.H., *J. Am. Chem. Soc.* **78**, 4926, (1956).
13. Gold, V., Jefferson, E.G., *J. Chem. Soc.* 1409 (1953).
14. Hudson, C.S., Brauns, D.H., *J. Am. Chem. Soc.* **37**, 2736 (1915).
15. Mehlenbacher, V.C., *Organic Analysis*, Vol. I, pp. 1–38, Interscience, New York, 1953.
16. Mesnard, P., Bertucat, M., *Bull. soc. chim. France* 307 (1959).
17. Morgan, K.J., *Anal. Chim. Acta* **19**, 27 (1958).
18. Pesez, M., *Bull. soc. chim. France* 1237 (1954).
19. Siggia, S., *Quantitative Organic Analysis via Functional Groups*, p. 9, Wiley, New York, 1954.
20. Smith, G.F., *Analytical Applications of Periodic Acid and Iodic Acid*, p. 61, G.F. Smith Chemical Co., Columbus, Ohio, 1950.
21. Toennies, G., Kolb, J.J., Sakami, W., *J. Biol. Chem.* **144**, 193–227 (1942).

CHAPTER 20

1,2-Dichloroethane as a Solvent for Perchloric Acid-catalyzed Acetylation†

J. A. MAGNUSON and R. J. CERRI

ETHYL ACETATE is the traditional solvent for the widely used Fritz Schenk [3] perchloric-acid-catalyzed acetylation method for determining organic hydroxyl groups. Their method is also applicable for the determination of amines and mercaptans, [6] alkoxy- [2,4] and mercaptosilanes, [1] and alkoxy- and mercaptogermanes. [5]

After testing some 25 low-dielectric-constant solvents, we find that 1,2-dichloroethane is superior to ethyl acetate as a solvent in many ways. In 1,2-dichloroethane, the acetylating agent can be prepared without cooling. Although the newly prepared reagent does become somewhat warm, it may be used within an hour's time. [With ethyl acetate, cooling to 5°C. [3] is necessary during one step of the acetic anhydride–perchloric acid mixing.]

The acetylating agent is virtually colorless, or a very light yellow tint at most. (The reagent in ethyl acetate is yellow to yellow-brown.) Indicator end points are sharp when the yellow color is absent.

† Reprinted from *Analytical Chemistry*, **38,** 1088 (1966). Copyright 1966 by the American Chemical Society and reprinted by permission of the copyright owner.

216

The acetylating agent has a useful life, at least two months, that is two or three times longer than reagents in ethyl acetate.

Presently, 1,2-dichloroethane is the only solvent besides ethyl acetate in which alkoxysilanes are quantitatively acetylated within 10 minutes. Table I shows typical results for the determinations of alcohols, phenols, and alkoxysilanes in 1,2-dichloroethane. Extensive use of the procedure below has shown that the relative precision (one std. dev.) is about $\pm 0.5\%$ for $\equiv$SiOC$\equiv$ linkages in monomeric or dimeric compounds, $\pm 1\%$ for alkoxy-containing poly(dimethylsiloxane) fluids of 5 to 20 dimethylsiloxy units, and ± 2–3% for similar fluids containing high amounts of trifunctionality ($RSiO_{1.5}$).

ACETYLATION METHOD

Acetylating Reagent

Acetic anhydride ($1\,M$) in 1,2-dichloroethane ($0.15\,N$ perchloric acid). Pour 420 ml. of 1,2-dichloroethane into a 500-ml. glass-stoppered flask and add 6.2 ml. of 72% perchloric acid and, slowly, while stirring, add 55 ml. of acetic anhydride. Colorless reagents are obtained more consistently in this laboratory if the flasks are first rinsed well with a 1:1 acetic anhydride: 1,2-dichloroethane solution.

Procedure

Pipet 10 ml. of the acetylating reagent into a 125-ml. glass-stoppered flask and add an accurately weighed 4–5 meq. of an acetylyzable sample. After a 5-minute reaction time, add 35 to 40 ml. of 6:3:1 dimethylformamide:pyridine:water hydrolyzing solution. Hydrolyze for 10 to 15 minutes, add 5 drops of 1% thymol blue indicator, and titrate with alcoholic $0.55\,N$ potassium hydroxide to the blue end point. Run an appropriate blank.

Dimethylformamide aids in solubilizing both the 1,2-dichloro-ethane and water. Its presence also sharpens the indicator end point.

REFERENCES

1. BERGER, A., MAGNUSON, J.A., *Anal. Chem.* **36**, 1156 (1964).
2. DOSTAL, P., CERMAK, J., NOVOTNA, B., *Collection Czech. Chem. Commun.* **30**, 34 (1965).
3. FRITZ, J.S., SCHENK, G.H., *Anal. Chem.* **31**, 1808 (1959).
4. MAGNUSON, J.A., *Ibid.*, **35**, 1487 (1963).
5. MAGNUSON, J.A., KNAUB, E.W., *Ibid.*, **37**, 1607 (1965).
6. SCHENK, G.H., FRITZ, J.S., *Ibid.*, **32**, 987 (1960).

CHAPTER 21

Micro Acid-catalyzed Acetylation of Organic Hydroxyl Groups†

GEORGE H. SCHENK and MILAGROS SANTIAGO

INTRODUCTION

Classical pyridine-catalyzed acetylation methods for hydroxyl groups are not ideal for adaptation to micro scale. The usual method[1] not only depends on the small difference between a blank and a sample titration, but also requires an excess of a fairly concentrated ($1–2M$) volatile acetylating reagent which must be measured carefully and refluxed carefully for 60 min.

If it is desired to determine the hydroxyl group at room temperature in pyridine, an inconveniently long time is required[2] since the ionization of acetic anhydride also becomes slow in the first step of the two-step reaction:

$$C_5H_5N + Ac_2O \rightleftharpoons C_5H_5NAc^{\oplus} + OAc^-$$

$$C_5H_5NAc^{\oplus} + ROH \xrightarrow{\text{slow}} ROAc + C_5H_5NH^+$$

At reflux temperatures the first step is rapid, but for a favorable rate of reaction for the second step, a high concentration of acetic anhydride is required to supply enough of the pyridine-acetylium ion to react with less basic (than pyridine) hydroxyl

† Reprinted from *Microchemical Journal* **VI,** 77 (1962). Reprinted by permission of the copyright owner.

219

compounds such as alcohols and phenols. Thus micro methods must use the same concentration of reagent as macro methods.

Acid-catalyzed acetylation in nonbasic solvents.[3, 4] has been shown to involve the reactive acetylium ion intermediate:

$$Ac_2O + H^+ \rightleftharpoons Ac^\oplus + HOAc$$

$$Ac^\oplus + ROH \xrightarrow{\text{fast}} ROAC + H^+$$

The second step of the reaction is not slow so that whatever effect dilution has on the first equilibrium step, is overcome by the irreversible nature of the fast second step: the acetylium ion intermediate reacts rapidly at room temperature with hydroxyl groups even when the acetylating reagent is reduced in concentration from 2 to $0.25 M$.[5] The method described below is based on the use of a $0.06 M$ reagent.

Table I compares several semimicro or micro methods with the proposed method.

Table I. Micro acetylation methods

Reagent, concentration	Reagent vol. used	Conditions, time	Reference
$2 M$ Ac_2O/C_5H_5N	0.4 ml.	Reflux, 30 min.	1
$0.4 M$ $AcCl/C_6H_5CH_3$	2 ml.	Reflux, 40 min.	6
$2 M$ Ac_2O/C_5H_5N	Weighed	R.T., 25 hr.	2
Ac_2O/C_5H_5N	—	60°, 2.5 hr.	7
$0.06 M$ $Ac_2O/EtOAc$	5 ml.	R.T., 20 min.	This paper

EXPERIMENTAL

Reagents

Ethyl acetate, reagent grade containing not more than 0.01 % water. If necessary dry over anhydrous potassium carbonate or phosphorus pentoxide.[8]

Acetic anhydride, ACS grade.

Pyridine, reagent grade.

Acetic anhydride, $0.06 M$ in ethyl acetate. Pipet 0.40 ml. of acetic anhydride into 50 ml. of ethyl acetate. Add 0.03 ml. of 72% perchloric acid. Stir or shake for 5 min. before use. Prepare fresh daily.

Sodium hydroxide, $0.05 N$ in methanol. To 20 ml. of saturated aqueous sodium hydroxide, add 50 ml. of water and 5400 ml. of absolute methanol. Store in a polyethylene bottle. Standardize against primary standard grade potassium acid phthalate.

Mixed indicator. Mix 37 parts of 0.1% neutralized thymol blue with 12 parts of 0.1% neutralized aqueous cresol red.

Procedure

In this procedure, the liquid samples were analyzed as received and checked if necessary by other acylation methods. Solid samples were vacuum sublimed if possible. The procedure below was then followed.

Weigh a sample containing from 0.05 to 0.1 meq. of hydroxyl group into a 50 or 125 ml. ground glass-stoppered flask. Pipet in 5 ml. of $0.06 M$ acetic anhydride in ethyl acetate and swirl gently after the sample is dissolved. Let stand 20 min. at room temperature until the sample is dissolved. Hindered hydroxyl compounds such as 2-substituted cyclohexanols or 2,6-di-*tert*-butylphenols require longer reaction times.

Add 0.5 ml. of water and 4.5 ml. of pyridine; let hydrolyze 10 min. at room temperature. The high concentration of pyridine and slight amount of heat generated from mixing permit rapid hydrolysis without external heating.

Add 4 drops of mixed indicator and titrate to a distinct red-violet with $0.05 N$ sodium hydroxide in methanol. Run a reagent blank under identical conditions, omitting the hydroxyl sample.

RESULTS AND DISCUSSION

The results for micro acetylation of alcohols and phenols as well as cholesterol are shown in Table II. A reaction time of 20 min. is recommended for most compounds except for hindered phenols containing 2,6-di-*tert*-butyl groups and for *o*- or *p*-nitro substituted phenols. Lauryl alcohol was acetylated in 10 min., being about 94% reacted in 5 min. Sterols such as cholesterol should not be acetylated any longer than 10 min. since they tend to degrade and give colors with perchloric acid.[9]

Cholesterol should not be acetylated longer than 10 min.; the recovery at 20 min. is 103%. Apparently this is not unusual as acetylation in pyridine of cholesterol at reflux temperatures gives results as high as 111%. Acetylation at room temperature in pyridine[2] gave 102% recovery. Acylation with 3,5-dinitrobenzoyl chloride[10] gave results of 99.9 and 100.1%, and acylation with pyromellitic anhydride[11] gives results of 100.5%.

Phenols with no more steric hindrance than one 2-*tert*-butyl group can easily be determined. However, 2,6-di-*tert*-butylphenols are quantitatively acetylated (as shown by infrared examination of the ester) only with macro reagents.[5] The purity of 2-*tert*-butylphenol was checked by acetylation at reflux temperatures in pyridine.

Oximes can be acetylated at room temperature with perchloric acid-catalyst in pyridine,[12] but an oxime such as cyclohexanone oxime reacts by this method to the extent of only 57–60% in 20 min.

Tertiary alcohols such as *tert*-amyl alcohol react about 3% after 1 hr. and about 33% after 24 hr.

Various concentrations of acetic anhydride with $0.006 M$ perchloric acid were used to acetylate lauryl alcohol and *p*-methoxyphenol. Both $0.25 M$ and $0.15 M$ anhydride were satisfactory, but $0.05 M$ anhydride required 60 minutes to react quantitatively with lauryl alcohol, and 0.03 M anhydride reacted with only 38 % lauryl alcohol in 15 min. or more. The perchloric acid concentration was increased to 0.007 M and the anhydride concentration to 0.06 M to remove the water added with the additional perchloric acid.

Some difficulty was encountered when hydrolysis of the anhydride was performed with 5 ml. of premixed 3:1 pyridine–water. When the ratio was increased to 9:1 pyridine–water and each was added separately, blank titrations were reproducible.

Apparently larger amounts of pyridine favor the ionization of the anhydride to the pyridine-acetylium ion which then reacts readily with water. It is known[13] that a high concentration of water accelerates pyridine-catalyzed hydrolysis of the anhydride by an enormous factor, but since water reduces the sharpness of the endpoint, more pyridine rather than more water is used to favor the catalysis.

Table III contains data on interferences and mixtures. Aldehydes and cyclohexanone interfere as they do in most acetylation procedures, but cyclopentanone does not. o-Nitrophenol did not react, and low results were obtained for m- and p-nitrophenol. Low results are also found for o- and p-nitrophenol after acetylation at room temperature in pyridine.[2]

REFERENCES

1. OGG, C. L., PORTER, W. L., and WILLITS, C. O., *Ind. Eng. Chem. Anal. Ed.*, **17,** 394 (1945).
2. PETERSON, J. W., HEDBERG, K. W., and CHRISTENSEN, B. E., *Ind. Eng. Chem. Anal. Ed.*, **15,** 225 (1943).
3. BURTON, H., and PRAILL, P. F. G., *J. Chem. Soc.*, 1203 (1950); 522 (1951).
4. KOSKIKALLIO, J., *Acta Chem. Scand.*, **14,** 1343 (1960).
5. SCHENK, G. H., and FRITZ, J. S., *Anal. Chem.*, **32,** 987 (1960).
6. KEPNER, R. E., and WEBB, A. D., *Anal. Chem.*, **26,** 925 (1954).
7. MA, T. S., *Microchem. J.*, **3,** 420 (1959).

8. FIESER, L., *Experiments in Organic Chemistry*, 3rd ed., Heath, Boston, 1957, p. 287.
9. SLACK, S.C., and MADER, E.J., *Anal. Chem.*, **33**, 625 (1961).
10. ROBINSON, W.T., CUNDIFF, R.H., and MARKUNAS, P.C., *Anal. Chem.*, **33**, 1030 (1961).
11. SIGGIA, S., HANNA, J.G., and CULMO, R., *Anal. Chem.*, **33**, 900 (1961).
12. SCHENK, G.H., *Anal. Chem.*, **33**, 299 (1961).
13. KOSKIKALLIO, J., *Suomen Kemistilehti*, **B32**, 41 (1959).

CHAPTER 22

Determination of Alkoxy Groups in Alkoxysilanes by Acid-catalyzed Acetylation†

J. A. MAGNUSON

ALKOXYSILANES are of considerable importance as intermediates in the manufacture of siloxane materials. Accurate alkoxy functional group analysis is necessary to ensure uniformity in the formulations to which these intermediates are added. For better product control, therefore, an attempt was made to develop a fast and quantitative alkoxysilane method suitable for routine use in a quality control laboratory. The method developed is also an aid for confirming the composition of newly created silanes by analysis of their alkoxy contents.

The alkoxy content of alkoxysilanes is often determined, following hydrolysis, by employing the conventional analytical methods for alcohols in aqueous solution.[5] There are several methods available for rapidly determining alcohols in this manner. The slow steps, however, are completion of the hydrolysis and separation of the alcohol from those silanes or siloxanes whose other functional groups (or the silanols formed) somewhat solubilize the alcohol. A modified Zeisel technique[1] has

† Reprinted from *Analytical Chemistry*, **35**, 1487 (1963). Copyright 1963 by the American Chemical Society and reprinted by permission of the copyright owner.

been used successfully for the analysis of methoxy-, ethoxy- and propoxysilanes. The limiting factors of this technique are a time-consuming procedure and the molecular weight of the alkyl group that can be distilled as the iodide. Accurate assays of aryloxysilanes capable of stoichiometric bromination have been reported.[7] Also, infrared spectrophotometry has been used to determine the methoxy content of siloxane polymers.[2]

All these methods, however, do not possess the versatility herein proposed. This method, incorporating the accuracy and speed of a simple titrimetric procedure is essentially that developed by Fritz and Schenk[6] for the determination of organic hydroxyl groups. Both monomers and soluble high molecular weight siloxanes containing a wide variety of alkoxy and aryloxy groups can be quantitatively determined with equal ease.

Acetylation of alkoxy groups bonded to silicon by acetic anhydride is perchloric acid-catalyzed in an ethyl acetate solvent. The acetylation is quantitative in less than 2 minutes at room temperature with $0.06 M$ perchloric acid catalyst.

EXPERIMENTAL

Reagents and Solutions

Acetic Anhydride ($2 M$) in Ethyl Acetate ($0.06 M$ in Perchloric Acid). Add 2.2 grams of 72% perchloric acid to 150 ml. of ACS grade ethyl acetate in a 250 ml. glass-stoppered flask. Add 5 ml. of ACS grade acetic anhydride to the flask and allow to stand at room temperature for 30 minutes. Cool the contents of the flask to 5°C. and add 45 ml. of cold acetic anhydride. Keep the flask at 5°C. for an hour, then allow the reagent to come to room temperature. A yellow color will develop which does not impair the usefulness of the anhydride reagent. The reagent has been used successfully for about 3 weeks.

Potassium Hydroxide (0.5 N). Dilute 170 ml. of aqueous 45%
potassium hydroxide solution to 4000 ml. with absolute methanol. Standardize against potassium acid phthalate using the mixed
indicator.

Procedure

Accurately weigh a sample containing 4 to 5 meq. of the alkoxysilane into a 125-ml. glass-stoppered flask. Pipet 5 ml. of
2 M acetic anhydride in ethyl acetate into the flask. Swirl the
solution. Allow the reaction to proceed for about 5 minutes.
(Organic-perchloric acid solutions must not be heated!) Then
add 1 or 2 ml. of water and swirl the mixture again for a few
seconds. Rinse the sides of the flask with 10 ml. of 3 to 1 pyridine–
water solution and allow the hydrolysis to proceed for about
10 minutes. Titrate with alcoholic 0.5 N potassium hydroxide.
The mixed indicator end point is the color change from yellow
to brownish-purple. The reagent blank is run in the same manner, but without the sample. The alkoxy content is calculated
from the difference in volume between the sample and blank
titrations.

RESULTS AND DISCUSSION

The following scheme of reactions is suggested for the acid-
catalyzed acetylation of alkoxy groups bonded to the silicon
atom:

$$Ac_2O + H^+ \rightleftharpoons Ac_2OH^+ \tag{1}$$

$$Ac_2OH^+ \rightleftharpoons Ac^+ + AcOH \tag{2}$$

$$Ac^+ + \equiv SiOR \rightarrow \equiv SiO^+R \tag{3}$$
$$\underset{Ac}{|}$$

$$\equiv SiO^+R + Ac_2O \rightarrow \equiv SiOAc + AcOR + Ac^+ \tag{4}$$
$$\underset{Ac}{|}$$

or

$$\equiv SiO^+R + AcOH \rightarrow \equiv SiOAc + AcOR + H^+$$
$$\overset{|}{Ac}$$

The formation of acetylium (Ac^+) from acetic anhydride and perchloric acid by steps 1 and 2 is reported by Burton and Praill.[3, 4] The first result in Table II illustrates that without the acid catalyst, acetylation of diphenyldimethoxysilane was not detected in a reaction time of 10 minutes. Acetoxysilanes from reaction mixtures, before hydrolysis, and after the perchloric acid had been adsorbed on activated charcoal, have been separated by gas chromatography and identified by infrared analysis. That acetates are formed is evidenced by the odor of the products resulting from proproxy- and butyoxsilane analysis. The formation of acetoxysilane does not interfere with the analysis since it is quantitatively and very rapidly hydrolyzed to silanol and acetic acid. Two reactions are proposed for step 4. These reactions, which may compete, would explain the necessary addition of only catalytic amounts of perchloric acid. The acetic anhydride reaction and the acetic acid reaction with the alkoxysilane acetylium species would regenerate acetylium ions and hydrogen ions, respectively.

Table II illustrates the extent of the reaction vs. concentration of catalyst over a reaction time of 10 minutes for diphenyldimethoxysilane. An increase in the perchloric acid concentration to $0.15 M$ showed neither further acetylation nor any deleterious effect. p-Toluenesulfonic acid, $0.15 M$, catalyzed the acetylation of dimethyldiethoxysilane by only 74% in 6 hours and 90% in 40 hours at room temperature. There was no detectable acetylation of the same silane in 30 minutes using $0.15 M$ trifluoroacetic acid as the catalyst.

The purity of the samples analyzed except where indicated, was assumed to be 98 to 100%. Following their preparation the alkoxysilanes were distilled at least once in a $^3/_{16}$-inch diameter glass-helices packed thermostated 24-inch column. The analyses may be considered quantitative. Apparently most alkoxy and phenoxy groups bonded to silicon may be analyzed by this method.

Table II. Effect of perchloric acid catalyst concentration upon extent of acetylation of diphenyldimethoxysilane

(10-minute reaction time; triplicate determinations)

M HClO$_4$ None	Reaction, % < 1
0.01	97.5 ± 0.6[a]
0.02	98.9 ± 0.6
0.04	99.2 ± 0.2
0.08	99.0 ± 0.3

[a] Average and standard deviation.

Limitations appear to be: solubility of the material to be analyzed, possible steric hindrance, and those expected for ordinary acetylation reactions. Substituted siloxysilyl, olefinic, nitrile, silicon hydride, γ-chloropropyl, or β-chloroethyl groups do not interfere. The two methoxyethoxysilanes in Table III illustrate that the perchloric acid does not appear to attack the methyl ether groups. Water and silanol within limits, as shown by Fritz and Schenk, do not interfere. Compounds containing acid groups however, must first be analyzed for titratable acid and appropriate corrections made in the alkoxy content calculations.

An alkenedioxysilane that resists acetylation, perhaps because of steric hindrance in step 4 of the proposed mechanism, is 2,2,4,4,5,5-hexamethyl-1,3-dioxa-2-silacyclopentane. A model of this silane suggests that the oxygen atoms are not sterically hindered from attack by acetylium as shown in step 3. Experimentally this attack appears to be successful as evidenced by a precipitation in the reaction mixture, which is presumably an alkenedioxysilane acetylium perchlorate. The salt dissolves immediately upon addition of polar and nonreactive solvents as acetone and pyridine. The reaction ceases, however, since upon dissolving, the salt does not quantitatively acetylate (even overnight).

Acetylation of 2,2,4,4,5,5-hexamethyl-1,3-dioxa-2-silacyclopentane proceeded, but to a small extent. It is believed that this occurs during hydrolysis. Acetic anhydride hydrolysis is not immediate. Some of the alkenedioxysilane is evidently hydrolyzed to its alcohol and subsequently acetylated before the hydrolysis of the acetic anhydride is complete.

Aminoalkyl side chains on alkoxysilanes can be quantitatively determined by acetic anhydride in the absence of acid catalysts because alkoxysilanes are inert to acetic anhydride unless certain acid catalysts are present. The nucleophilic amines, of course, require no acid catalysts for rapid acetylation by acetic anhydride

REFERENCES

1. *Analytical Chemistry of Polymers*, G. M. Kline, Ed., p. 372, Interscience, New York, 1959.
2. BROWN, P., SMITH, A. L., *Anal. Chem.* **30,** 549 (1958).
3. BURTON, H., PRAILL, P. F. G., *J. Chem. Soc.* 1203 (1950).
4. *Ibid.,* 522 (1951).
5. EABORN, C., *Organosilicon Compounds*, p. 502, Butterworths, London, 1960.
6. FRITZ, J. S., SCHENK, G. H., *Anal. Chem.* **31,** 1808 (1959).
7. SMITH, B., *Acta Chem. Scand.* **11,** 558 (1957).

CHAPTER 23

Epoxy Acids from Oleic and Elaidic Acids†

BEN H. NICOLET and THOMAS C. POULTER

THE PRESENT work was undertaken to throw light on the effect of a long aliphatic chain on the reactivity of the ethylene oxide grouping. It also offered an opportunity to compare a pair of epoxides which were geometrical isomers.

Our experience confirms the results of Albitzki, that both the chlorohydrin and the epoxide derived from oleic acid give on alkaline hydrolysis only the low-melting 9,10-dihydroxystearic acid. The corresponding derivatives from elaidic acid gave only the high-melting dihydroxy acid. It appears, however, that the epoxides are formed with such relative ease that with *these particular compounds* the hydrolysis of the chlorohydrins by alkali must take place almost exclusively by way of the epoxides.

While these epoxides react with water in the presence of alkali or of dilute acids only after hours of boiling, they add hydrogen chloride or sulfuric acid rather readily in ether solution at room temperature. When $0.1 N$ hydrogen chloride in dry ether was used, the reaction with elaidic acid epoxide was 90% complete after one hour at 20°; the oleic acid epoxide disappeared 3 or 4 times as rapidly. The products were chlorohydrins, each of

† Reprinted from *Journal of the American Chemical Society* **52**, 1186 (1930). Reprinted by permission of the copyright owner.

which with alkali regenerated the same epoxide from which it had been formed. They were, however, readily obtained as solids, and appear to differ from the chlorohydrins formed by the addition of HOCl to the unsaturated acids. The latter (IIa, b) are presumably 9-chloro-10-hydroxystearic acids. It is considered probable that the products obtained from the epoxides and hydrogen chloride are the isomeric 9-hydroxy-10-chlorostearic acids (IVa, b).

An analytical method for the determination of the epoxides in mixtures was based on the reaction with hydrogen chloride in ether just described. By using a standard acid solution, allowing the reaction to go to completion and then determining the total acidity of the final solution, it was possible to determine the amount of hydrogen chloride which had disappeared in the reaction, and therefore the amount of epoxide initially present. Results consistent within 1 % or less were readily obtained, and as neither the chlorohydrins nor the dihydroxystearic acids interfered, this method was very useful in following the reactions to be reported below.

EXPERIMENTAL

Quantitative Determination of the Epoxides

The absorption of hydrogen chloride by the epoxides in dry ether has been discussed. An analytical method was based on this reaction.

A 0.1–0.2N solution of hydrogen chloride in dry ether was prepared and standardized. The sample of epoxide was dissolved in a measured volume of this solution containing at least twice the amount of hydrogen chloride theoretically necessary, allowed to stand for two hours at room temperature in a stoppered flask, then poured into neutralized alcohol and titrated with standard potassium hydroxide solution, using phenolphthalein. The alkali equivalent of the fatty acid used must be separately determined on another sample. The acid which disappears in the reaction (hydrogen chloride) is reported as moles of epoxide. The dihydroxystearic acids and 10-ketostearic acid do not interfere. Results within 1 % could be obtained with known mixtures.

This method was used to determine the epoxides in the various experiments to be reported on the (approximate) rates of reaction of these substances.

Relative Reactivities of the Two Epoxides toward Hydrogen Chloride

Appropriate titrations showed that in 0.1 N ethereal hydrogen chloride at 20°, elaidic acid epoxide reacted to the extent of 90 % in one hour. The oleic acid epoxide reacted at least three times as rapidly.

Relative Rates of Hydrolysis to Dihydroxystearic Acids

On boiling with 1 % aqueous hydrochloric or sulfuric acid, the epoxides of oleic and elaidic acids gave the dihydroxystearic acids (m.p. 96 and 133°, respectively). The oleic epoxide reacted decidedly the more rapidly, but the hydrolysis requires many hours even in this case.

CHAPTER 24

Direct Titration of Oxirane Oxygen
with Hydrogen Bromide in Acetic Acid†

A. J. DURBETAKI

EPOXY compounds have assumed commercial importance in recent years with the advent of resins, epoxy plasticizers, epoxy stabilizers, and epoxy insecticides. This has focused increased attention on analytical methods for oxirane oxygen. Until now oxirane oxygen has been determined by indirect methods.[1-3, 5, 6, 8, 9, 11] The methods that have found the widest applicability because of their specificity employ hydrogen chloride in ether, dioxane, and pyridine.[2, 6, 9, 11] All these methods are based on the addition of hydrogen chloride to oxirane oxygen to form the corresponding chlorohydrin. The difference between the amount of unconsumed hydrochloric acid and that of the corresponding blank is a measure of the epoxy content. As carboxylic acids interfere with these determinations, a correction for the amount of acid present in the sample has to be made. In general, these methods require appreciably more time and operations and involve errors of three, as compared with one, separate titrations to obtain the oxirane oxygen content.

The first direct titration procedure for oxirane oxygen[4] employed an acetic acid–hydrochloric acid reagent. Titrations were

† Reprinted from *Analytical Chemistry*, **28**, 2000 (1956). Copyright 1956 by the American Chemical Society and reprinted by permission of the copyright owner.

performed potentiometrically. The method presented here is an improved and simplified procedure, which utilizes an acetic acid–hydrobromic acid reagent. Visual end points can be employed and the general range of applicability is considerably extended. Hydrogen bromide is a much stronger acid than hydrogen chloride in glacial acetic acid [7] and reacts to a faster rate with the α-epoxy group.

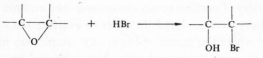

REAGENTS

Crystal violet indicator solution, 0.1 % crystal violet (Eastman) in glacial acetic acid.

Hydrogen bromide, anhydrous, Matheson Co.

Hydrogen bromide in Acetic Acid, 0.1 N. Bubble anhydrous hydrogen bromide at a slow rate through 1 liter of glacial acetic acid, until the desired normality is attained. Standardize against 0.1 gram of sodium carbonate, dissolved in 5 ml. of glacial acetic acid, and titrate to the blue-green end point of the crystal violet indicator.

APPARATUS

Reservoir Buret, Karl Fischer Type, Arthur H. Thomas Co., No. 2484-B. Fill the drying tubes of the reservoir and buret with Todd universal absorbent. Replace the drying tube of the reservoir with a ball joint stopper when the buret is not in use.

PROCEDURE

Weigh accurately a sample of 0.3 to 0.6 gram in a 50-ml. Erlenmeyer flask. Dissolve epoxy resins in chlorobenzene, other compounds in chlorobenzene or benzene. Add 5 drops of 0.1 %

crystal violet indicator solution, place the rubber stopper in position, and lower the buret tip to a point just above the solution. Titrate the sample to the blue-green end point while stirring at a slow speed with the magnetic stirrer.

RESULTS AND DISCUSSION

A variety of purified epoxy compounds and commercial epoxy plasticizers were analyzed. In order to evaluate the method, especially where the purity of the epoxy sample was not known, the results were compared with those obtained by the hydrochloric acid–ethyl ether method[11] or the pyridinium chloride–pyridine method.[2] The oxirane oxygen content obtained by the acetic acid–hydrobromic acid method is in excellent agreement with those obtained by the other two methods (Table I). The reaction with all compounds tested so far is almost instantaneous and proceeds at a speed equal to that of aqueous acid–base titrations. Epoxides, such as styrene oxide, which isomerize readily in acid media cannot be titrated quantitatively by this method. This is also true of other methods employing acidic reagents.[5]

Although glacial acetic acid can be used as a solvent, in the presence of chlorobenzene or benzene sharper end points are obtained without sacrificing the speed of the reaction. Because of its greater polarity, chlorobenzene is preferable, especially in the titration of epoxy resins. In cases where desired, the titration can be followed potentiometrically using the glass-calomel electrode system as in the acetic acid–hydrochloric acid method.[4] The sample is dissolved in 10 ml. of glacial acetic acid and a mechanical stirrer is used. Three potentiometric titration curves for a plasticizer, epoxy resins, and an epoxy compound are given in Fig. 1.

The specificity of the reagent to the α-epoxy group was checked by investigating the possible interference of other functional groups. With peroxides such as oleyl peroxide, lauroyl peroxide, and benzoyl peroxide, the end points were stable for more than 5 minutes. A slow reaction of hydroperoxides was noticed but with no observable interference, as indicated by the study of mixtures of varying concentrations of cumene hydroperoxide and 9,10-epoxystearic acid and similar mixtures of *tert*-butyl peroxide and 9,10-epoxystearic acid (Table II). The end point is sharp and stable for about half a minute. The apparent reaction rate of hydroperoxides is slower than that of the oxirane oxygen and no apparent reaction of the hydroperoxide prior to the complete reaction of the epoxy group was observed.

REFERENCES

1. BLUMRICH, K., *Angew. Chem.* **54,** 374 (1941).
2. BRADLEY, T.F. (to Shell Development Co.), U.S. Patent 2,500,-600 (1950).
3. DECKERT, W., *Z. anal. Chem.* **82,** 297 (1930); **109,** 166 (1937).
4. DURBETAKI, A.J., *J. Am. Oil Chemists' Soc.* **33,** 221 (1956).
5. JUNGNICKEL, J.L., PETERS, E.D., POLGÁR, A., WEISS, F.T., *Organic Analysis*, Vol. I, pp. 127–54, Interscience, New York–London, 1953.
6. KING, G., *J. Chem. Soc.* 1980 (1931).
7. KOLTHOFF, J.M., WILMAN, A., *J. Am. Chem. Soc.* **56,** 1014 (1934).
8. METZGER, K., *Beitrag zur quantitativen Bestimmung des Äthylenoxyds*, U.S. Technical Oil Mission, Reel 15, Bag 3043, p. 2266 (1938).
9. NICOLET, B.H., POULTER, T.C., *J. Am. Chem. Soc.* **52,** 1186 (1930).
10. RIDDICK, J.A., *Anal. Chem.* **24,** 41 (1952).
11. SWERN, D., FINDLEY, T.W., BILLEN, G.N., SCANLAN, J.T., *Ibid.*, **19,** 414 (1947).

CHAPTER 25

Direct Titration of Epoxy Compounds and Aziridines†

R. R. JAY

SIR: THE determination of the oxirane ring in organic compounds has generally involved reaction with excess hydrochloric acid in a variety of solvents. Because the reaction is slow, at least a 15-minute reaction time is generally allowed before back titrating the excess acid. The determination of aziridines also requires back-titration techniques.[1, 4] Durbetaki[2] described a direct titration of epoxies with anhydrous hydrogen bromide in acetic acid. While this method is rapid and capable of good results, the reagent, which fumes profusely in air, requires special handling and frequent restandardizations for accurate analyses.

The following method employs a stable, readily available, titrant which can be used for the direct titration of oxiranes and certain aziridines. The sample is dissolved in chloroform and titrated to a crystal violet end point with standard perchloric acid (in acetic acid or dioxane) in the presence of an excess of a soluble quaternary ammonium bromide or iodide.

For epoxides either reagent can be used, but the quaternary bromide is satisfactory for virtually all the materials usually en-

† Reprinted from *Analytical Chemistry*, **36**, 667 (1964). Copyright 1964 by the American Chemical Society and reprinted by permission of the copyright owner.

countered and is recommended over the iodide because of economy and better storability. With aziridines, however, the iodide is preferred as it gives more rapid reactions and sharper end points.

EXPERIMENTAL

Reagents

Standard $0.1 N$ $HClO_4$ in glacial acetic acid. Mix 8.5 ml. of 72% $HClO_4$ with 300 ml. of glacial acetic acid and add 20 ml. of acetic anhydride. Dilute to 1 liter with glacial acetic acid and allow to stand overnight. Standardize against potassium acid phthalate.[3]

Tetraethylammonium bromide reagent. Dissolve 100 grams of NEt_4Br in 400 ml. of glacial acetic acid. Add a few drops of crystal violet indicator. Compensate for any slight indicator blank by titrating dropwise with the standard $HClO_4$ to the end point color change.

Tetrabutylammonium iodide reagent, 10% in chloroform. Dissolve 50 grams of NBu_4I (Eastman white label grade, or equivalent) in 500 cc. of reagent grade chloroform. This reagent is stable providing it is not preneutralized with perchloric acid reagent, or exposed to light. Store in the dark.

Procedure

Into a 50-ml. Erlenmeyer flask weigh a sample estimated to contain 0.6 to 0.9 meq. of oxirane or aziridine. Dissolve in about 10 ml. of chloroform. Acetone, benzene, and chlorobenzene may also be used as solubility considerations warrant. Add 10 ml. of the quaternary bromide or iodide reagent and 2 or 3 drops of crystal violet indicator. Titrate to a definite color change with standard $0.1 N$ perchloric acid using a 10-ml. micro buret. Very sharp visual end points are generally obtained, especially for epoxides, but in some cases a potentiometric correlation using glass *vs.* calomel electrodes, may be desirable. The reagent blank is usually negligible, but should be checked occasionally.

DISCUSSION AND RESULTS

In the above titrations, hydrogen bromide (or iodide) generated *in situ* by the addition of perchloric acid to the quaternary ammonium halide rapidly opens the oxirane or aziridine ring

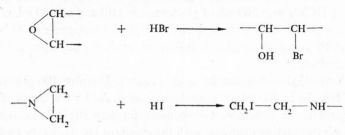

The large excess of bromide and the higher acid strength of perchloric acid afford somewhat more rapid oxirane titrations and sharper end points than those obtained with the HBr acetic acid titrant. A wide variety of epoxy compounds have been titrated by the tetraethylammonium bromide procedure with good results. In particular, it should be noted that epoxy resins Epon 1031 and ERRA 0153 were readily analyzed by the quaternary bromide technique whereas the HBr–acetic acid method failed to give discernible end points with these solid essentially tetrafunctional resins.

Work with both oxiranes and aziridines demonstrated that HI is a more energetic ring opening agent than HBr and accordingly the quaternary iodide gives sharper end points in the perchloric acid titrations. With oxiranes this is of relatively little practical importance as the quaternary bromide system is adequate. However, for the aziridines, the more vigorous quaternary iodide–

perchloric acid system is recommended. Likewise, for especially unreactive epoxides the iodide method is preferred, and in extraordinary cases an excess of perchloric acid may be added and back titrated with sodium acetate in acetic acid.

The use of acetic acid as a solvent for aziridines sometimes gives low results because of a competing proton catalyzed reaction. Only a limited number of aziridines have been investigated, but by using a solution of tetrabutylammonium iodide in chloroform the acetic acid introduced by the perchloric acid reagent did not interfere with the assays of tris-[1-(2-methyl)-aziridinyl]-phosphine oxide or phenyl bis[1-(2-methyl)aziridinyl]phosphine oxide.

REFERENCES

1. ALLEN, E., SEAMAN, W., *Anal. Chem.* **27,** 540 (1955).
2. DURBETAKI, A.J., *Ibid.*, **28,** 2000 (1956).
3. FRITZ, J.S., *Acid Base Titrations in Nonaqueous Solvents*, The G.F.Smith Chemical Co., Columbus, Ohio, 1952.
4. SCHLITT, R.C., *Anal. Chem.* **35,** 1063 (1963).

CHAPTER 26

An Improved Direct Titration
of α-Epoxy Compounds
using Crystal Violet as the Indicator†

R. DIJKSTRA and E. A. M. F. DAHMEN

MOST methods for the determination of α-epoxy compounds are
indirect titrations based upon the formation of chlorohydrin by
the relatively slow reaction of the epoxy group with an excess of
hydrogen chloride. For hydrogen bromide the addition reaction
is far more rapid; DURBETAKI's method[1] for the determination
of epoxides by direct titration with 0.1 N hydrobromic acid in
glacial acetic acid takes advantage of this.

On titrating glycidyl esters in this manner we found that the
reaction may still be annoyingly slow, especially towards the end
of the titration: after each addition of titrant a fairly long wait
was necessary before the colour of the indicator no longer
changed.

The course of the titration could be made more clearly visible
by means of potentiometric titration combined with a recorder.
A Dow Precision Recordomatic Titrometer was modified in such
a way that a 0.2-ml portion of titrant was added in 10 sec, after
which there was a pause of 50 sec before the next portion was
added. The titration of epichlorohydrin with 0.1 N hydrobromic

† Reprinted from *Analytica Chimica Acta* **31**, 38 (1964). Reprinted by
permission of the copyright owner.

acid in glacial acetic acid using glass and calomel electrodes thus yielded the curve reproduced in Fig. 1. The peaks in the Fig. correspond to the potential changes caused by each portion of titrant. The smooth curve—drawn in later—is the normal titration

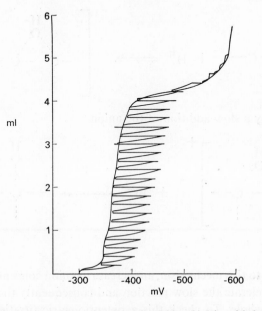

Fig. 1. Intermittent titration of epichlorohydrin with hydrogen bromide. Electrodes: glass/calomel.

curve. Apparently, DURBETAKI's method can be used successfully, but the slow reaction prevents expeditious titrations.

A closer look at the reaction mechanism suggested modifications in the titration procedure which should speed it up. These modifications, the principle of which was published already some years ago,[2] and the results are discussed in the following sections.

Mechanism of the addition reaction

The mechanism of the addition of hydrogen bromide to epoxy compounds is well known. It involves two steps:[3] a rapid protonation

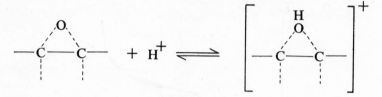

followed by a slow addition of the anion

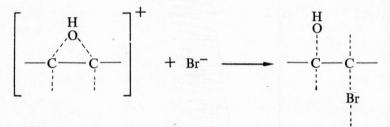

According to this mechanism, an increase in anion concentration should accelerate the slow reaction and consequently the addition as a whole. To check this a potentiometric titration was carried out in the presence of 3 equivalents of tetrabutylammonium iodide. Figure 2 shows the curve obtained. Not only has the addition of the iodide eliminated the peaks, but at the same time the potential jump at the equivalence point has increased, which favourably influences the accuracy of the titration.

A further conclusion to be drawn from the reaction mechanism is that any sufficiently strong acid should be able to effect the protonation. *p*-Toluenesulfonic acid and perchloric acid can indeed replace hydrogen bromide in the titration. In practice, the highly stable solution of perchloric acid in acetic acid is to be preferred, because with this titrant the jump in potential at the equivalence point is about the same as for hydrogen bromide. Figure 3 shows the curve for the titration of the glycidyl ester of cyclohexane carboxylic acid with perchloric acid in the presence of 3 equivalents of tetrabutylammonium iodide.†

The solvent also influences the rate of the addition reaction. Acetic acid proved to be the most suitable medium in combination with the titration technique described here; addition of chlorobenzene or benzene slows the reaction down.

For routine application tetrabutylammonium iodide is too expensive, and accordingly a cheap substitute was sought. Cetyltrimethylammonium bromide, which is sold under a variety of trade names, gave satisfactory results, provided that the amount of anion-supplying salt was increased from 3 to nearly 6 equivalents (Fig. 4). Lithium bromide, which is fairly readily soluble in acetic acid, is another possible substitute, although in this case the potential jump at the equivalence point is relatively small.

Titrations with crystal violet as an indicator

If, for a titration with perchloric acid in acetic acid in the presence of cetyltrimethylammonium bromide, crystal violet is used as an indicator, its colour towards the end of the titration first changes slowly from violet to blue. On further addition of titrant it exhibits the familiar colour change to blue-green. At *ca.* 600 mV potential difference there is a third change, from blue-green to bright green. This last change provides a suitable visual endpoint for the epoxy titration.

Here another advantage of the cheaper quaternary bromide

† Later experiments have shown that when the added anion is iodide and the titrant $HClO_4$ one should protect against direct light. Otherwise, decomposition occurs yielding a yellow colour and high results. This can easily be prevented by coating the titration beaker externally with a black paint, and covering the beaker with a piece of black paper with holes for the electrodes.

over the tetrabutylammonium iodide comes to the fore: the iodide, which in this case cannot be protected from light, would cause yellow products to appear, interfering with the observation of the colour change.

The above-mentioned colour change to bright green does not coincide exactly with the potentiometrically determined equivalence point of the titration. The titration will only give reliable values for glycidyl ethers and esters, if a blank titration is performed. The perchloric acid can be accurately standardized against sodium biphthalate with tropaeolin oo as an indicator.

EXPERIMENTAL

Method summary

The glycidyl ester is dissolved in glacial acetic acid at room temperature. Immediately after addition of an excess of cetyltrimethylammonium bromide, this solution is titrated with $0.1 N$ perchloric acid in acetic acid, using crystal violet as an indicator.

Reagents

Solvent. Glacial acetic acid, analytical reagent quality.

Cetylmethylammonium bromide, commercial grade "Cetavlon" (ICI) or similar product sold as cationic detergent and antiseptic.

0.1 N Perchloric acid in acetic acid. Mix 8.5 ml of concentrated perchloric acid (s.g. 1.70; 70%) with 1 l of glacial acetic acid. A sufficient quantity of acetic anhydride should be added to bind the water contained in the concentrated perchloric acid.

Procedure

Weigh to the nearest 0.1 mg a quantity of sample containing not more than 0.5 mequiv of epoxide into a 50-ml beaker. Add to the sample 25 ml of glacial acetic acid, 2 g of cetyltrimethylammonium bromide and 5 drops of a 0.1 % (w/v) solution of crystal violet indicator in glacial acetic acid.

Start the magnetic stirrer and rapidly titrate, immediately after dissolution of the sample and the cetyltrimethylammonium bromide, with standardized perchloric acid solution until the bright green colour persists. The titrant should be added from a 10-ml microburet, *e.g.* a Metrohm piston buret E274. Although the correct visual end-point in this determination occurs at the first colour change of the indicator from blue to blue-green, the colour change from blue-green to bright green is much sharper and easy to observe. In this procedure distinct colour changes are caused by 0.01–0.02 ml of 0.1 N perchloric acid.

Make a blank test in exactly the same way as described above, but omit the sample. With "Cetavlon", blanks of not more than 0.1–0.2 ml are obtained.

REFERENCES

1. DURBETAKI, A.J., *Anal. Chem.* **28**, 2000 (1956).
2. DAHMEN, E.A.M.F., *Chem. Weekblad* **57**, 259 (1961).
3. MOUSSERON, J.J., and PEYRON, A., *Bull. Soc. Chim. France*, 1093 (1958).

CHAPTER 27

The Volumetric Determination of Anthracene with Maleic Anhydride†

I. Ubaldini, V. Crespi, and F. Guerrieri

The old methods for the analysis of anthracene in technical products, as anthracene pastes and commercial anthracene of various grades, are based on the conversion of the hydrocarbon considered into anthraquinone by treatment with chromic acid in acetic acid.

For many years, the most widely used process has been that of Luck,[1] which is always given in the best-known books on analysis,[2] in spite of the criticisms raised against it by, in particular, J. Sielisch[3] and Sielisch and Koeppen.[4]

A quite new direction in the analysis of anthracene appeared with the investigations of O. Diels and K. Adler [sic],[6] who showed the capacity of the hydrocarbon considered for reaction with maleic anhydride, crotonic acid, and similar unsaturated compounds.

The first allusion to the use of maleic anhydride in the determination of anthracene was given in 1936 by H. P. Kaufmann and J. Baltes.[8]

The method of analysis is generally applicable to compounds containing conjugated double bonds and consists in heating the

† Reprinted from *Annali di Chimica Applicata* **39**, 77 (1949). Reprinted by permission of the copyright owner.

substance with maleic anhydride dissolved in acetone for 26 hr at 100° in a glass tube and then titrating the excess of anhydride in the presence of phenolphthalein. In the cold, the addition compound of anthracene and maleic anhydride does not react with alkalis so that the titration of the excess of maleic anhydride can be carried out without its being necessary to separate it first from the anthracene derivative.

Subsequently, Kaufmann et al.[9] replaced the alkalimetric titration of maleic anhydride by an iodometric titration and reduced the reaction time to 4 hr by using a $^3/_5$-molar solution of maleic anhydride in boiling toluene.[10]

But the most decisive step forward in the analysis of anthracene was taken by Postovskii and Khmelevskii[11] with the proposal to carry out the maleic anhydride treatment in boiling xylene, then removing the solvent by steam-distillation, and finally titrating the aqueous solution of maleic acid in excess.

Having had occasion to apply this procedure to the analysis of samples of anthracene of various grades, we have, however, easily been able to find in some cases marked discrepancies in the results of determinations carried out in parallel so that the results obtained could not be accepted even in the case of tests of a technical nature.

On examining the tests carried out to identify the causes of error, we have found that on working under the conditions suggested by the authors of the method there are never losses of any kind with respect to the maleic anhydride but there is often a partial hydrolysis of the addition compound with the anthracene so that the acid derived from the hydrolysis considered is also titrated as maleic acid. The compound is, therefore, not absolutely inert to the action of boiling water, as Posstowski and Chmelewski state, but part of it, depending mainly on the volume of water with which it is in contact, is converted into the corresponding dibasic acid and passes into the aqueous solution.

If the solubility mentioned above is taken into account and the volume of the aqueous solution resulting from the steam treatment is measured, satisfactorily concordant results are obtained, as we shall prove by means of the data given below.

Nevertheless, in the circumstances it seemed to us to be worthwhile to further modify the process by simply eliminating the process of boiling in a current of steam through the use of a water-immiscible solvent with which it would be possible to extract the maleic anhydride on simple shaking with hot water.

A solvent that satisfies this fundamental requirement is chlorobenzene. In the hot it readily dissolves both anthracene and maleic anhydride and it has a boiling point sufficiently high for the reaction to take place in it at a rate practically equal to that in xylene, but has the great advantage over the latter that the titration of the excess of maleic anhydride does not require its preliminary removal from the aqueous liquid. After the reaction with maleic anhydride has completed, it is sufficient to add hot water to the flask in which the operation is carried out, to shake for a few minutes, to cool the mixture, and then to titrate the excess of maleic anhydride. When simplified in this way, a determination of anthracene requires about 30 minutes and always gives results that are much more concordant and reliable than those obtained either by the laborious oxidation methods or by the original Posstowski method.

EXPERIMENTAL

Determination of the excess of maleic anhydride without elimination of the solvent

The necessity for removing the solvent in Posstowski and Chmelewski's method is due to the fact that if the reaction mixture is taken up with hot water and titrated with alkali, not all the maleic anhydride passes immediately into the aqueous liquid so that the end of the titration is always slow and uncertain.

By using chlorobenzene in place of xylene, it has been found that the reaction between the maleic anhydride and anthracene takes place equally fast and, in addition, the considerable advantage is obtained that the neutralization of the excess of maleic anhydride can be carried out in the presence of the same solvent without any interference.

Titration tests carried out by first dissolving the maleic anhydride in boiling chlorobenzene and then extracting the mixture with water have always given results in perfect agreement with those of the titration of the maleic anhydride dissolved directly in water.

The anthracene addition compound easily dissolves in boiling chlorobenzene and when the resulting solution is shaken for a short time with hot water the partial hydrolysis found in the case of boiling in a current of steam does not take place.

To extract the maleic anhydride from the chlorobenzene it is in fact sufficient to shake the mixture with hot water for about 1 minute, and in this short time the anthracene derivative undergoes practically no change.

The reaction between maleic anhydride and anthracene in boiling chlorobenzene is sufficiently rapid if the concentration of the anhydride in the solvent is kept in a ratio of about 1 g of the former per 5 cm^3 of the latter. With more dilute solutions, there is no certainty of completing the operation in 20–25 minutes.

For the practical performance of the determination, therefore, we recommend the following procedure:

1 or 2 grams of anthracene, according to whether its titre is greater or less than 50%, respectively, 1 g of maleic anhydride, and 5 cm^3 of chlorobenzene are boiled gently for 20–25 minutes in a 250-cm^3 long-necked flask provided with an air condenser 50–60 cm long. Then the heating is stopped and with a funnel

about 100 cm³ of previously-boiled hot water is poured into the flask through the air condenser, the mixture is shaken vigorously for about 1 minute, and immediately afterwards is cooled by the immersion of the flask in running water. When the mixture has been brought almost to room temperature in this way, the excess of maleic anhydride is titrated with N/5 NaOH in the presence of phenolphthalein until a permanent pink coloration is obtained. The colour change is usually very sharp even with low-titre samples of anthracene giving highly coloured solutions in chlorobenzene. Simultaneously, a blank test is carried out with maleic anhydride and chlorobenzene, and the difference in the amounts of N/5 NaOH consumed gives the anthracene content of the sample on the basis that 1 cm³ of this caustic soda corresponds to 0·01782 g of anthracene.

REFERENCES

1. LUCK, Z. anal. Chem. 12, 347 (1873); Ber. 6 (1847).
2. VILLAVECCHIA, G. V., Chimica Analitica Applicata, Vol. 1, p. 774, Hoepli, Milan, 3rd Ed., 1936.
3. SIELISCH, J., Z. angew. Chem. 39, 682, 1248 (1926).
4. SIELISCH, J., KOEPPEN, Ibid. 39, 1249 (1926).
5. RHODES, NICHOLAS, MORSE, Ind. Eng. Chem. 17, 839 (1925).
6. DIELS, O., ALDER, K., Ann. 486, 191 (1931).
7. CLAR, E., Ber. 64, 2198 (1931).
8. KAUFMANN, H.P., BALTES, J., Fette u. Seifen 43, 93 (1936).
9. KAUFMANN, H.P., BALTES, J., BUTER, H., Ber. 70, 903 (1937); KAUFMANN, H.P., BALTES, J., HARTWEG, L., Ber. 70, 2559 (1937).
10. KAUFMANN, H.P., BALTES, J., BUTER, H., Ibid., 70, 905 (1937).
11. POSTOVSKII, I.Y.Y., KHMELEVSKII, V.I., Chem. Zentr. II, 2042 (1937).

CHAPTER 28

Determination of Diels–Alder
Active Dienes with Tetracyanoethylene†

MARA OZOLINS and GEORGE H. SCHENK

FEW GENERAL titrimetric methods have been developed for determining dienes by the Diels–Alder reaction, although a number of methods have utilized maleic anhydride for the determination of anthracene. Ubaldini, Crespi, and Guerrieri[17] determined anthracene by adding an excess of maleic anhydride, refluxing in chlorobenzene, and extracting the excess away from the water-insoluble adduct with hot water. Funakubo, Matsumoto, and Hiroike[3] modified this method by performing a two-phase titration of the excess maleic anhydride as maleic acid, using water at 55° as the second phase.

Polgar and Jungnickel[10] reviewed diene determinations by the addition of maleic anhydride and recommend an iodine-catalyzed method, especially for isomeric mixtures.

One general diene method is that of Putnam, Moss, and Hall.[11] which utilizes β-elimination of chloride ion from the adduct of the diene and chloromaleic anhydride. However, chloromaleic anhydride is, unfortunately, less reactive than maleic anhydride.

† Reprinted from *Analytical Chemistry*, **33,** 1035 (1961). Copyright 1961 by the American Chemical Society and reprinted by permission of the copyright owner.

p-Nitrobenzenediazonium salts have also been used for the general determination of 1,3-dienes by colorimetric[1] and titrimetric methods.[16]

Tetracyanoethylene (TCNE) has been reported by Middleton, Heckert, Little, and Krespan[9] to react quantitatively with various dienes. TCNE has been used by Schenk and Ozolins for the indirect colorimetric determination of anthracene.[15]

The procedures described below use pure TCNE as the reference standard. A weighed excess of TCNE and the diene to be determined are mixed in methylene chloride and the Diels–Alder reaction is allowed to proceed at room temperature. Then the excess TCNE is back-titrated slowly with 0.05 M cyclopentadiene in alcohol to form the colorless Diels–Alder adduct:

$$C_5H_6 + TCNE \xrightarrow{\text{fast}} C_5H_6{=}TCNE \qquad (1)$$

A warning indicator of 20 % phenanthrene in benzene indicates the approach of the equivalence point, with the disappearance of the red-violet color of the TCNE-phenanthrene complex.

$$C_5H_6 + TCNE[C_{14}H_{10}] \xrightarrow{\text{fast}} C_5H_6{=}TCNE + C_{14}H_{10} \qquad (2)$$
(Red violet)

Then a 1 % pentamethylbenzene indicator is added and the disappearance of the red color of the TCNE-pentamethylbenzene complex is taken as the equivalence point.

$$C_5H_6 + TCNE[C_6H(CH_3)_5] \xrightarrow{\text{slow}} C_5H_6{=}TCNE + C_6H(CH_3)_5 \qquad (3)$$
(Red)

The photometric titrations follow the same procedure, except that the disappearance of the colors of both indicator complexes as shown in Equations 2 and 3 is followed at 525 mμ.

EXPERIMENTAL

Apparatus

To perform the photometric titrations, use a Bausch & Lomb Spectronic 20 with a 125-ml. Erlenmeyer flask equipped with inlet and outlet tubes as directed by Rehm, Bodin, Connors, and Higuchi.[12] Use a 25- or 50-ml. buret equipped with a Teflon stopcock.

Reagents

0.05 M CYCLOPENTADIENE. Crack dicyclopentadiene at 160° to the monomer, redistill the monomer, and collect the fraction boiling at 40° in a receiver cooled in a dry ice–acetone bath. Weigh about 0.8 gram of the cyclopentadiene at the dry ice–acetone temperatures as accurately as possible and dissolve in 250 ml. of absolute ethyl alcohol.

Although the freshly prepared reagent need not be standardized for routine work, it can be standardized for careful work against pure TCNE, following the back-titration procedure below. As shown in Table I, its molarity decreases 12% in 4 days.

Table I. Stability of cyclopentadiene titrant
at room temperature

Day	M-Cyclo-pentadiene, M	% Decrease
0	0.0600	...
1	0.0580	2.9
2	0.0560	6.7
3	0.0539	10.1
4	0.0527	12.1

To check its stability, the cyclopentadiene titrant can be used in a direct titration of TCNE alone, using a photometric end point. Typical results are shown in Table I. It is apparent that the titrant must be standardized each day or freshly prepared each day.

TETRACYANOETHYLENE (TCNE). Synthesize from malononitrile[2] or obtain from Distillation Products Industries. Sublime under vacuum at bath temperature of 120°C. to obtain a white solid. Recrystallize from chlorobenzene or methylene chloride. Store in a desiccator over sodium hydroxide pellets.

20% PHENANTHRENE INDICATOR. Dissolve 10 grams of recrystallized phenanthrene in 40 ml. of reagent grade benzene.

1% PENTAMETHYLBENZENE INDICATOR. Dissolve 1 gram of Eastman White Label pentamethylbenzene in 100 ml. of reagent grade methylene chloride.

PROCEDURES

Visual Indicator Titration

Weigh between 0.32 and 0.39 gram of TCNE into a stoppered 250-ml. flask, add 50 ml. of distilled methylene chloride, and dissolve with heating. Then weigh 1.25 to 1.5 mmoles of diene into the flask. Allow to react 10 minutes at room temperature for most dienes (consult Table II for special cases). Add 10 drops of phenanthrene warning indicator. Titrate slowly, allowing time for complete reaction, with 0.05 M cyclopentadiene until the red-violet color disappears. Add 5 drops of pentamethylbenzene indicator and continue the titration dropwise until the red color disappears.

To determine as little as 20 mg. of anthracene and semimicro amounts of other dienes, use 60 mg. of TCNE, 0.1 mmole of diene, 50 ml. of methylene chloride, and 0.05 M cyclopentadiene in a 10-ml. buret in the above procedure.

To determine a reactive diene such as anthracene in the presence of a less reactive diene, or an aromatic hydrocarbon such as indene, prepare a solution of between 0.32 and 0.39 gram of TCNE in 100 ml. of distilled methylene chloride. Heat to dissolve, if necessary. Prepare a slush of carbon tetrachloride by freezing in dry ice–acetone. Then cool the solution to $-20°C$. in the slush, add the diene or anthracene-indene mixture, and allow to react 20 minutes at $-20°$. Titrate the excess TCNE as above. If the unreacted diene forms a strong, colored complex with TCNE as does indene, take the end point as the disappearance of the color of this complex rather than adding either of the above indicators. Since anthracene reacts only to about 96% at $-20°$, run a blank on it alone and correct for this.

Photometric Titration

Weigh between 0.32 and 0.39 gram of TCNE into a beaker or, if necessary, a 250-ml. stoppered flask. Add 75 ml. of distilled methylene chloride and weigh 1.25 to 1.5 mmoles of diene into the beaker or flask. After a 10-minute reaction at room temperature for most dienes, transfer to a 250-ml. Erlenmeyer flask equipped with inlet and outlet tubes,[12] which is connected to the test tube supplied with the Bausch & Lomb Spectronic 20, and circulate the solution through the flask and cell by magnetic stirring.

Then adjust the transmittance to read 100% at 525 mμ. Add 10 drops of the phenanthrene warning indicator and titrate slowly with 0.05 M cyclopentadiene from a 25- or 50-ml. buret, until the transmittance is between 80 and 90%. Add 0.1 gram of pentamethylbenzene and continue the titration until the transmittance is about 50%. Thereafter record the absorbance at 0.2-ml. intervals and allow 30 seconds between successive additions. Stir thoroughly after each addition. Correct absorbance readings for dilution[4] if desired and plot these data against milliliters of 0.05 M cyclopentadiene. Determine the end point graphically.

REACTION CONDITIONS

Solvents

Since aromatics solvents complex TCNE to varying degrees,[8] they cannot be used as the solvent in the determination.

Because chlorinated alkanes do not measurably complex TCNE with reference to ethers, the former appear to be ideal solvents. Methylene chloride dissolves TCNE most rapidly; chloroform can be added to reduce volatility of the solvent if desired.

Indicators

The pentamethylbenzene-TCNE π complex is the second strongest complex reported by Merrifield and Phillips.[8] Its K value is 123. Pentamethylbenzene appears to complex the last traces of TCNE strongly enough to provide an accurate end point. However, the reaction of cyclopentadiene with the complexed TCNE, as shown in Equation 3, is too slow to permit a reasonable initial titration rate.

The weaker π complex of phenanthrene-TCNE is therefore used as a warning indicator, since the reaction of cyclopentadiene with this complex, as shown in Equation 2, is fast enough to be useful initially. The K value is probably close to the value of 18 reported for the fluorene-TCNE complex.[8] The TCNE remaining after the breakup of the colored TCNE-phenanthrene complex is then complexed upon addition of pentamethylbenzene.

Although Sausen, Engelhardt, and Middleton[13] found that phenanthrene is alkylated by TCNE in pyridine catalyst at the macro level, this reaction is slow relative to Equations 1 and 2. In the absence of pyridine, TCNE could be recovered by the above procedure to the extent of $100.0 \pm 0.4\%$ at phenanthrene-TCNE ratios varying from 0.1 to 10.

TCNE

This compound is used as a reference standard for cyclopentadiene, since it can be readily purified. This is a more reliable method than the secondary method of Unger.[18]

Anthracene of 99.8% purity can be used to check the effect of further purification of TCNE, by the above procedure. After the reaction, the excess TCNE is back-titrated photometrically with the cyclopentadiene titrant. A typical analysis of the recrystallized and sublimed TCNE used routinely gives 99.5% recovery of anthracene; after a second recrystallization, the recovery is 99.6% after a second sublimation instead of a second recrystallization, the recovery is 99.5%. Although this assumes that the cyclopentadiene molarity is correct, the consistency of the results using the same cyclopentadiene titrant proves that TCNE used routinely is pure enough for the accuracy and precision within 1% that are claimed for the method.

RESULTS

Quantitative results for the determination of a number of aromatic and cyclic and acyclic aliphatic dienes are given in Table II. Both visual and photometric methods of end point detection can be employed.

Mixtures

Anthracene can be determined in relatively large amounts of phenanthrene. The recovery of anthracene in 75 mole % phenanthrene is 101.0%; in 90 mole % phenanthrene, 100.2%. The recovery of anthracene in 98 mole % phenanthrene is only 97.4%, which may be due to the slow breakup of the phenanthrene-TCNE complex which indicates the end point. (No pentamethylbenzene indicator was used in these cases, since a tenfold excess of phenanthrene indicates the end point satisfactorily.)

Table II. Determination of 1.5 mmoles of dienes

Diene	Reaction time at room temp., min.	% Purity found
Aromatic		
Anthracene	10	99.9
Anthracene	20	99.4
1,2-Benzanthracene	60	102
1,2,5,6-Dibenzanthracene	96 hr.	99.4
9-Methylanthracene	5	99.4
Naphthacene	15	100.9
Pentacene	30[c]	118.2
Pyrene	72 hr.	27
Indole	48 hr.	99.9
Aliphatic		
Cyclohexa-1,3-diene (78.9%)	10	78.1
Cyclopentadiene	Instant	100.4
2,3-Dimethylbutadiene	Instant	98.2
trans-Penta-1,3-diene (69.0%)	20	70.5
Sorbic acid	24 hr.	35.6

REFERENCES

1. ALTSHULLER, A.P., COHEN, I.R., *Anal. Chem.* **32,** 1843 (1960).
2. CARBONI, R.A., *Organic Syntheses*, Vol. **39,** p. 64, Wiley, New York, 1959.
3. FUNAKUBO, E., MATSUMOTO, Y., HIROIKE, S., *J. Chem. Soc. Japan, Ind. Chem. Sect.* **56,** 798 (1953).
4. GODDU, R.F., HUME, D.N., *Anal. Chem.* **26,** 1740 (1954).
5. HINE, J., BROWN, J.A., ZALKOW, L.H., GARDNER, W.E., HINE, M., *J. Am. Chem. Soc.* **77,** 594 (1955).
6. KLOETZEL, M.C., *Organic Reactions*, Vol. **IV,** p. 47, Wiley, New York, 1948.
7. MCKUSICK, B.C., HECKERT, R.E., CAIRNS, T.L., COFFMAN, D.D., MOWER, H.F., *J.Am . Chem. Soc.* **80,** 2806 (1958).
8. MERRIFIELD, R.E., PHILLIPS, W.D., *Ibid.*, **80,** 2778 (1958).
9. MIDDLETON, W.J., HECKERT, R.E., LITTLE, E.L., KRESPAN, C.G., *Ibid.*, **80,** 2783 (1958).

10. POLGAR, A., JUNGNICKEL, J.L., *Organic Analysis*, Vol. **III**, pp. 310–15, Interscience, New York, 1956.
11. PUTNAM, S.T., MOSS, M.L., HALL, R.T., *Ind. Eng. Chem. Anal. Ed.* **18**, 628 (1946).
12. REHM, K., BODIN, J.T., CONNORS, K.A., HIGUCHI, T., *Anal. Chem.* **31**, 483 (1959).
13. SAUSEN, G.N., ENGELHARDT, V.A., MIDDLETON, W.J., *J. Am. Chem. Soc.* **80**, 2815 (1958).
14. SAWICKI, E., ELBERT, W., STANLEY, T.W., HAUSER, T.R., FOX, F.T., *Anal. Chem.* **32**, 811 (1960).
15. SCHENK, G.H., OZOLINS, M., *Talanta* **8**, 109 (1961).
16. TERENT'EV, A.P., VINOGRADOVA, E.V., HAL'PERN, G.D., *Compt. rend. abad. sci. U.R.S.S.* **4**, 267 (1935).
17. UBALDINI, I., CRESPI, V., GUERRIERI, F., *Ann. chim. appl.* **39**, 77 (1949).
18. UNGER, P., *Analyst* **80**, 820 (1955).

CHAPTER 29

Precise Determination of the Molecular Weight of Trinitrobenzene Complexes†

JOHN C. GODFREY

CAREFUL determination of the molecular weight of compounds of unknown structure is often of considerable value in establishing their structures. An ebullioscopic method employing highly specialized apparatus has been described, by which the maximum reported error is 0.7%.[4] However, the usual ebullioscopic, tensimetric, and cryoscopic (Rast) methods yield results which are reliable only to within a few per cent of the true value. Recently a spectrophotometric method has been reported[3] which gives the molecular weight of picric acid complexes to within 1%. It employs Equation 1, which follows from Beer's law.

$$\text{Molecular weight} = \varepsilon_\lambda \times c \times b \times n / A_\lambda \tag{1}$$

In this equation ε_λ is the molar absorptivity of the pure complexing agent at wave length λ, c is the concentration of the complex in grams per liter, b is the length of the light path in centimeters, n is the number of molecules of complexing agent associated with one molecule of unknown, and A_λ is the absorbance of the solution at the same wave length. The wave length is so chosen that interference from absorption by the unknown is

† Reprinted from *Analytical Chemistry*, **31**, 1081 (1959). Copyright 1959 by the American Chemical Society and reprinted by permission of the copyright owner.

avoided. The value for n is usually 1, or occasionally a small integer, but it can be determined by comparing the carbon, hydrogen, and nitrogen analyses of the pure substrate (unknown) with those of the complex.

Andrews[1] has noted that symmetrical trinitrobenzene (TNB) forms many more complexes than picric acid. Condensed aromatic and heteroaromatics systems invariably form complexes with trinitrobenzene. These complexes are generally considered to be of the electron donor–electron acceptor type, which are usually described as π complexes.[1] Molecules such as stilbene, which complex with more than one molecule of trinitrobenzene, nearly always have present two or more structurally independent coordination sites.[1] Although picric acid and trinitrobenzene adducts are completely dissociated in very dilute solutions,[7] trinitrobenzene itself is colorless in such solutions, and spectrophotometric measurement of its concentration in the presence of other organic substances is not practical. There are reports that in the presence of excess strong base, trinitrobenzene is converted to highly colored substances of unknown structure.[9, 14]

Investigation of the spectrum of highly purified trinitrobenzene in 95 % ethyl alcohol in the presence of a 100-fold excess of potassium hydroxide revealed absorption bands at 428 to 429 mμ ($\varepsilon = 26,600$ at t_0, the moment of addition of base) and 501 to 503 mμ ($\varepsilon = 17,910$). The absorption band at 429 mμ decays rapidly, falling to about 26,000 after 20 minutes, and the rate of decay appears to depend upon the concentration of the base. On the other hand, the absorption band at 502 mμ is constant, within experimental error, over a period of 30 minutes. This band has been chosen as a reference point for a method of determining molecular weights which involves.

Formation and isolation of a trinitrobenzene adduct.

Preparation of a dilute alcoholic solution from a weighed sample of the adduct.

Conversion of all the trinitrobenzene present to a highly colored complex with excess potassium ethoxide.

Spectrophotometric determination of the concentration of the trinitrobenzene–potassium ethoxide complex.

REAGENTS

1,3,5-Trinitrobenzene (Eastman Kodak White Label) was crystallized twice from hot 95% ethyl alcohol to a constant melting point of 123.5–124.0°C.

PROCEDURE

Absorptivity of 1,3,5-Trinitrobenzene

Duplicate determinations of ε_{502} of solutions of trinitrobenzene in 95% ethyl alcohol containing a 100-fold excess of potassium hydroxide (one pellet in 50 ml. of solution) gave identical values of 17,910. As confirmation, an average "best value" for ε_{502} was back-calculated from the nine most reliable determinations, and found to be 17,910 ± 40.

Preparation of Adducts

(Preparation of the carbazole complex illustrates the general method.) To a boiling solution of 0.3 gram of carbazole in 30 ml. of absolute ethyl alcohol were added 10 ml. of a saturated solution of trinitrobenzene in absolute ethyl alcohol (ca. 2% solution at 25°C.). The solution was boiled for 1 minute and set aside to crystallize. The complex was recrystallized to a constant melting point from absolute ethyl alcohol containing a small excess of trinitrobenzene. It was usually necessary to add to the recrystallization liquid about 5% by volume of the saturated trinitrobenzene in absolute ethyl alcohol solution in order to prevent dissociation of the complex. The product was then filtered, washed with cold absolute ethyl alcohol, and vacuum-dried over phosphorus pentoxide at room temperature.

Molecular Weight

A solution was prepared from a carefully weighed (microbalance) amount of complex so that the concentration was 20 to 30 mg. per liter (ca. $10^{-4} M$). Fifty milliliters of the solution were measured in a graduated cylinder and added to one crushed potassium hydroxide pellet (ca. 0.15 gram) in a glass-stoppered 125-ml. Erlenmeyer flask, which had previously been flushed with nitrogen. (Sodium hydroxide gives identical results, but is very slow to dissolve.) The spectrum of the deep orange solution was observed over the range 475 to 525 mμ about 12 times in the course of 20 minutes, and the average value of the maximum absorbance (at 501 to 503 mμ) was employed in Equation 1 to calculate the molecular weight of the complex.

RESULTS

Determinations were carried out on 15 complexes. Ten of the 15 results are within 0.5% of the expected value, and obvious sources of uncertainty may account for most of the errors greater than 0.5%. The complex containing two molecules of 1-naphthoic acid and one of trinitrobenzene is unusual in several respects. Aromatic molecules having only electronegative substituents seldom form adducts with trinitrobenzene. Furthermore, formation of complexes containing more than one molecule of trinitrobenzene per aromatic molecule is not uncommon, but the reverse is very rare.

DISCUSSION

This determination is subject to several types of uncertainty, some of which may be minimized. The most common source of error is the occasional instability of the organic substrate–trinitrobenzene complex. Two types of instability were observed. Most of the complexes tended to dissociate during purification by recrystallization, but this difficulty was easily avoided by adding a small excess of trinitrobenzene to the recrystallization liquor. Such dissociation, if not overcome, would give high results. Certain volatile organic compounds quickly evaporate from the solid complex, leaving behind excess trinitrobenzene which leads to low results. Such evaporation is difficult to suppress, and the consequences are exemplified by the very low value obtained for N,N-dimethylaniline.

The greatest uncertainty is in the value at 502 mμ for ε_{TNB} = 17,910 $\pm$ 40. The weight of sample and the absorbance are good to at least 0.001. In practice, the absorbance could always be read to $\pm$0.001. The greatest probable error is therefore $\pm$0.5%, neglecting possible error in dilution. Most of the values reported fall within these limits.

The dissociation constant of the complex trinitrobenzene–potassium ethoxide was determined at various total concentrations of trinitrobenzene in 95% ethyl alcohol in order to demonstrate that the excess of base used in the molecular weight measurements was sufficient to repress the dissociation of the colored complex, and to determine the stability of the solution of trinitrobenzene–potassium alkoxide toward decomposition, as opposed to dissociation of the complex. If the dissociation constant were "constant", it could be concluded that the dissociation of trinitrobenzene–potassium alkoxide was the only reaction occurring. Measurement of $K_{diss.}$, reported in Table II, showed that it is not in fact constant, nor does it depend in any simple way upon the concentration of the base. The lack of constancy may be considered to be a result of base-catalyzed reactions which occur at a slow rate in the essentially neutral solutions employed in determining K_{diss}. Fortunately, the rate at which side reactions occur in ethyl alcohol at room temperature is small enough that it does not affect the determination of molecular weight when carried out as described.

Table II. Dissociation constant for reaction
$$TNB.KOC_2H_5 \rightarrow TNB + KOC_2H_5$$

c Complex, $\times 10^4 M$	$A_{502}{}^a$	$K_{diss.} \times 10^3 M$
1.20	0.150	1.48
1.42	0.254	1.15
1.57	0.328	1.05
1.95	0.600	0.84
2.14	0.674	0.82
3.65	1.930	0.61

^{a} To assure uniform comparisons, values of A_{502} were read 15 minutes after solution of sample.

These observations suggested that the colored from of trinitrobenzene upon which the molecular weight determination depends might be an equilibrium mixture of π- and σ-complexes,[1] structures I and II, respectively. Support for this view was found upon investigating the visible spectra of a large number of compounds which complex with trinitrobenzene. (These data will be reported in detail elsewhere.) In 95% ethyl alcohol containing trinitrobenzene, aromatic nuclei which carry electron-donating substituents and which are not capable of significant hydrogen-bonding with the solvent, induced the trinitrobenzene to show only a single low intensity broad maximum, corresponding to the 502 mμ absorption band of trinitrobenzene in the presence of strong base. On the other hand, aliphatic amines which are capable of hydrogen-bonding with solvent induced trinitrobenzene to show both the sharp, intense, short wave length band near 430 mμ, and the broad, less intense band near 505 mμ. It seems clear therefore that the 502 mμ band of trinitrobenzene in basic ethyl alcohol is due to the π-complex, while the 429 mμ band is characteristic of the σ-complex.

REFERENCES

1. ANDREWS, L.J., *Chem. Revs.* **54**, 713–76 (1954).
2. ASAHINA, TEICHI, SHINOMIYA, CHIRO, *J. Chem. Soc. Japan* **59**, 341–51 (1938).
3. CUNNINGHAM, K.G., DAWSON, W., SPRING, F.S., *J. Chem. Soc.* 2305–6 (1951).
4. DIMBAT, MARTIN, STROSS, F.H., *Anal. Chem.* **29**, 1517–20 (1957).
5. FIESER, L.F., FIESER, M., *Organic Chemistry*, 1st ed., pp. 574–5, Heath and Co., New York, 1944.
6. HIBBERT, H., SUDBOROUGH, J.J., *J. Chem. Soc.*, 1334–42 (1903).
7. JONES, R.C., NEUWORTH, M.B., *J. Am. Chem. Soc.* **66**, 1497–9 (1944).
8. KENT, ANDREW, MCNEIL, DONALD, COWPER, R.M., *J. Chem. Soc.* 1858–62 (1939).
9. KORTUM, GUSTAV, *Ber.* **74B**, 409–16 (1941).
10. LOBRY DE BRUYN, C.A., *Red. trav. chim.* **14**, 89–94 (1895).
11. LOBRY DE BRUYN, C.A., VAN LEENT, F.H., *Ibid.*, **13**, 148–54 (1894).
12. *Ibid.*, **14**, 150–5 (1895).
13. MARVEL, C.S., BATEMAN, D.E., *Organic Syntheses*, pp. 219–20, Col. Vol. **I**, Wiley, New York, 1941.
14. MUDGE, C.S., *Food Ind.* **1**, 613–15 (1929).
15. Natl. Bur. Standards, Circ. **C-434**.
16. NOLLER, C.R., *Chemistry of Organic Compounds*, 2nd ed., p. 460, Saunders Co., Philadelphia, 1957.
17. OSTROMISSLENSKIĬ, I., *J. prakt. Chem.* **84**, 495–506 (1911).
18. PFEIFFER, PAUL, *et al.*, *Ann.* **412**, 253–63 (1916).
19. SEN GUPTA, S.C., CHATTERJEE, D.N., *J. Indian Chem. Soc.* **31**, 285–90 (1954).
20. SUDBOROUGH, J.J., *J. Chem. Soc.* 522–33 (1901).
21. *Ibid.*, 1339–43 (1916).
22. SUDBOROUGH, J.J., BEARD, S.H., *Ibid.*, 773–98 (1910).
23. *Ibid.*, 209–17 (1911).
24. WELLER, L.E., REBSTOCK, T.L., SELL, H.M., *J. Am. Chem. Soc.* **74**, 2690 (1952).
25. WHITMORE, F.C., *Organic Chemistry*, 2nd ed., p. 636, Van Nostrand, New York, 1951.

CHAPTER 30

A Study of the Pi Complexes of Tetracyanoethylene with Phenols, Aromatic Hydrocarbons and Aryl Ethers†

GEORGE H. SCHENK, MILAGROS SANTIAGO, and PATRICIA WINES

USE OF ethylenediaminetetraacetic acid (EDTA) as a general complexometric reagent requiring mild reaction conditions (room temperature, neutral pH) is one of the chief tools of the inorganic analytical chemist. Furthermore, it is possible to render EDTA complexation more selective by reduction, masking, kinetic masking, and pH control. Lastly, the chemist can readily calculate the effects of pH and masking.

Until recently no similar reagent had the same potential for the organic analytical chemist.

In 1958 Merrifield and Phillips[8] published a study of the intensely colored π complexes of tetracyanoethylene (TCNE) with aromatic hydrocarbons. The potential of TCNE soon became apparent as Tarbell and Huang[19] used TCNE for color development in paper chromatography, Peurifoy and Nager[11] utilized TCNE for the estimation of nitrogen compounds, and

† Reprinted from *Analytical Chemistry*, **35,** 167 (1963). Copyright 1963 by the American Chemical Society and reprinted by permission of the copyright owner.

Schenk and Ozolins[10, 16] used TCNE for the colorimetric estimation of anthracene and the titrimetric estimation of dienes via the Diels–Alder reaction. Recently, Bauer[3] showed that the substitution of unconjugated olefins could be determined with TCNE.

Selectivity

TCNE was thus shown analytically to complex under mild conditions, but approaches such as reduction, pH control, and masking have not been established to eliminate interferences to make TCNE more specific. Phenols, aromatic hydrocarbons, aryl ethers, mercaptans, amines, thiophenes, and Diels–Alder–active dienes as well as many unconjugated alkenes are among the many organic species that react or π complex with TCNE. Because most of the spectral bands that result from these reactions are too broad to be eliminated by spectrophotometry, approaches such as solvent control, acidity, and functional group reactions are explored for possible elimination of interferences, and the results reported herein.

Beer's Law-I

Another object of this work was to study the conditions and make calculations for adherence to Beer's law for the π complexes formed according to the reaction:

$$\text{TCNE} + \text{aromatic base} \rightleftharpoons \text{complex} \qquad (1)$$

To obtain formation (or pseudo stability) constants for the above reaction, Merrifield and Phillips[8] plotted the molarity of TCNE divided by absorbance *vs.* the reciprocal of the mole fraction of aromatic hydrocarbon (under conditions where the concentration of aromatic was large compared to TCNE) and obtained straight lines.

This indicated that plots might be obtained which, although not strictly obeying Beer's law, might not deviate seriously from Beer's law over a small concentration range and under standardized conditions. Such plots indeed have been obtained for the colorimetric determination of aromatic rings where TCNE is present at lower concentrations than the aromatic π base. This method appears best for phenols and some aromatics where K is fairly large ($\geqslant 20$) since a small amount of a weak aromatic base does not form enough of the complex to measure spectrophotometrically.

Beer's Law-II

The more sensitive method involves TCNE at concentrations appreciably higher than the concentration of aromatic or phenol. The formation constant expression for this situation[15] is:

$$K = \frac{(C)}{\{(B) - (C)\}\{[TCNE] - [C]\}} \tag{2}$$

in which (C) is the concentration of the complex at equilibrium, (B) is the initial concentration of the π base, [TCNE] is the initial mole fraction of TCNE, and $[C]$ is the mole fraction of the complex at equilibrium.

Because most of the π complexes are very weak, [TCNE] $- [C]$ will approximate [TCNE] within 5%, and Equation 2 rearranges to:

$$(B) = \frac{(C)\{1 + K[TCNE]\}}{K[TCNE]} \tag{3}$$

The absorbance, A, of a given solution in a 1-cm. cell will equal $\varepsilon(C)$, where ε is molar absorptivity. The lower limit of (B) that can be measured accurately ($A = 0.1$) will depend on ε, which is of the order of 2000 for most of the complexes in methylene chloride, on [TCNE], which is 0.0032 for the convenient 0.05 M TCNE solutions in methylene chloride, and on K.

Substituting A/ε for (C) in Equation 3 gives:

$$(B) = \frac{A\{1 + K[TCNE]\}}{\varepsilon K[TCNE]} \simeq \frac{A}{\varepsilon K[TCNE]} \simeq \frac{0.016}{K} \quad (4)$$

Where K is of the order of 1, the lower limit of (B) that can be determined accurately is about $1.6 \times 10^{-2} M$; where K is of the order of 100, the lower limit is about $1.6 \times 10^{-4} M$.

Plots which did not deviate seriously from Beer's law are also obtained for this method, but since K's and molar absorptivities are not available to delineate all lower limits of (B) that can be accurately measured in different solvents and at different concentrations of TCNE, still a further object of the study was to determine some of these experimentally. For this purpose and for the purpose of investigating adherence to Beer's law, a five- to tenfold excess of TCNE over aromatic or phenol appeared sufficient to ensure a constant slope, $\Delta A/\Delta(B)$, for all but the strongest π bases.

EXPERIMENTAL

Reagents

Tetracyanoethylene (TCNE) was obtained from the Eastman Kodak Co., sublimed to obtain a white solid, and stored in a desiccator over sodium hydroxide pellets.

TCNE solutions were prepared, for example, by dissolving 6.4 mg. of TCNE per ml. with heating for 0.05 M TCNE in methylene chloride.

The 0.06 M acetylating reagent was prepared from ethyl acetate, acetic anhydride, and perchloric acid by the method of Schenk and Santiago.[17] If chloroform was used as solvent instead of ethyl acetate, 1.5 ml. of acetic anhydride per 50 ml. of chloroform was used to acetylate the 0.75% ethanol in the chloroform.

The 0.1 M perchloric acid in glacial acetic acid was prepared by the method of Fritz.[5]

Procedures

Solvent effects were determined by mixing 1 ml. of 0.05 M TCNE in methylene chloride with 0.3 mmole of durene and diluting to 25 ml. with the appropriate solvent.

Adherence to Beer's law was investigated by first selecting chlorinated solvents for making up the sample as well as dissolving TCNE.

Acetic anhydride was used for the same purpose; 1 ml. of acetic anhydride was added to the above mixtures in 10 ml. of chloroform and the solution was allowed to stand 30 minutes at room temperature. TCNE in methylene chloride was added in excess of the aromatic or phenol or in smaller amounts than either. The solution was diluted to 25 ml. with chloroform, and the absorbance was measured at the appropriate wavelength, such as 520 mμ for 2,6-dimethylphenol. The blank (no amine) was treated similarly.

The use of the 0.06 M acetylating reagent (0.007 M in perchloric acid) was investigated to prevent the interference of amines, phenols, and mercaptans in the complexation of aromatic hydrocarbons or aryl ethers. A threefold excess (5 ml.) of the acetylating reagent was added to 0.1 mmole of amine, phenol, or mercaptan and 0.5 mmole of 1,3-dimethoxybenzene in 0 to 3 ml. of methylene chloride. After 20 minutes reaction at room temperature, the solution was diluted to about 20 ml. with chloroform, 1 ml. of 0.05 M TCNE in methylene chloride was added, the solution was diluted to 25 ml. with chloroform, and the absorbance was read at 575 mμ. The blank (no phenol, amine, or mercaptan) was treated similarly.

DISCUSSION

Solvent Effects

Table I gives the solubility of TCNE in a number of solvents, and shows the effect of solvent on the absorbance of the durene-TCNE π complex. Solvent effects were also investigated for some solvents for the π complexes of 1,3-dimethoxybenzene, 2,6-dimethylphenol, and naphthalene, and rough agreement was

Table I. Solubilities of TCNE and solvent effects

Solvent	Solubility	0.012 M durene, 0.002 M TCNE, $A_{480m\mu}(b = 22$ mm.)
CCl$_4$	...	Approx. 2 (pptn.)
CHCl$_3$	0.01 M (slow)	0.63
CHBr$_3$	< 0.004 M (slow)	1.05
CH$_2$Cl$_2$	0.1 M (heat)	0.38
CCl$_2$:CCl$_2$	...	Approx. 1 (pptn.)
CHCl$_2$CHCl$_2$	Approx. 0.002M	0.57
CH$_2$ClCH$_2$Cl	0.15M	0.15
HOAc	0.3 M	0.17
EtOAc	> 0.5 M	0.06
Ac$_2$O	...	0.06
0.06 M Ac$_2$O/EtOAc	...	0.08
CH$_3$CN	> 0.5 M	0.07
(CH$_3$)$_2$CO	...	0.03
p-Dioxane	...	0.02
CH$_2$OH	...	0.01

noted. This supplements the excellent work of Cram and Bauer[4] on the shift of absorbance maxima with solvent for 3,4-para-cyclophane–TCNE π complexes. They suggested that one or two solvent molecules were bound in the π complex, giving rise to the solvent effect.

The change in absorbance from solvent to solvent for the TCNE-durene π complex reflects not only a change in K, but also possibly a change in ε, as seen from Equation 4. The data of Merrifield and Phillips[8] indicate that only K decreases appreciably with a change from chloroform to methylene chloride but that K decreases appreciably and ε increases appreciably with a change from chloroform to diethyl ether.

Where there is no π complexation possible to assist in solvation, the minimum requirement for solvation of TCNE appears to be compounds of the type HCR_3, where the R's are all electron withdrawing groups—e.g., chloroform or bromoform. The hydrogen of bromoform is inductively less acidic and more sterically hindered than that of chloroform, probably forms a weaker hydrogen bond (Equation 5) and is therefore a poorer solvent than chloroform, as shown in Table I.

$$\text{(NC)}_2\text{C:C(CN)}_2 + HCR_3 \rightleftharpoons \overset{\text{CN}}{\text{(NC)}_2\text{C:CCN:}} \rightarrow HCR_3 \qquad (5)$$

However, the hydrogen of bromoform or chloroform can also hydrogen bond to an aromatic π electron system (Equation 6 and Table I), as shown by Tamres.[18] Thus chloroform, the better solvent for TCNE, forms a stronger hydrogen bond to π electron systems according to Tamres,[18] competes with TCNE more favorably than bromoform, and therefore favors π complexation of TCNE less than bromoform.

$$Me_4C_6H_2 + HCR_3 \rightleftharpoons (Me_4C_6H_2) \xrightarrow{\pi} HCR_3 \qquad (6)$$

A compound of the type H_2CR_2, such as methylene chloride, possesses less acidic hydrogens than the type HCR_3, but does have a statistical advantage and a smaller steric bulk. The equilibria in Equations 5 and 6 are more favorable for methylene chloride than for chloroform, making it a better solvent but a less favorable media for π complexation of TCNE with an aromatic such as durene in Equation 6.

Acid, Base, and Salt Effects

Table I indicates that acetic acid as solvent favors complexation more than nonhalogenated solvents. Table III indicates that 0.1 M perchloric acid in acetic acid and 0.05 M periodic acid in 90% acetic acid–10% methanol apparently do not disturb the equilibrium in acetic acid. (Tables VII and VIII elaborate on the effect of perchloric acid in the presence of amines.)

In contrast, most bases tend to catalyze the decomposition of TCNE, giving rise to yellow colors.

Agreement with Beer's Law

Table IV lists various complex systems (containing an aromatic, a phenol, or an aryl ether) which do not deviate significantly from Beer's law from zero concentration to the upper limit of concentration stated. An absorbance of 0.07 is obtained for $5 \times 10^{-4} M$ pyrene and for $4 \times 10^{-3} M$ 2,6-dimethylphenol.

Table IV illustrates both the use of TCNE in excess over the π base as well as the use of the aromatic π base in excess over TCNE (plots II and I). Several plots are listed in which interferences such as nitrophenols or resorcinol are present.

Lower Limit of Concentration

Table V contains data on lower limits of concentration for which absorbance can be measured accurately (0.10) for four different solvents and for one solvent mixture. The data were found directly or calculated from data such as in Table I, using Equation 4 with the approximation that (B) is equal to $A/\varepsilon K$ [TCNE]. This corresponds to an error of 16% for durene in methylene chloride when the exact solution is used in Equation 4. Since this is the strongest complex listed and since the data are the result of a single determination of εK, the error for any value is estimated to be no more than 20 to 30%. The data in Table V are calculated for 1-cm. cells in the Spectronic 20 since the theoretical lower limit is calculated on a 1-cm. basis using molar absorptivities determined on a prism spectrophotometer (Cary).[8] It is estimated that the data would be about 15% lower on a prism spectrophotometer such as a Beckman spectrophotometer because of correspondingly higher molar absorptivities.

Table V. Lower limits of concentration
($A = 0.10$, $b = 1$ cm.)

Solvent	(TCNE)	[TCNE]	Durene $(K)=(54)$	Pyrene (29.5)	2,6-Dimethyl-phenol (~ 20)
CH$_2$Cl$_2$ (theory)	0.050	0.0032	3.5×10^{-4}	1.0×10^{-3}	7×10^{-4}
CH$_2$Cl$_2$	0.050	0.0032	3×10^{-4}	1×10^{-3}	8×10^{-4}
CHCl$_3$	0.01	0.0008	8×10^{-4}	...	3×10^{-3}
70% CH$_2$Cl$_2$– 30% CHCl$_3$	0.70	0.0047	...	5×10^{-4}	...
HOAc	0.30	0.018	3×10^{-4}	6×10^{-4}	3×10^{-4}
EtOAc	0.50	0.051	2×10^{-4}	9×10^{-4}	2×10^{-4}

INTERFERENCES AND SELECTIVITY

Effect of Water

Since water hydrolyzes TCNE slowly even where a solvent such as acetonitrile[1] has been rigourously dried, the effect of water on the absorbance of the TCNE-2,6-dimethylphenol complex with time was checked. After an hour, the absorbance of a "wet" chloroform solution did not change although it decreased from 0.67 to 0.60 after 24 hours. The absorbance of a similar "wet" methylene chloride actually increased from 0.50 to 0.56 in an hour and to 0.61 in 24 hours. Obviously the effect of water is small in chlorinated solvents; the use of acetic anhydride or acid-catalyzed acetylation should minimize hydrolysis of TCNE in any solvent.

Acetic Acid as Solvent

The use of glacial acetic acid as solvent provides no selectivity but should retard the reactions of some amines with TCNE; the more reactive amines still interfere somewhat as shown in Table VII.

Table VII. *Acetic acid as solvent*
0.004 M 2,6-dimethylphenol, 0.026 M
TCNE, absorbance constant for 40 min.

0.002 M amine	$A_{520\,m\mu}$ (b = 22 mm.)
None (blank)	0.25
Et$_3$N	0.24
PhNMe$_2$	0.265
Bu$_2$NH	0.25
PhNHMe	0.31
BuNH$_2$(0.004 M)	0.38
PhNH$_2$(0.004 M)	Approx. 1

Table VIII. *0.1 M perchloric acid/acetic acid as solvent*
0.004 M 2,6-dimethylphenol,
0.026 M TCNE

0.012 M amine	$A_{520\,m\mu}$ (b = 22 mm.)
None (blank)	0.26
PhNH$_2$	0.255
BuNH$_2$	0.24
PhNHMe	0.245
PhNMe$_2$	0.27

Acetic acid prevents the interference of tertiary amines and secondary alkyl amines. This is useful since tertiary amines cannot be acetylated and interfere in chlorinated solvents containing acetic anhydride (Table IX).

Perchloric Acid in Acetic Acid

Table VII indicates that 0.1 M perchloric acid in acetic acid prevents the interferences encountered in acetic acid alone even when the interfering amines are present at 3 to 6 times the concentration used in Table VII. It appears that protonation by the perchloric retards N-alkylation of the primary and secondary amines as well as perhaps 4-tricyanovinylation of N,N-dimethylaniline.

Uncatalyzed Acetylation

It is well known that acetic anhydride reacts rapidly with most primary and secondary amines even without a catalyst. Vogel[20] uses pyridine as catalyst for their determination at room temperature in 30 minutes reaction time. The data in Table IX demonstrate that the interference of most primary and secondary amines can be removed after uncatalyzed acetylation (no pyridine) at room temperature.

*Table IX. Uncatalyzed acetylation
at room temperature*
2,6-Dimethylphenol (2,6-DMP),
amine in $Ac_2O/CHCl_3$ for 30 minutes

0.004 M amine	$A_{520\,m\mu}$ ($b = 22$ mm.)
0.002 M 2,6-DMP, 0.02 M TCNE, 48% $CHCl_3$–48% CH_2Cl_2	
None (blank)	0.22
$PhNH_2$	0.30
p-$BrC_6H_4NH_2$	0.26
$BuNH_2$	0.22
PhNHMe	0.24
Bu_2NH	0.22
Ph_2NH	0.27
Et_3N	0.05

Acid-catalyzed Acetylation

Acetic anhydride alone at room temperature reacts rapidly only with amines, but acetylation catalyzed by pyridine at reflux temperatures[20] occurs with phenols and mercaptans as well and would be a way to some selectivity. However, TCNE is not necessarily stable at reflux temperatures, and pyridine would complex the TCNE strongly enough to prevent complexation in most cases.[8]

Table X illustrates the usefulness of the micro acid-catalyzed acetylating reagent of Schenk and Santiago.[17] Not only does acetylation take place rapidly at room temperature, but only a minimal amount ($0.06 M$) of acetic anhydride is introduced so as not to disturb the complexation equilibrium in halogenated solvents (Table I). In addition, the perchloric acid ($0.007 M$) has no effect on the complexation as would the large amount of pyridine necessary for catalysis. Finally the solvent can be varied from chloroform to ethyl acetate, etc., depending on the sensitivity desired.

The results should not be taken to indicate that the interference of all phenols may easily be removed since resorcinol is

Table X. Acid-catalyzed acetylation
at room temperature

($0.02 M$ 1,3-dimethoxybenzene, $0.002 M$ TCNE,
$0.06 M$ $Ac_2O/CHCl_3$)

0.004 M interference	$A_{575 m\mu}$ ($b = 22$ mm.)
None (blank)	0.21
Resorcinol (no $0.06 M$ Ac_2O)	0.27
Resorcinol	0.20
Aniline (filtered)	0.21
Dodecyl mercaptan	0.22
p-Methoxyphenol	0.225

acetylated twice and its π basicity is correspondingly reduced. Stronger π bases such as p-methoxyphenol may interfere somewhat after acetylation.

Strength of π Bases

Some aromatic hydrocarbons and phenols may be determined in the presence of others by virtue of being much stronger π bases. Table IV lists Beer's law conditions for the determination of 2,6-dimethylphenol and 3,5-dimethylphenol in o- and p-nitrophenol. Table XII lists other selective determinations that are possible. The magnitude of these interferences would be expected to increase if a weaker π base than 2,6-dimethylphenol were being complexed.

Table XII. Complexation of a stronger
π base in weaker π bases
0.008 M 2,6-Dimethylphenol,
0.002 M TCNE, $CHCl_3$

Weaker π bases, M	$A_{520 \, m\mu}$ ($b = 22$ mm.)
None (blank)	0.16
Salicylic acid 0.016 M	0.165
Benzene, 0.032 M	0.145
m-Chlorophenol, 0.004 M	0.155
Anisole, 0.004 M	0.16
Acetophenone, 0.032 M	0.17
p-Nitrophenol, 0.016 M	0.17
m-Nitrophenol, 0.016 M	0.16
o-Nitrophenol, 0.016 M	0.16
Thiophene, 0.024 M	0.175

REFERENCES

1. ABRAHAMSON, E. A., E. I. du Pont de Nemours & Co., Wilmington, Del., private communication, 1962.
2. ADLER, E., MAGNUSSON, R., *Acta Chem. Scand.* **13**, 505 (1959).
3. BAUER, R. H., *Anal. Chem.* **35**, 107 (1963).

4. CRAM, D.J., BAUER, R.H., *J. Am. Chem. Soc.* **81,** 5971 (1959).
5. FRITZ, J.S., *Acid-Base Titrations in Nonaqueous Solvents,* p. 13, G.F. Smith Chemical Co., Columbus, Ohio, 1952.
6. INGBERMAN, A.K., *Anal. Chem.* **30,** 1003 (1958).
7. MCKUSICK, B.C., HECKERT, R.E., CAIRNS, T.L., COFFMAN, D.D., MOWER, H.T., *J. Am. Chem. Soc.* **80,** 2806 (1958).
8. MERRIFIELD, R.E., PHILLIPS, W.D., *Ibid.,* **80,** 2778 (1958).
9. MIDDLETON, W.J., LITTLE, E.L., COFFMAN, D.D., ENGELHARDT, V.A., *Ibid.,* **80,** 2795 (1958).
10. OZOLINS, M., SCHENK, G.H., *Anal. Chem.* **33,** 1035 (1961).
11. PEURIFOY, P.V., NAGER, M., *Ibid.,* **32,** 1135 (1960).
12. REILLEY, C.N., CRAWFORD, C.M., *Ibid.,* **27,** 1716 (1955).
13. SAUSEN, G.N., ENGELHARDT, V.A., MIDDLETON, W.J., *J. Am. Chem. Soc.* **80,** 2815 (1958).
14. SAWICKI, E., *Rec. Chem. Prog.* **22,** 249 (1961).
15. SCHENK, G.H., OZOLINS, M., *Anal. Chem.* **33,** 1562 (1961).
16. SCHENK, G.H., OZOLINS, M., *Talanta* **8,** 109 (1961).
17. SCHENK, G.H., SANTIAGO, M., *Microchem. J.* **VI,** 77 (1962).
18. TAMRES, M., *J. Am. Chem. Soc.* **74,** 3375 (1952).
19. TARBELL, D.S., HUANG, T., *J. Org. Chem.* **24,** 887 (1959).
20. VOGEL, A.I., *Elementary Practical Organic Chemistry,* Part 3, p. 694, Longmans, Green, London, 1958.
21. WILSON, J.R., NUTTING, M.D., BAILEY, G.F., *Anal. Chem.* **34,** 1331 (1962).
22. WINSTEIN, S., SMITH, S., DARWISH, D., *J. Am. Chem. Soc.* **81,** 5511 (1959).
23. WRONSKI, M., *Z. Anal. Chem.* **174,** 280 (1960).

CHAPTER 31

Diphenylpicrylhydrazyl as an Organic Analytical Reagent in the Spectrophotometric Analysis of Phenols†

G. J. PAPARIELLO and M. A. M. JANISH

THIS is the second report devoted to studying the utility of diphenylpicrylhydrazyl, a stable free radical, as a colorimetric analytical reagent. The initial work on this reagent dealt with the use of the reagent in the colorimetric analysis of amines.[7] Knowledge about the reagent uncovered during the prior study can be applied with some modifications to this work. The advantages that this reagent was found to bring to amine analysis, it also brings to the analysis of phenols. The reagent's intense color and the great differences in reaction rate between various phenols enables both sensitivity and selectivity to be obtained when using this reagent.

This phenol work benefits from studies by a number of workers[4−6, 8] on the mechanism and kinetics of reaction of phenols with diphenylpicrylhydrazyl. McGowan et al.[6] suggested that the rate-determining step in the reaction involves the removal of hydride from the phenolic hydroxyl group with the formation of

† Reprinted from *Analytical Chemistry*, **38**, 211 (1966). Copyright 1966 by the American Chemical Society and reprinted by permission of the copyright owner.

an ion with a positive charge. They base this contention on a comparison of the relative rates (the ratio of the rates for substituted to unsubstituted compound) of solvolysis of substituted α,α-dimethylbenzyl chlorides in 90% aqueous acetone to the relative rates of reaction for the corresponding substituted phenols with diphenylpicrylhydrazyl. The great similarity found in the relative rates suggest that the mechanism of reaction is similar. The rate of solvolysis of α,α-dimethylbenzyl chlorides almost certainly involves the formation of the carbonium ion(I). Thus, they conclude the reaction of diphenylpicrylhydrazyl with phenol involves the formation of the cation(II).

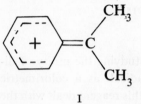

I

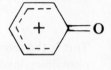

II

Hogg, Lohmann, and Russell,[4] on the other hand, contend that the reaction involves the abstraction of a hydrogen atom from the phenol to give diphenylpicrylhydrazine and a phenoxy radical, as follows:

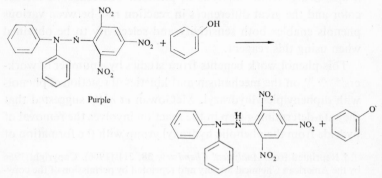

Although there is some disagreement as to the exact mechanism of reaction, there is general agreement that the reaction is usually a second-order reaction, that is, rate of disappearance of hydrazyl = k_2 [hydrazyl] [phenol].

EXPERIMENTAL

Reagents

Phenolic substances were used as received commercially. With the exception of the solvent study, methanolic solutions of the phenols were always used in this work at phenol concentrations of 2×10^{-2} mmoles/ml. to 2×10^{-5} mmoles/ml.

2,2-Diphenyl-1-picrylhydrazyl (Eastman, No. 7703) was used as received. A 2×10^{-4} mmoles/ml. methanolic solution of diphenylpicrylhydrazyl was used as the reagent solution except in the solvent study where a solution of the reagent was prepared in the solvent in question. The reagent solution should be prepared fresh daily.

An aqueous $1 N$ acetate buffer system, adjusted to a pH of 5.0, was used to control the pH.

Analytical Procedure

Pipet into a glass-stoppered test tube 4 ml. of phenol sample solution, 1 ml. of methanol, 1 ml. of acetate buffer solution, and 4 ml. of diphenylpicrylhydrazyl reagent. In another test tube prepare a reagent blank using 5 ml. of methanol, 1 ml. of buffer, and 4 ml. of reagent. After mixing, allow test tubes to stand at room temperature or 60°C. for 15 minutes to 1 hour. (The time and temperature of reaction depend on the rate of reactivity of the particular phenol being considered.) The absorbance of the sample and the reagent blank are measured against a methanol blank at 155 mμ in 1-cm. cells in a suitable spectrophotometer.

The analysis value is obtained by finding the difference between the absorbance values of the blank and sample. The concentration corresponding to this difference value is then read on a calibration curve made with known concentrations of the same phenol.

Table I. Reactivity of various phenols[a]

Compound	Phenol:reagent ratio	Reactivity[b]
Monohydric phenols		
Phenol	100:1	Good
p-Methoxyphenol*	1:2	Good
o-Methoxyphenol (guaiacol)*	1:2	Good
m-Methoxyphenol	10:1	Good
p-Bromophenol	100:1	Fair
2,6-Dichlorophenol	100:1	Good
8-Hydroxyquinoline	10:1	Good
3-Hydroxypyridine	100:1	Fair
4-Hydroxypyridine	100:1	No reaction
α-Naphthol*	1:5	Good
Dihydric phenols		
Hexachlorophene	100:1	Good
Diethylstilbestrol	1:1	Good
4-Hexylresorcinol	1:1	Good
Resorcinol	10:1	Good
Hydroquinone*	1:5	Good
Chlorohydroquinone*	1:5	Good
Pyrocatechol*	1:10	Good

[a] All compounds were run at 60°C., with the exception of those marked with an asterisk, which were run at 25°C.

[b] Evaluation of the reactivity of a phenol with the reagent is based on per cent discoloration caused by the phenol during a 30-minute reaction period using indicated mole ratio. Descriptive terms used are defined as follows: no reaction, 0–5% discoloration; poor, 5–10% discoloration, fair, 10–30% discoloration; and good 30–100% discoloration.

RESULTS AND DISCUSSION

Phenol Reactivity

The reactivity of a number of phenols with the reagent was determined by periodically sampling and reading the absorbance of a solution of the phenol and the reagent under various assay conditions. In this manner it was found that the mole ratios of phenol to reagent, the temperature, and the time were all factors which influence the reactivity of the phenols with diphenylpic-rylhydrazyl. As with the amine work, 30 minutes' reaction time was found to be adequate for most compounds encountered and it is chosen as the usual reaction time for analysis.

The results of the reactivity study are tabulated in Table I. The ring substituents affect the reactivity of the phenols in a manner similar to that of the amines. Thus, ring-activating groups such as methoxy or alkyl groups increase the reactivity of phenols with the reagent, and, conversely, ring-deactivating groups such as nitro, carboxyl, or halogen groups decrease the reactivity. Explanations for this behavior can be obtained by referring to the amine paper[7] and to the work of Hogg et al.[4] which correlates Hammett σ values and the rate of reaction.

Influence of Solvent

A quantitative description of the solvent influence on the reaction of the reagent with phenolic compounds was attempted.

The derived relationship for reaction rate and dielectric constant of the reaction medium can be expressed as follows:

$$\ln k = \ln k_0 - \frac{N(D-1)}{RT(2D+1)} \sum \frac{u^2}{r^3} \tag{1}$$

where k is the rate constant in the medium of dielectric constant D and k_0 is the rate constant in a medium of dielectric constant unity; μ represents the dipole moment, and r, the molecular radius; N, R, and T are Avogadro's number, the gas constant, and absolute temperature, respectively.[1] The equation predicts that if the activated complex is more polar than the reactants, the reaction increases with an increase in dielectric constant. A plot of $\log k$ vs. $(D - 1)/(2D + 1)$ for reactions involving charged species in mixtures of two solvents should be linear, assuming there are no interfering influences. Consequently, a study was made to determine whether or not this relationship, Equation 1, was followed for the phenol-hydrazyl reaction in an ethanol-benzene system. An ethanol-benzene system was chosen because it offers the possibility of covering a wide dielectric constant range. This approach parallels that used by Hanna and Siggia in their study of the rates of bromination of unsaturated compounds.[2]

To make this study, it was necessary to obtain kinetic data. The collection of reliable quantitative data for this reaction was difficult, for, as others have pointed out,[4] the reaction product, diphenylpicrylhydrazine, retards the reaction. The use of initial rates of reaction where the concentration of the retarding product is low is imperative. The method chosen to obtain the required kinetic data is a graphical one suggested by Wilkinson.[10]

With this method, rate data in ethanol-benzene mixtures were collected for p-methoxyphenol and 8-hydroxyquinoline.

Plots of $\log k$ vs. $(D - 1)/(2D + 1)$ for 8-hydroxyquinoline and p-methoxyphenol reactions in the ethanol-benzene system were found to be linear over a great part of the dielectric constant range. There is, however, some deviation from linearity as one approaches the lower ethanol concentration, that is, below 10% ethanol. A possible explanation for this behavior is that ethanol forms a strong association with the reagent, enabling a small percentage of the ethanol in a benzene solution to complex with the reagent and consequently retard the reaction with the phenol. Once all the hydrazyl present has been complexed, however, further addition of ethanol will have no greater retarding effect, but it will increase the polarity of the medium. This hypothesis gains support from the fact that the reaction rate in benzene alone is greater than that of the lower ethanol-benzene mixtures. This work indicates that Equation 1 is followed for the phenol-hydrazyl reaction as long as complications such as association reactions are not met. It should be emphasized that dielectric constant is not the only factor which influences the rate of reaction of hydrazyl with a given phenol, but it is an important factor and one which can most readily be quantitatively correlated.

Table II. Room temperature rate data for reaction of 8-hydroxyquinoline with diphenylpicrylhydrazyl in various solvents

Solvent system	Dielectric constant[a]	Rate constant liters mole^{-1} minute^{-1}
Methanol	32.6	193
Ethanol	24.3	89
1-Propanol	20.1	49
1-Butanol	17.1	45
2-Propanol	18.3	28
2-Methyl-1-propanol	17.7	17
Benzyl alcohol	13.1	47
1-Octanol	11.3[b]	24
9.1% Ethanol–90.9% benzene[c]	4.2	5
18.3% Ethanol–81.7% benzene[c]	6.1	13
37.3% Ethanol–62.7% benzene[c]	10.1	48
57.2% Ethanol–42.8% benzene[c]	14.7	76
78.1% Ethanol–21.9% benzene[c]	21.1	83

[a] Values obtained from references [3] and [9].

[b] This value was determined in this laboratory at 25°C. using a Sargent Model V Chemical Oscillometer.

[c] Weight-weight percentages.

*Table III. Room temperature rate data for reaction
of p-methoxyphenol with diphenylpicrylhydrazyl
in various solvents*

Solvent system	Dielectric constant[a]	Rate constant liters mole^{-1} minute^{-1}
Methanol	32.6	5760
Ethanol	24.3	5000
1-Propanol	20.1	4630
1-Butanol	17.1	3400
2-Propanol	18.3	900
9.1% Ethanol–90.9% benzene[b]	4.2	910
18.3% Ethanol–81.7% benzene[b]	6.1	1550
37.3% Ethanol–62.7% benzene[b]	10.1	4240
57.2% Ethanol–42.8% benzene[b]	14.7	5700
78.1% Ethanol–21.9% benzene[b]	21.1	6440
88.9% Ethanol–11.1% benzene[b]	22.9	7350
94.4% Ethanol– 5.6% benzene[b]	24.4	10,415

[a] Values obtained from references [3] and [9].

[b] Weight-weight percentages.

Further quantitative indications of solvent effects on the rate of hydrazyl reaction with phenols were considered. When a variety of solvents are being considered, however, Equation 1 is not applicable and, hence, a simple plot of log k *vs.* dielectric constant must be made. If one plots the rate data listed for the various alcoholic solvents in Tables II and III, one finds that there is an increase in the reactivity for both the 8-hydroxyquinoline and the *p*-methoxyphenol as the dielectric constant increases. As a matter of fact, if only the normal chain alcohols are considered, a linear relationship is obtained.

Practical Applicability in Phenol Analysis

The results of the analyses of a number of phenols are summarized in Table IV. The reproducibility and accuracy of these results are all one could ask for. However, use of a calibration curve prepared from standards run along with the samples was necessary to achieve such results. It was found that a sensitivity down to 10^{-3} to 10^{-5} mmoles of phenol could be obtained.

Attempts were made at assaying one phenol in the presence of another. Successful analysis of such mixtures depends upon the difference in the rate of reaction between the phenols in question. The analysis of o-methoxyphenol in the presence of vanillin was the first determination attempted. o-Methoxyphenol is a starting material in the synthesis of vanillin and could very well be a contaminant of the vanillin. Because the reaction of o-methoxyphenol with the reagent is rapid at room temperature, whereas the vanillin reaction is only appreciable at elevated temperatures, viz., 60°C., o-methoxyphenol in vanillin could be determined, see Table V. Successful analyses of pyrocatechol in phenol were also accomplished, see Table V.

Table V. Results of phenol analyses in phenol mixtures

Mixture	Theo-retical, %	Found %
o-Methoxyphenol	50	50, 50, 49
Vanillin	50	
o-Methoxyphenol	75	76, 75, 74
Vanillin	25	
Pyrocatechol	50	50, 50, 50
Phenol	50	
Pyrocatechol	75	76, 75, 75
Phenol	25	

REFERENCES

1. FROST, A.A., PEARSON, R.G., *Kinetics and Mechanism*, 2nd ed., p. 140, Wiley, New York, 1961.
2. HANNA, J.G., SIGGIA, S., *Anal. Chem.* **37**, 690 (1965).
3. HODGMAN, C.D., *Handbook of Chemistry and Physics*, 42nd ed., p. 2513 to 2522, The Chemical Rubber Publishing Co., Cleveland, Ohio, 1961.

4. HOGG, J.S., LOHMANN, D.H., RUSSELL, K.E., *Can. J. Chem.* **39,** 1588 (1961).
5. MCGOWAN, J.C., POWELL, T., *J. Chem. Soc.*, 2106 (1961).
6. MCGOWAN, J.C., POWELL, T., RAW, R., *Ibid.*, 3103 (1959).
7. PAPARIELLO, G.J., JANISH, M.A.M., *Anal. Chem.* **37,** 899 (1965).
8. VENKER, P., HERZMANN, H., *Naturwissenschaften* **47,** 133 (1960).
9. WASHBURN, E.W., *International Critical Tables of Numerical Data, Physics, Chemistry and Technology*, Vol. 6, p. 102, McGraw-Hill, New York, 1929.
10. WILKINSON, R.W., *Chem. & Ind. (London)* 1395 (1961).

Index

Made in Great Britain